# Roses

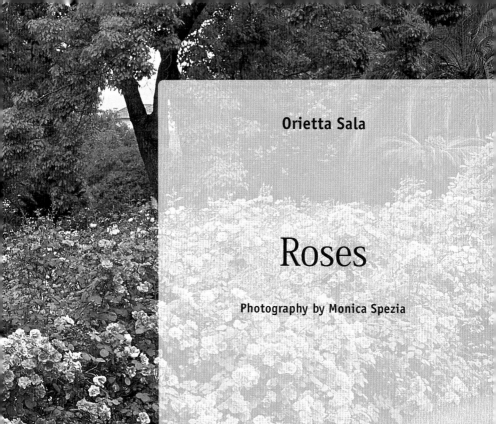

Orietta Sala

# Roses

**Photography by Monica Spezia**

FIREFLY BOOKS

Inside photographs:
Page 1: *Rosa banksiae lutea*,
Alhambra, Granada, Spain.
Pages 2-3: 'Flora,' Parc Phoenix,
Nice, France.
These pages: 'Graham Thomas,'
Regent's Park, London, England.
Pages 6-7: 'Parkjuwel'
(syn. 'Parkjewel').
Pages 10-11: 'Purezza.'
Pages 242-243: Rose garden of the
Associazione Italiana della Rosa,
Villa Reale, Monza, Italy.


*Editorial Director*
Mariella De Battisti

*Art Director*
Giorgio Seppi

*Editorial Production*
Progetto Media, Milan

*Layout*
Isabella Gianazza

*Editor*
Claudia Vassallo

*Watercolors and Drawings*
Orietta Sala

*Photography*
Barbara Monica Spezia

*Translation*
Jay Hyams

*Editor of English Edition*
Mary Patton

Published in Canada in 2003 by
Firefly Books Ltd.
3680 Victoria Park Avenue
Willowdale, Ontario M2H 3K1

Published in the U.S. in 2003 by
Firefly Books (U.S.) Inc.
P.O. Box 1338
Ellicott Station
Buffalo, New York 14205

**A FIREFLY BOOK**

Published by Firefly Books Ltd.
2003

Copyright © 2001 Arnoldo
Mondadori Editore S.p.A.
English translation © 2002 Arnoldo
Mondadori Editore S.p.A.

First printing 2002


Sala, Orietta.
   Roses : a Firefly guide /
Orietta Sala ; photography by
Monica Spezia. – 1st ed.
[304] p. : col. ill. , photos. ;  cm.
Includes bibliographical
references and index.
Summary: A comprehensive guide
to 150 modern and antique roses
including
photographs, dimensions,
origins and cultivation tips.
ISBN 1-55297-627-0 (pbk.)
1. Roses. I. Spezia, Monica.
II. Title.
21          635.933734 21
QK495.R78.S25  2003

Printed in Spain
D.L. TO: 1234-2002

# CONTENTS

## Symbols

### Flower Size

 Large: 3.5–6.5 inches
(9–16 cm)

Medium: 2–3 inches
(5–8 cm)

Small: 0.75–1.5 inches
(2–4 cm)

### Flower Shape

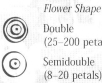 Double
(25–200 petals)

Semidouble
(8–20 petals)

Single
(fewer than 7 petals)

### Type of Flowering

Reflowering

Not reflowering

Perpetual flowering

### Fragrance*

Slight

Moderate

Strong

*Absence of a symbol means the rose is
without scent.

## NOTE TO THE READER

Gardening is not an exact science, and although the information in this book is both accurate and up-to-date, it can only offer guidelines. The size and behavior of a rose and the color of its flowers depend in large part on the quality and nature of the soil in which it is planted, on the fertilizers and treatments it is given and even on the water; the quality of the original stock is also of importance. The rose's fragrance is affected by heat and humidity. The time of flowering depends on climate.

### Rose Names

Plants are given botanical names based on the binomial system of classification created by the Swedish naturalist Carolus Linnaeus. This system gives each plant a Latin name composed of two parts: The first is the genus to which the plant belongs (all roses are in the genus Rosa); the second is the species (such as canina); if there is a third Latin name, it denotes a subspecies (Rosa canina inermis). An x inserted between the genus and species names indicates a hybrid or a sport, an artificial or spontaneous cross between two species.

The cultivars (cultivated varieties) created by hybridizers since the 19th century bear registered coded names and are protected by copyright to prevent unauthorized reproduction. The coded name usually includes the first three letters of the name of the hybridizer or the company that put the rose on the market: Meiviolin (Meilland), Harubasil (Harkness), Barlev (Barni), Ausvelvet (Austin). When they are put on the market, these plants are given fanciful names that appear between single quotation marks. The made-up names are sometimes odd, sometimes evocative. Roses have been dedicated to film stars, to leading lights of politics, science and culture and even to heroes and heroines of novels and plays: 'Toulouse Lautrec,' 'Charles de Gaulle,' 'Hiawatha,' 'Shakespeare,' 'Ophelia.' And then there are the likes of 'Nostalgia,' 'Old Port' and 'Marmalade Mist' as well as those named for their creators or for relatives of their creators: 'Albéric Barbier,' 'Papa Meilland.'

## ACKNOWLEDGMENTS

The author and editor wish to thank the Associazione Italiana della Rosa, David Austin, Vittorio Barni, Peter Beales, André Eve, W. Kordes and Antonio Pennati for their kind help in providing illustrations for this book.

# PREFACE

Roses are the world's most talked about flowers. They are the unrivaled heroines and centers of attention in any garden. Stacks of books and magazines relate the stages of the rose's long history, provide rules and guidelines for keeping roses healthy and describe in abundant detail the thousands upon thousands of varieties that have been created. Without doubt, enormous pleasure can be derived from investigating the nooks and crannies of the personal life of this flower, getting to know it intimately.

But there is one point that should be cleared up before all others. Of all the many roses, which do we want to plant in our gardens? Answering that question is the primary aim of this book. Anyone who wants to buy, plant and learn about a rose, or many roses, always has his or her special problem: "I need a small rose for a small garden," "I have three planters on my balcony; are there any roses I could put in them?" "I want a large hedge that is always in flower," "I want a big yellow rose."

This book has been organized according to the practical needs of cultivation, making it simple to locate the answers to all such questions. The roses are divided on the basis of the uses to which they are best put in a garden: roses that climb and ramble; roses for beds, borders and hedges; roses for espalier and groundcover; roses for patios and balconies.

Each rose described in the book has its own "identity card," a description of its characteristics and needs accompanied by one or more color photographs. Since not all cultivars are available everywhere, good alternative selections are given for each rose, thus greatly enlarging the already vast selection presented in the book. In some cases, suggestions are made for roses or other flowers that make good garden companions.

This detailed rose-by-rose treatment is preceded by an introduction that includes a brief history of the rose from antiquity to today—certainly the most fascinating flower history there is—and a guide to the techniques of rose cultivation, from buying plants to soil preparation, fertilizers, pruning, methods of propagation and measures for handling diseases and insect pests.

Those who wish to learn more can begin with the classification of roses at the back of the book, in which all the classes of roses are listed—antique roses and many of the more recent creations. Also given are names and addresses of leading nurseries from which roses can be bought.

# INTRODUCTION

# A LOOK AT THE PAST

## WILD ROSES AND THE CULTIVATION OF ROSES FROM ANTIQUITY TO THE 18TH CENTURY

There are about 150 species roses, meaning those that grow in the wild. Of these, 95 are indigenous to Asia, 18 to North America, about 20 to Europe and a few others to northern Africa. The highest concentration, fully 85 percent, is found between western China and the mountainous regions of the Himalayas. Among the most important of these are *Rosa gallica, canina, sempervirens, arvensis, villosa, rubrifolia, eglanteria* and *pimpinellifolia.*

These wild roses are not, however, the roses that grow in our gardens. The roses we cultivate are the result of the ongoing efforts of humans, the fruit of scientific operations, products that come to us signed by their creators and protected by trademarks.

### Origins

Wild roses were known to the Chinese 5,000 years ago. The ancient Egyptian queen Hatshepsut sent expeditions to the region of Punt in search of them. They were cultivated in the gardens of the Medes and the Persians. Between those roses and today's runs a long history full of adventure and travel. It is a history of research, experimentation, discovery and hard work. Knowing the broad outlines of this history will help you understand why roses are so different from other flowers and will also reveal some of the mystery behind their fascination.

Roses appeared on Earth during the Tertiary era, as indicated by the many fossil roses found in various areas of the world—the Baltic region, India, Oregon and Colorado. By about 2000 B.C., the history of the rose had become interwoven with the history of humans. Art, literature, poetry, myth and legend slowly took possession of the rose. Stories were invented to explain why roses were as white as sea foam or as red as blood; prophets, deities and kings were called on to explain the origin of roses or to help sing their beauty. The rose became a symbol. Vishnu, supreme divinity of Hinduism, created his bride using 108 large rose petals and 1,008 small ones. Roses decorate the stone jars of the Hittites and the friezes of the palaces of Nineveh; they appear around a blue bird in a fresco in the palace of Knossos. Homer describes Aphrodite anointing the body of Hector with oil of roses, and the shield of Achilles was adorned with roses. Rhodes, as its name indicates, is the island of roses. Sappho, the poet who delighted in weaving "soft garlands of roses and violets," was the first to call the rose the queen of flowers.

There is evidence that roses were being cultivated in China as early as 500 B.C.; according to Confucius, there were roses in the imperial gardens of the Chou Dynasty. The ancient Greeks also grew roses, but it was the Romans who exalted them and set them on their path to future fame. The Romans adored them. The well-to-do had the floors of their banquet halls carpeted with rose petals or had them rain down from the ceiling onto their dinner guests; roses were strewn

*Opposite: detail of the David Austin rose garden in Albrighton, England.*

*Ancient designs based on the rose: top, from the hem of a gown worn by a statue of Artemis from Ephesus; above, from a Hittite stone cup from Elbistan, Turkey.*

Rosebud depicted on a Chaldean jar, or krater.

Above: rosette from a detail of a temple dedicated to Demeter at Eleusis; center: rosette from a fragment of the palace of Knossos on Crete; right: double rose on the Tudor coat of arms.

over city streets so that the feet of emperors would not have to come into contact with the ground; they were thrown into baths to perfume the water and used to decorate homes. Hedges encircled Roman gardens. The Romans cultivated roses with such enthusiasm that they had to import plants from Egypt to meet the enormous demand.

## Science and Legend

Throughout history, scholars, botanists and historians have written about roses. Herodotus refers to a "60-petaled" rose that grew in Macedonia in the garden of King Midas; it was probably a damask. Virgil speaks of *Rosa* x *bifera*, the autumn damask, as the "twice-bearing rose" of Paestum (a former Greek colony in southern Italy). Pliny described many types of rose: the rose of Praeneste and the rose of Miletus, the same one Linnaeus later called the gallica; the rose of Campania with its pale, scented flowers and glaucous leaves, an alba; the rose of Paestum; and a rose with "a hundred petals," probably once again the damask.

The most scientific among the early writers was the Greek Theophrastus. He even provided important advice on cultivation, recommending the elimination of deadwood to improve flowering and the use of cuttings as a more rapid and effective method of propagation than seeding.

In Roman times, the rose was surrounded by an aura of luxury exaggerated almost to the level of depravity, and like the rest of Roman culture, it followed step by step the decline of the empire. With the fall of the Roman Empire, the rose, too, fell into a dark age.

Like other aromatic and medicinal herbs, the rose ended up in the cloistered gardens of monasteries. The most important rose of this period was probably the pharmacist's rose, *Rosa gallica officinalis*, which was believed to possess many medicinal properties.

All this time, the Persians had been embellishing their gardens with roses, placing them alongside splashing fountains; such Persian poets as Omar Khayyám sang praises to the beauty of the rose and the sweetness of its fragrance. By the close of the first millennium, vast areas of Syria were being used to grow the damask rose, the essence of which, as reported by the philosopher and physician Avicenna, was extracted to create attar. As the Arabs extended their dominion over the regions of the Mediterranean world, they took the rose with them. Thus the rose reached Morocco, invaded Spain and triumphed in the gardens of the Alhambra. The Crusades brought the rose from the Middle East to Europe; the gallica conquered France, most of all in the region of Provins, to the south of Paris, which became a center of its cultivation. Both the gallica and the alba crossed the English Channel to take root in England.

By then, the image of the rose had begun to undergo some changes. No longer merely an aspect of luxury and pleasure, it was taking on symbolic value. The red rose became a symbol of passion, the white of innocence. Christianity took hold of this in representations of the Virgin Mary, the mystic rose, pure love. In Dante's *Divine Comedy*, the heavenly host of the blessed are given the form of a pale rose. The dukes of York and Lancaster chose white and red roses as the emblems for their warring houses.

## An Irresistible Rise

The queen of flowers was coming into her own. Nothing stood in her way as her emblematic power grew and expanded in art and in daily life. The rose appeared in the stained-glass windows of cathedrals, in jewels, on coins, in friezes, in tapestries, in paintings, in books of hours, in chivalric romances and in the poetry of love. It stood for beauty and youth, fragility and chastity.

Precisely which roses were known to the Europeans and used in their gardens is unclear until the time of the Renaissance. Dioscorides, the ancient Greek physician, makes many references to *Rosa gallica officinalis*. William Turner, known as the father of English botany, describes several varieties; John Gerard grew nine types in his garden and described sixteen in his *Herbal*, the compendium of Renaissance botany. But the definitive and most reliable text of the period was *Paradisus Terrestris* by John Parkinson, in which 24 roses are described, including the date of their introduction, and many are illustrated, although sometimes under other names than those we use today: *Rosa gallica*, simple and double, *alba*, *incarnata*, *damascena* and *damascena versicolor*, *francofurtensis*, *moschata*, *lutea*, *cinnamomea* and *sempervirens*. Parkinson also refers to *R. spinosissima* and mentions a rose only recently arrived from America, *R. virginiana*.

A different rose made its appearance in the 16th century; it had a hundred petals (centifolia), and the flowers were so heavy that they bent back languidly onto the petioles. The guarantor of its existence was Gerard, who called this rose the Grand Rose of Holland, or the Provence Rose. In fact, the Dutch and French, having recognized the enormous commercial potential of the centifolias, dedicated themselves to the serious work of

Rosa centifolia (hollandica), from *John Gerard's* Herbal *(1597).*

crossing species, giving birth to the profession of hybridization. Between 1580 and 1710, the Dutch alone seem to have created 200 varieties. At the end of the 17th century, the moss roses came into being, mutations of the centifolias; their great moment would arrive later, in the Victorian age.

At the close of the 1700s, the château of Malmaison, near Paris, became a setting of central importance to the cultivation of roses. There, Empress Josephine dedicated herself to spreading the popularity of the rose. Her personal collection included 167 types, many of them gallicas, a collection known to us through the stupendous images created by Pierre-Joseph Redouté, the empress's painter.

## A Marriage of East and West

The Chinese were likely the first to cultivate flowers in their gardens, although roses were far less popular in the East than were chrysanthemums and peonies. The only source we have for this is Confucius, who aside from reporting that there were roses in the imperial gardens of Peking, says that the emperor's library had 600 volumes on the subject. There must have been many varieties: We have ancient illustrations that show roses such as *Rosa laevigata*, *rugosa* and *banksiae*, which was called by the evocative name "fragrance woods." The most common rose in these gardens was almost certainly *R. odorata*, which has probably been cultivated for 2,000 years.

The exact history of Chinese roses is of less importance to our story than the dates and the consequences of their appearance in the West. The marriage of Oriental roses to those cultivated until then in the West led to the birth of the types of roses that dominated 19th-century gardens. Those roses in turn were the parents of all modern roses. The Chinese roses brought two important qualities to the western roses: reflowering (only the autumn damask was able to flower twice) and a brilliant red, much different from the dark violet-red of the gallica.

*Chinese rose in a watercolor (ca. 1800) by an anonymous artist in an album found in Canton.*

*Opposite: detail of a still life by H. Neergard, ca. 1850. Copenhagen, Staten Museum for Kunst.*

As early as 1733, a Chinese rose had appeared in a European herbal. In 1789, a rose arrived in England destined to take the name of 'Parson's Pink China' (the rose is also known as 'Old Blush,' among other names). In 1792, a captain of the East India Company brought home a red rose, 'Slater's Crimson China.' These were hybrids between *Rosa chinensis* and *R. gigantea*, and in texts, they are always cited as the "stud roses." To these, in 1810 and 1824 respectively, two more were added: 'Hume's Blush Tea-Scented China,' which was pink, and 'Park's Yellow Tea-Scented China,' both, of course, with the scent of tea.

*Top to bottom: 'Alfred de Dalmas,' 'Kazanlik,' 'Belle des Jardins.'*

*Opposite:* Rosa damascena, *painted by P.J. Redouté.*

## THE GREAT ROSE CLASSES OF THE 19TH CENTURY

The first result of the arrival of the Chinese roses was the birth of the Portland roses, named for a duchess who returned home to England from Italy with a red rose; another specimen of the same rose came into the possession of Monsieur Dupont, gardener to Empress Josephine.

The 'Duchess of Portland' rose, as it came to be called, was the object of immediate interest and study. Its origin seemed to involve a Chinese rose (although some experts strongly doubt it), a damask and a gallica. It eventually became the basis of a small family. The honor of being the parent goes to the 'Rose du Roi' from the gardens of St. Cloud.

Another, more important group is the Noisettes. Around the time 'Parson's Pink China' reached London, another specimen arrived in Louisiana. (Yet another ended up in the Indian Ocean on the island of Bourbon, today Réunion.) Around 1820, a South Carolina rice planter named John Champneys crossed it with *Rosa moschata*, and the resulting plant ('Champneys' Pink Cluster') ended up in the hands of his neighbor Philippe Noisette. Noisette sent it off to his brother Louis, who worked in Paris, which ultimately led to the birth of 'Blush Noisette,' one of the first of the group. Several others soon followed and quickly conquered Paris. A new class of rose had been born, delightful and exciting, with large bunches of small musk-scented flowers and great zeal for continuous flowering.

The third and most important group is the Bourbons. They made their appearance at the same time as the Noisettes and resulted from seeds sent to A. Jacques, gardener of the duc d'Orléans in Paris, by the director of the botanical garden of the island of Bourbon. The seeds had been collected from a rose that was probably a spontaneous cross between a descendant of 'Pink China' and one of the autumn damasks that grew in the garden in thick hedges. The most active French horticulturists of the period, such as Lacharme, Laffay and Garçon, recognized the importance of this event and got busy with the patient work of crossing the crosses. The results are splendid roses: highly scented, sensual and romantic, with rich flowers and guaranteed reflowering.

Yet another class is the tea roses, born in

*Rosa Damascena.*        *Rosier de Cels.*

*Rosa bifera officinalis.*　　　　*Rosier des Parfumeurs.*

P.J. Redouté pinx.　　　　Imprimerie de Rémond　　　　Langlois sculp.

Europe from the two Chinese hybrids imported early in the century, 'Hume's Blush Tea-Scented China' and 'Park's Yellow Tea-Scented China,' varieties of *Rosa* x *odorata*, which was probably a hybrid of *R. chinensis* and *R. gigantea*. These roses came to be called tea roses in Europe because of their fragrance and also because they were brought to Europe on the same ships that bore that other precious cargo.

Because of the beautiful shape of their flowers, their strong scent and the delicacy of their colors, the tea roses came to be highly valued in the more temperate zones of Europe. According to the catalog of the horticulturist Despotes, 27 varieties were created between 1821 and 1830; by the year 1900, when they gave way to more robust descendants, the hybrid teas, they had come to number 1,382. Of these, 188 were attributed to Nabonnand, Laffay was credited with almost 400 varieties, and several important ones go to the Englishman William Paul, creator of the celebrated 'Ophelia' and author of an important catalog, *The Rose*.

## New Hybrids

Today, roses are available in enormous variety, highly diversified and inviting; there are all these remarkable classes, and other roses have meanwhile arrived from the Orient and from the Americas: *Rosa multiflora, wichuraiana, rugosa, banksiae* and *bracteata*.

Hybridizers have dedicated themselves to the enormous and still somewhat mysterious process of hybridization. Thanks to the science of genetics, the techniques of cross-breeding have been increasingly perfected. As the work has become more scientific, greater care has been dedicated to the process; all possibilities of interference are excluded, so family lines are defined with greater accuracy. Breeders experiment, putting this plant together with that, always with the aim of obtaining roses that are more vibrant, more beautiful, more heavily scented, better at reflowering and more robust.

Production has become large-scale, and the different classes of roses, now mixed up together, have begun to lose their natures. The roses obtained by hybridizers often come without clear characteristics. Efforts are made to keep things in order, to catalog and classify, so when various new roses seem to possess similar characteristics, the authorities decide that a new class has been born. This is what happened with the hybrid perpetuals, a group that is not completely homogeneous but does have one important common characteristic. The first dates to 1837, the most recent to 1900, and they represent the bridge between 19th-century roses and roses classified as "modern." The parent plant is 'Rose de la Reine,' created by Laffay in 1842.

The new hybrid perpetuals reaped immediate success. They quickly came to dominate contests, becoming the vogue roses of the second half of the 19th century. They took over gardens and delighted an increasingly large public with their scent, showy blossoms and robustness.

*Opposite:* Rosa x bifera (autumn damask), also called 'Quatre Saisons,' painted by P.J. Redouté.

## Hybrid Teas

The first of the modern roses were the hybrid teas, whose history begins in the 19th century. Although they are conventionally said to have begun with the creation of 'La France' by J. G. Gullot in 1867, it seems more logical to date them back to a rose with a more definite character, such as 'Madame Caroline Testout' of 1890, a rose that enjoyed great

fame and popularity in its time, existed in hundreds and hundreds of specimens and is still found in gardens. Essentially, a hybrid tea is a rose born of the seed of a tea crossed with a rose from another class, most frequently one of the hybrid perpetuals. The enthusiastic descriptions of hybrid teas in books and catalogs and their enormous popularity have fixed their image as the classic, ideal rose. And for many people, the hybrid tea has held onto that role to this day. Its most striking characteristics are the stupendous shape of the bud, the typical high-centered flower held high at the end of a long stem, the ever-blooming habit and the extraordinary variety of colors, the shades of which have gradually become quite sophisticated.

Owing to the work of Pernet Ducher, father of the Pernettian roses, for which he used *Rosa foetida*, the hybrid teas possess the brilliant yellow that was missing in other classes. The only color now lacking is the true blue that roses can never have because their genetic code does not include delphinine, the necessary pigment.

## Floribundas

The most cultivated roses in our century besides the hybrid teas are the floribundas. They began with crosses made with *Rosa multiflora* (or *polyantha*) and two varieties obtained from these by Gullot in Lyons, 'Pâquerette' and 'Mignonette,' which gave birth to a group of roses called the Polypoms.

No sooner had botanists identified sufficient common elements in about 200 subjects than they declared them to be a new class, baptized dwarf polyanthas: small bushes with very small flowers in pretty bunches, very floriferous and vigorous. Danish hybridizer Svend Poulsen crossed polyanthas with hybrid teas to obtain such crosses as 'Else Poulsen' and 'Kirsten Poulsen,' which attracted enthusiastic

*Top:'Westerland'; bottom: 'Princesse de Monaco.'*

recognition. Many horticulturists soon followed Poulsen's example, creating interesting roses, hybrids of polyanthas, which for greater clarity and in honor of their extraordinary flowering, have come to be called floribundas. Over the course of the last century, they became legion, second in number and popularity only to the hybrid teas. There was nothing surprising about their success: More versatile than the hybrid teas, easier to place in the garden, easier to cultivate, highly

22

colored, always in flower and with a better-shaped shrub, they fully deserved their popularity. All the greatest hybridizers competed in the creation of the most, the best, the most beautiful: Le Grice, Dickson, Harkness, Kordes, Tantau and the Americans Boerner, Lammerts, Swim and many others.

## Other Roses

What other roses compete with these two popular classes for a place in our gardens? Today we are seeing a return to the antique roses. As for modern roses, the selection has become truly enormous. There is the great number of roses known generically as modern shrub roses, a miscellaneous grouping of roses of diverse origin, often with spectacular flowers, that can be placed in all areas of the garden except for beds. There are also the miniature roses, ideal for balconies and small terraces.

*'La Rossa.'*

Two categories of steadily increasing interest are the groundcover roses and the patio roses. The groundcovers originated with roses that are prostrate by nature, such as *Rosa rugosa* 'Max Graf,' which was developed in the United States in 1919, and the Japanese *R. wichuraiana.* The patio roses are all small roses. They are robust, take up little space and are wonderfully graceful. Climbers and ramblers have attracted increasing interest because the vertical dimension is needed in any garden but is particularly necessary in small ones, and vertical roses are often far easier to grow in the limited space of a balcony. Climbers have large flowers and dependable reflowering; almost all of them are modern, for they create the most effect and offer the most color. Ramblers are almost equally valued, being more adaptable, more discreet and more natural.

## Antique Roses or Modern Roses?

Even among rose lovers, one finds partisan disputes. In particular is the dividing line between the supporters of antique roses and the fans of the modern. In antique roses, the bloom is ephemeral but delicate, emotionally moving, scented; the bushes have a more natural and freer growth habit. Modern roses offer reflowering and brightly colored flowers in a wide range of colors, but their shrubs are more rigid and angular. There is one very easy solution to the problem, of course: Plant both kinds. From among the first group, take the best that is offered, such as the Bourbons; from among the second, select the roses that best preserve the beauty of the past, such as the English roses.

# CULTIVATION

## BUYING ROSES

The best time to buy roses is between early spring and early summer, but you can buy the plants in pots and bring them home at any time of the year except the coldest months of the winter. Even so, experts agree that you'll get the best results by doing your planting in autumn and buying rosebushes with bare roots or in plastic containers with the roots wrapped in a material that guarantees good preservation. Growers usually make shipments in the fall. Buying plants that have been in containers for too long is not recommended, since the roots lose vitality and the plants may have difficulty getting established.

It is of paramount importance that you buy the plants from a nursery that specializes in roses and is known for being dedicated and professional. Buying from such nurseries guarantees not only the quality and healthy state of the plant but also its authenticity, meaning that you can be sure it comes from good stock.

## CLIMATE, POSITION AND SOIL

Roses grow wild over a vast area of the world, including the northern hemisphere, the temperate zones and the Mediterranean. All varieties of roses can be grown in those areas, the spontaneous varieties and hybrids as well as those created by humans. The areas where roses won't grow are those with extreme temperatures—regions with tropical climates, which are too humid and too warm, and those with very cold climates. Altitude is also important; for example, roses can flourish in equatorial zones provided they are grown in gardens as high as 6,500 feet (2,000 m). The ideal climate for roses is one in which the summer is not too hot, winter temperatures do not dip below 10 degrees F (–12 degrees C), the rain is intermittent, and the humidity

*A healthy plant needs at least three main branches, a reasonably thick bud union where the graft is, and a well-developed root system.*

24

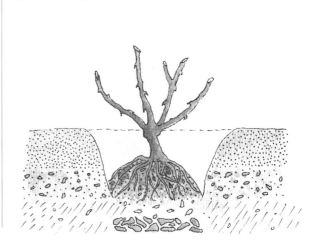

*Right: planting a shrub rose with bare roots.*

is moderate. Roses are usually best positioned in full sun, but in areas with warm, dry summers it is best to locate them in half-shade, protected by light branches of trees. Some roses will grow in partial shade, places that receive sun for only part of the day, but they can never be grown in total shade; in such positions, they grow foliage but do not flower. Roses are equally tolerant in terms of the soil they're planted in, which can be either alkaline or acidic, provided that the extremes of either are avoided. The ideal soil has a pH of 6.5 (7 is neutral; higher numbers mean that the soil is alkaline). Overly acidic soil will prevent proper growth, and in overly alkaline soil, which is calcareous or clayey, the plants will suffer iron chlorosis, a condition marked by precocious yellowing of the leaves followed by leaf fall. As for the type of soil, the best is one with a medium mixture—when squeezed in the palm of the hand, it remains compact, forming a ball.

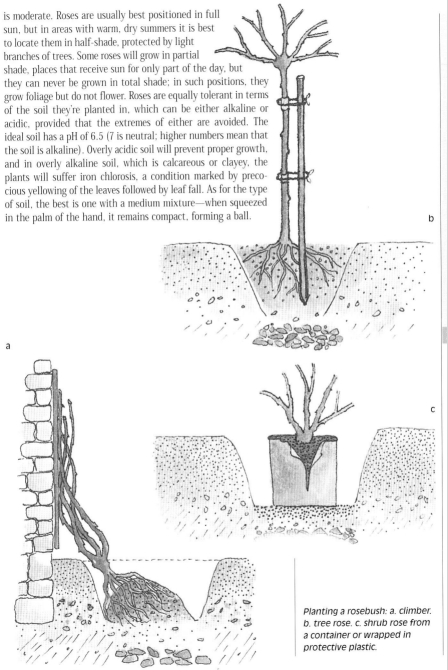

a

b

c

Planting a rosebush: a. climber. b. tree rose. c. shrub rose from a container or wrapped in protective plastic.

# SELECTING ROSES FOR POSITION AND CLIMATE

| ANTIQUE ROSES | Partial shade | Temperate climates or on verandas | Cold climates |
|---|---|---|---|
| BOTANICAL SPECIES AND THEIR VARIETIES | *Rosa arvensis, bracteata, brunonii, californica, canina, ecae, eglanteria (rubiginosa), farreri persetosa (elegantula* 'Persetosa'), *filipes, glauca, helenae,* x *kordesii, laevigata, micrugosa, moschata* and its hybrids, *pimpinellifolia, rugosa, sempervirens, virginiana* | *Rosa banksiae, bracteata, brunonii,* 'Canary Bird,' *R. laevigata* and its hybrids, 'Mermaid,' *R. murtola* | *Rosa pimpinellifolia* and its hybrids |
| GALLICAS | Moderate shade, in particular: 'Assemblage des Beautés,' 'Complicata,' 'Empress Josephine,' 'Sissinghurst Castle' | | |
| DAMASKS | 'Kazanlik' | | |
| ALBAS | All | | All |
| CHINESE | 'Mutabilis,' 'Old Blush' | 'Anna Maria de Montravel,' 'Cécile Brünner,' 'Comtesse du Cayla,' 'Hermosa,' 'Madame Laurette Messimy,' 'Perle d'Or' | |
| PORTLANDS | 'Jacques Cartier,' 'Rose de Rescht' | | 'Rose de Rescht' |
| BOURBONS | 'Gipsy Boy,' 'Great Western,' 'Kathleen Harrop,' 'Honorine de Brabant,' 'Louise Odier,' 'Madame Isaac Pereire,' 'Zéphirine Drouhin' | | |
| NOISETTES | All those with small flowers; 'Desprez à Fleurs Jaunes' | Large-flowered: 'Céline Forestier,' 'Cloth of Gold,' 'Desprez à Fleurs Jaunes,' 'Maréchal Neil,' 'Madame Alfred Carrière,' 'Rêve d'Or' | |
| TEAS | | 'Anna Olivier,' 'Archiduc Joseph,' 'Belle Lyonnaise,' 'Devoniensis,' 'Duchesse de Brabant,' 'Gloire de Dijon,' 'Lady Hillingdon,' Madame Jules Gravereaux,' 'Niphetos,' 'Rosette Delizy,' 'Safrano,' 'Sombreuil,' 'Souvenir d'un Ami' | |
| HYBRID PERPETUALS | | 'Mrs. John Laing,' 'Paul Neyron' | 'Dupuy Jamain' |

| MODERN ROSES | Partial shade | Temperate climates or on verandas | Cold climates |
|---|---|---|---|
| FLORIBUNDAS | 'Escapade,' 'Glenfiddich,' 'Iceberg,' 'Lichtkönigin Lucia,' 'Mountbatten' | 'Apricot Nectar,' 'Dearest,' 'Elizabeth of Glamis,' 'Fragrant Delight,' 'Trumpeter,' 'Sexy Rexy' | |
| HYBRID TEAS | | 'Anna Pavlova,' 'Etoile de Hollande,' 'Kordes Perfecta,' 'Ophelia,' 'Pascali,' 'Peace,' 'Peer Gynt,' 'Royal Sunset,' 'Silver Jubilee,' 'Sir Frederick Ashton,' 'Sonia,' 'Super Star,' 'Sweet Surrender,' 'Virgo' | |
| SHRUB ROSES | 'Fritz Nobis,' 'Pearl Drift,' 'Red Blanket,' 'Rokoko,' 'Rosy Cushion,' 'Yesterday' | | 'Bonica 82' |
| GROUNDCOVER AND PATIO ROSES | 'Grouse,' 'Little White Pet,' 'Smarty,' 'Swany,' 'The Fairy,' 'Yvonne Rabier' | | 'Nozomi,' 'Sea Foam' |
| CLIMBERS | 'Clair Matin,' 'Constance Spry,' 'Danse du Feu,' 'Golden Showers,' 'Gloire de Dijon,' 'New Dawn,' 'Parade,' 'Pink Perpétue,' 'Souvenir du Dr. Jamain' | 'Étoile de Hollande' | 'Alchymist' |
| RAMBLERS BASED ON ROSA MULTIFLORA | 'Bleu Magenta,' 'Bobbie James,' 'Francis E. Lester,' 'Ghislaine de Féligonde,' 'Rambling Rector,' 'Seagull,' 'The Garland,' 'Veilchenblau,' 'Violette' | 'Lauré Davoust' | |
| RAMBLERS BASED ON ROSA WICHURAIANA | 'Albéric Barbier,' 'Alexander Girault,' 'American Pillar,' 'Crimson Shower,' 'Débutante,' 'Gardenia,' 'Gerbe Rose,' 'May Queen' | | |
| SHRUBS, CLIMBERS AND GROUNDCOVERS CREATED BY KORDES | | | 'Dortmund,' 'Flammentanz,' 'Friesia,' 'Ilse Krohn Superior,' 'Lavaglut,' 'Mariandel,' 'Rokoko,' 'Rosarium Uetersen,' 'Sommerwind,' 'The Times Rose' |
| RUGOSAS | | | All |

## Planting and Drainage

The first step in planting a rosebush is to dig a hole. The hole should be wide and deep; for a medium-size bush, it should be 20 inches deep and 20 inches in diameter (50 x 50 cm) and, for a large bush, 32 inches deep and 24 inches in diameter (80 x 60 cm). Mix plenty of compost into the soil taken from the hole or use a prepared soil mixture that already contains fertilizer; add a good dose of bone meal. Form a little mound at the bottom of the hole, and rest the bush on it so that the roots are fully spread and have room to grow. Shovel over the roots the soil you've set aside or the prepared soil mixture, being careful to leave the bud union, or graft, just barely covered. Press down firmly with your feet to remove any air pockets around the roots, and water abundantly. Repeat the watering over the next few days.

All new rose plants should be cut back, even if they appear to have been pruned when you buy them, because it is important that they achieve good root growth before the foliage starts growing.

Whether planted in the garden or in containers, roses need good drainage; stagnant water damages their roots. If your soil has a heavy clay content, dig the hole deeper than usual, and line the bottom with pebbles or shards of crockery or bricks.

## Transplanting an Old Rosebush

You can transplant a rosebush with relative ease even if it's a few years old. Moving a mature climber or rambler will prove quite difficult, of course, given the size of the growth and the number of branches. Whatever kind of rose it is, moving it is a task to perform in early spring, before the plant has begun its new growth. The absolutely necessary first step is to cut back the top growth of the plant, drastically pruning away the branches and also cutting off a good part of the fibrous root mass. Use delicacy, and be sure to cover the roots with fresh soil, soft and full of humus, tamping it down all around the plant. Water generously, and repeat the watering over the following days.

## Rose Sickness

Rose sickness is a condition of the soil; the term refers to the difficulty sometimes encountered when trying to grow a rose where another has grown for several years. The scientific explanation seems to involve antibodies in the soil that keep new roots from taking hold. To avoid the problem, the soil in which a rose has been growing should be allowed to rest for three to four years before a new rose is planted in the same place. Of course, if the garden is large enough, you can avoid the problem by alternating the areas used for roses. But there are ways to get around it altogether. The simplest way is to replace the soil, digging a very wide, deep hole—at least 32 inches (80 cm) deep—and filling it with new soil blended with plenty of compost. If you have mechanical means available—ideally a backhoe—you could remove quite a large area of soil, fill the hole with new soil and plant the area with new rosebushes. Rose expert John Mattock suggests yet another way to avoid rose sickness—plant annuals of the *Tagetes* genus (such as marigolds), and when they reach the end of their growing cycle, incorporate them into the soil to disinfect it.

## Watering

Roses are not fond of being dry, although several recently created varieties show more tolerance than others. The amount of water you should give your roses will depend on the season, the amount of rain and the temperature. From spring to autumn, the soil should not be allowed to stay dry for long. When watering, be sure to use enough water to pen-

etrate the soil all the way down to the deep taproots, which absorb most of the moisture. The best times of day for watering are early morning before the sun climbs too high and evening around sunset. Direct the water at the ground; a good rule is to avoid wetting the leaves, since wet leaves can create the kind of humidity in which the spores of fungal diseases proliferate. If you can't avoid wetting the leaves, do your watering early enough to give the leaves time to dry in the daytime because the spores find conditions favorable for reproduction during the night. As the growing season draws to a close, excessive watering can increase the growth of weak foliage that can be winter-killed. Plants in containers should be watered more often than those in garden soil.

*Roses protected with coarse mulch, left, and with low-growing plants, right.*

## Mulch

In nature, soil is almost never bare for very long. The same should be true of the soil in gardens. In place of grass or weeds, leaves or snow, garden soil can be covered with a protective layer of mulch. The practice of mulching, of particular importance in warm, dry temperate climates, involves covering the soil around the base of roses and other plants in order to limit evaporation and erosion as much as possible and to control the growth of weeds; aside from these reasons, there are also aesthetic concerns.

Winter mulch, applied at the onset of the cold season, should be of well-rotted manure or fertilizer. Spread it around the base of each

*Indications of mineral deficiencies. a. Lack of potassium: the young leaves are reddish, the margins of mature leaves become fragile and dry, buds fail to open, flowers are misshapen. Caused by overly sandy soil. b. Lack of iron: loss of color due to lack of chlorophyll, yellowing of leaves (chlorosis). Caused by excess lime in soil. c. Lack of manganese: leaves yellow but veins remain green. Caused by excess calcium in soil.*

plant after carefully raking the soil and removing dry leaves. Besides serving as a mulch, this is also part of the plant's nutrition program, because you will work it into the soil in spring.

Shortly after the spring reawakening, after the manure or fertilizer has been worked into the soil and the prescribed amount of spring fertilizer applied, it is time to cover the soil with a mulch of organic matter: straw and the remains of plant material, including partially decomposed pieces of branches from pruning, leaf compost and wood shavings. From all points of view, including the aesthetic, the best mulch is well mixed and finely broken up. Of course, the material should be completely free of poisonous chemicals—shavings of chemically treated wood as well as grass clippings and other materials that may contain herbicides. Furthermore, if plant material is used, take care that it does not include the seeds of weeds or other invasive plants.

Another way to cover the soil around rosebushes and keep it fresh is to plant prostrate, or ground-cover, plants in the area. Well suited to this use are bugleweed (*Ajuga reptans*), which has metallic foliage and purple flowers; speedwell (*Veronica prostrata*) and Siberian bugloss (*Brunnera macrophylla*), with its pretty minute foliage, both with blue flowers; lily-of-the-valley and strawberries, with white flowers; creeping jenny, or moneywort (*Lysimachia nummularia*), with yellow flowers, which should be planted near white or yellow roses; periwinkle, violets and sweet alyssum (*Lobularia maritima*), with white, yellow or violet flowers; and even creeping thyme (*Thymus serpyllum*).

### Fertilizers and Compost

An abundant application of well-rotted manure at planting time and once a year afterward early in the autumn is the type of fertilization roses need most. It will also be necessary to add fertilizer to supply the vitamins and trace elements necessary to the well-being of the plant and to good growth and flowering. Large numbers of suitable products are available on the market, and many of them are specifically for roses. Slow-release and water-soluble fertilizers are the most useful.

The principal elements necessary for the cultivation of roses are nitrogen (in the form of nitrogen compounds), phosphorus (in the form of phosphates) and potassium. Nitrogen helps in plant growth, but an excess will cause excessively green, unnatural coloration and abundant foliage growth but few flowers. Phosphorus is involved in the formation of healthy root growth. Potassium helps the plants absorb iron and favors resistance to drought, cold and disease. The normal

a

b

c

proportion of these three elements in a good fertilizer is 1 part nitrogen, 1 part phosphorus and 2 parts potassium.

Other essential elements include iron, which helps maintain the good appearance and health of the leaves; it should be applied in the form of iron chelates, especially in alkaline soil, to avoid chlorosis, or green sickness. Magnesium is also necessary for maintaining healthy branches. Plants that show an inclination to disease should be treated with applications of potassium and magnesium (5 parts potassium to 1 part magnesium). Trace elements are present only in tiny amounts, but they are no less necessary for the health of plants because they carry out important functions in many vital processes; they include boron, manganese, molybdenum and zinc. Sulfur is another; a lack of it shows up in excessive branching of roots and poor formation of buds, which become woody and fail to open. A lack of calcium shows up only in highly acidic soils; this should be corrected by adding calcareous material; the most striking symptoms of calcium deficiency are leaves that droop, hanging limply as though thirsty, and poor bud growth.

A good program of nutrition includes two annual applications of fertilizer containing all the elements mentioned above—as granules, liquid or powder—once at the beginning of spring before applying mulch and again right after the first, most abundant flowering. An application of potassium sulfate at the end of winter or the beginning of spring will help the roses resist disease. Always welcome and helpful for improving the structure of the soil are such old-style fertilizers as bone and fish meal; these can be applied to the base of each bush and worked into the soil slightly at planting time and in spring.

## Deadheading

Removing faded or spent flowers is an operation of fundamental importance that many people, unfortunately, tend to overlook. Deadheading frees the plant of useless weight and urges it to prepare for new flowering. Obviously, this applies to reflowering roses; no other roses, in particular those that produce decorative hips, should be deadheaded.

The best course of action is to cut the spent flowers off below the first three complete leaves (a, page 32); you can make the cut lower if the flower stems are particularly long. If the bush is on its first flowering, it is best to cut off only the stem bearing the flower in order to avoid depriving the plant, still not fully developed, of too

*d. Lack of magnesium (infrequent): leaves yellow at the center with areas of dryness, reduced leaf size. e. Lack of phosphorus: insufficient growth of canes and buds, purple spots on lower sides of leaves. f. Lack of nitrogen: overly pale leaves, poor foliage growth.*

a–b. *Points at which spent flowers can be deadheaded.*

many leaves. With many roses, especially those that are very quick to repeat their bloom—groundcover types, shrub roses such as 'Red Coat' and floribundas such as 'Class Act' and 'Iceberg'—the best place to cut the stem will be apparent because the plant will already have developed new buds to produce future blooms. In roses that bear flowers in large corymbs, such as 'The Fairy,' 'Surrey,' 'Essex' and 'Little White Pet,' the entire flower stem should be removed (b).

At the end of the flowering season, ramblers, meaning roses that do not produce hips, will be covered with hundreds of spent flowers that look like pitiful rags. Rather than trying to cut these off with shears, which would be a superhuman undertaking, you can get rid of them simply by blasting them off with a hose.

### Blind Shoots and Suckers

Blind shoots (or blind wood) are canes, often vigorous, that grow very tall but do not produce flowers. Many reasons have been given for this behavior, but in truth, there is no single explanation. Some roses send out blind shoots more readily than others (among the English roses, for example, are 'Gertrude Jekyll,' 'Graham Thomas,' 'Sweet Juliet' and 'Brother Cadfael'), and the phenomenon is more frequent in places with warm temperate climates than where summers are cool. Just as there is no agreement on the causes of blind shoots, there is no agreement on what do about them, even when they develop to such a degree that they threaten to unbalance a plant without offering any possible advantage. Many experts simply ignore the problem. Indeed, one possible solution is to leave them be and give them support as needed, despite the fact that they may spoil the appearance of the shrub. The most drastic and effective response is to cut them off at the base, but doing so goes against the advice that it will damage the plant if done during the summer, particularly in a region with a very warm climate. The one suggestion that must be ruled out is precisely the one most often given: cutting off the blind shoot halfway. Doing so may well relieve the bush of its unbalanced appearance, but the cut branches will be unproductive and will also generate more blind shoots.

Blind shoots are not to be confused with suckers, which are branches that grow from below the bud union, or graft, directly from the rootstock; they are easily recognized because they bear a different number of leaves than the plant and are very pale in color. Left to grow, they could eventually overwhelm the plant. They should be removed at the base, sliced off as close to the root as possible. Of course, this applies only to hybrid roses, those that are grafted onto rootstock.

Some species roses such as *Rosa gallica, pimpinellifolia* and *rugosa* tend to form new shoots from the roots. Sending out these shoots is the way the plant grows in width; the shoots will generate flowers of the same quality as the mother rose. They can be left alone or eliminated, depending on available space.

c

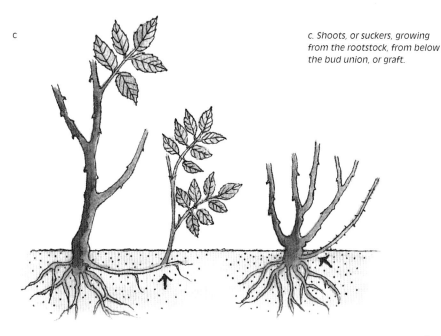

c. Shoots, or suckers, growing from the rootstock, from below the bud union, or graft.

## PRUNING

Pruning is without a doubt the most delicate and at the same time the most important single operation in the cultivation of roses. Wild roses have no need of pruning, but the roses we grow in gardens are highly sophisticated plants, manipulated by humans to increase the quality of their flowers, their ability to flower and the duration of their flowering. Pruning is necessary to maintain the desired qualities. With the passage of time, rosebushes tend to accumulate much wood, and if it is not removed, it can end up suffocating the plant and preventing good flowering. This is the first objective of pruning. The second is that of reducing the volume of the bush by cutting down the highest part, meaning all the canes that have produced flowers and need to be replaced. But it must always be kept in mind that with the exception of the hybrid teas and other roses cultivated in beds—whose size must be strictly controlled and which are grown expressly to produce high-quality flowers—it is never a good idea to struggle with a rose's natural inclination. Put simply, a rose is a bush like any other, and its structure should not be deformed merely to favor the production of flowers. It must also be said that pruning does not follow precise rules and is most of all a matter of common sense. It is more a matter of intuition than reason and leaves plenty of room for personal choice.

Roses are plants with widely differing origins and characters, and each type or class requires a different kind of pruning. This is one reason why it is a good idea to plant roses in groups according to

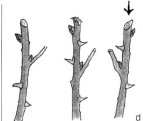

d. Make the cut with a sharp knife or secateurs. The cut should be clean, at an angle, about half an inch (1 cm) above a bud and directed outward. In the illustrations above, the arrow indicates the correct cut.

their common needs (such groupings also facilitate the application, when necessary, of chemical treatments particular to each type).

Some advice applies to all types of roses: Use very sharp secateurs because they will make a clean cut. This is important not only because work well done gives satisfaction but because a clean wound heals more rapidly. The cut should be made at an angle, because an angled cut is more likely to follow the arrangement of the cells, which is longitudinal, without cutting them in half; it also favors healing and prevents harmful elements such as fungus spores from collecting on the surface of the cut. The cut should be directed outward and made about half an inch (1 cm) above an outward-facing bud (d, page 33).

When to do your pruning? The advice here is valid for all plants: Never prune in winter. With regard to roses, it is a good idea to divide them into two categories: those which flower once and those which reflower. Those that flower once should be pruned at the end of the flowering period and reshaped at the end of winter, just before the spring awakening. With reflowering roses, the trend among experts today is to recommend a moderate pruning of the foliage at the end of autumn to prevent wind and extreme weather from breaking branches. In moderate and warm climates, the autumn pruning should be particularly modest so as to avoid stimulating the production of buds and shoots during a mild winter, for they would only be lost in the spring pruning. The real pruning is done at the end of winter, when there is no longer danger of frost but before the spring reawakening, usually between the end of January and March, according to the climate. It should be neither too late, when the buds are already elongated, nor too early, so as not to expose new growth to damage from a late cold spell.

Deadheading is itself a form of pruning, one that should be practiced all year long. For some small roses, it is all the pruning that will ever be needed.

## Antique and Shrub Roses

Antique roses, which have a single flowering and grow flowers on canes produced the preceding year, require far less drastic pruning

a. Pruning antique shrub roses.
b. Pruning hybrid teas.
c. Pruning floribundas.

a

b

c

than do modern roses. It should be quite light (a). The cuts have a triple aim: to remove deadwood, meaning branches too old to stimulate new growth; to eliminate branches growing in undesired directions, growing crooked or growing crosswise, as well as those that are too thin to produce flowers; and to shorten, cutting off a fifth to a third of the canes that have flowered in order to stimulate the growth of new canes that will flower the next year. This pruning should be performed at the end of the flowering season. Antique perpetuals such as Bourbons and hybrid perpetuals can be treated as floribundas, taking into consideration their larger size.

## Modern Roses

### Hybrid Teas and Floribundas

Hybrid teas, which are grown exclusively for their flowers, require drastic pruning (b); it is necessary to eliminate almost the entire bush, which often becomes angular, rigid and unattractive, by cutting the branches back to three to four buds from the ground. Doing so guarantees orderly growth of the bushes and copious flowering with blooms of maximum quality and size.

With floribundas, more moderate pruning is recommended (c), given that over time, this class of rose usually produces a graceful bush with good structure. The branches should be cut back by a third to half their height at most; always cut away branches that are old, damaged and thinner than a pencil as well as those that cross others. The finished bush should look round and well balanced from every side.

### English Roses and Modern Shrub Roses

These classes include roses that sometimes have very different shapes and habits. For those with upright habits, up to half the plant must be eliminated to maintain the desired compactness and to prevent the flowers from forming at too great a height (d). In the case of those with open habits and arching branches, the pruning should be relatively light, directed at maintaining the natural shape of the plant, shortening the canes only by a fifth or a quarter, although, as always,

*Pruning English roses and shrub roses. d. With upright habit. e. With open habit and arching branches. f. With very dense, bushy habit.*

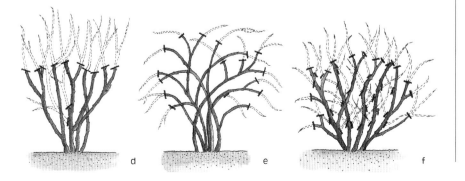

d          e          f

it will be necessary to cut out all canes that are too old in the hope of stimulating new growth (e, page 35). Finally, for roses that have dense, bushy habits and are packed with internal branches, the goal of pruning should be to clear out all the internal branches that cross or are too thin and to cut the bush back by a third to a half (f, page 35).

## Climbers

Modern reflowering climbers, especially those with large flowers, and the climbing forms of antique roses such as Bourbons and teas usually flower on side branches produced during the growing season, so the growth of those branches needs to be promoted.

When you plant the rose, fix the branches to a support or wall in such a way that they form a fan (a); the external branches should run in a direction almost horizontal to the ground so that flowering will take place in the lower areas, which tend to lack coverage. Over the coming years, it will be best not to prune the main branches but to gradually eliminate them entirely so that they will be replaced by new shoots (b–c). All the side branches, however, should be shortened by two to three buds. To carry out this operation, it is best to detach the plant from its support, prune it and then reattach the branches. The younger branches should not be touched; the more mature branches—the ones you are not eliminating—should be tied down horizontally so as to favor the growth of side branches that will flower on the lower part of the wall.

## Ramblers—Species and Their Varieties

Given the exuberant nature of these roses, it is best to let them grow without restrictions. Either they should not be pruned at all or they should be pruned for practical and aesthetic reasons, which means cutting away any parts of the plant that grow in inconvenient directions, are damaging one another, are poorly formed, diseased or excessively awkward. In general, you should not deadhead these roses, since they almost always produce colored hips that brighten up the autumn. *Rosa banksiae* types, which flower better as their wood ages, should never be touched. Leave them alone to grow into big, intertwined trees or

*Pruning climbers*
*a. Arrangement of branches at planting.*
*b. Arrangement of branches and pruning points two years after planting.*

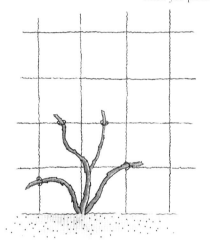

a

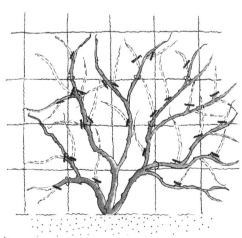

b

to stretch along the length of a wall until they become truly majestic. Hybrids of *R. eglanteria*, luxurious shrubs, should be allowed to grow like wild roses; they can be controlled by means of a noose wrapped around their lower branches (d). *R. rugosa*, too, prefers to be left in peace; if after a few years, a plant shows signs of exhaustion, you can cut it back very low to stimulate renewed growth.

## Polyanthas

This type of rose, with its continuous, very abundant flowering, is pruned practically all year by way of the process of deadheading. The deadheading applies both to those which produce single flowers and to those which produce flowers in bunches or corymbs. Nothing need be done before the spring awakening except clean the bush and prune it lightly.

## Miniature and Patio Roses

These roses, like the polyanthas, require little pruning, but since they are expected to flower only once, their branches should be cut back before the spring reawakening so that the flowering will occur at the desired height. Since they tend to accumulate a great many large and small interior branches, they also require a careful cleaning-out.

## Groundcover Roses

Groundcover roses that form low, orderly bushes can be treated in the same way as polyantha and miniature roses. For groundcover roses with long branches, there are two methods. You can leave the branches at their full length and cut away dry or damaged parts or branches that intertwine—a kind of pruning well suited to plants growing above walls or on low supports as well as those you want to cover the ground or are growing with their branches wrapped around one another to form a kind of flowering pillar (in which case, you will want to shorten or eliminate side branches). Or you can prune the plant short, leaving the branches at a height of about a foot (30 cm), treating them like bushes you want contained so that they will renew themselves every year.

*c. Removal of dead branches four to five years after planting to renew the bush.*
*d. How to tie hybrid eglanterias and musk roses to keep them orderly.*

## Rose Standards

Hybrid teas and floribundas grown as standards, or tree roses, should be pruned according to their class. If they are patio or miniature roses, the pruning will be drastic—leaving only three to four buds on the branches. If they are ramblers or ground-cover roses with long branches or shrub roses, the pruning should be limited to cleaning the plant and shortening any branches that grow in undesired directions.

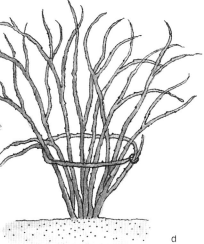

## Hybrid Musk Roses

The class of hybrid musks produces very long branches that tend to arch and bears flowers on both terminal and lateral corymbs. Careful deadheading, cutting back and elimination of the lateral canes as they flower will maintain flowering for the entire season. These roses should never be subjected to pruning that might alter their character, which is that of large, bushy shrubs. If cut back by a third to a half, the branches will become unsightly and the foliage will take off in all directions. The advice is to eliminate them gradually, cutting them off at the base as new ones form. There are various suggestions about how to keep these highly vigorous roses orderly: You can let them grow without any interference; you can wrap the branches around supporting stakes so that the side branches will display their flowers to best advantage; or you can support the branches with a ring of wire at a pleasing height and let their ends fall forward in a harmonious way (d, page 37).

## FUNGAL DISEASES AND INSECT PESTS

Like all plants, roses have natural enemies, the most fearsome of which are fungi. Fungal diseases are not usually deadly for the plant, and most roses can survive one attack or more. But these diseases spoil the plant's beauty and damage the leaves, which interferes with the vital process of photosynthesis and brings the plant to a poor state of health. Experience shows that it is far easier to prevent fungal diseases than it is to battle them once they become established.

When making crosses among plants, hybridizers put much effort into the search for disease-resistant varieties; before a plant can be listed as resistant, it must pass stringent tests. Despite such efforts and despite the fact that roses in general are hardy, adaptable plants capable of overcoming many obstacles, roses get sick constantly. Many of the reasons for these problems are well known to all of us— pollution and the overuse of chemical substances, for example. But there are other factors: A climate with high temperatures, high humidity and cool nights favors the growth of powdery mildew, and plants that have been given excessive amounts of nitrogen-heavy fertilizer and an imbalanced program of nutrition are more subject to blackspot. Furthermore, some rosebushes are known to be predisposed to certain diseases: The gallicas and Bourbons are vulnerable to powdery mildew, just as roses descended from *Rosa foetida* are vulnerable to blackspot. On the other hand, roses with small, very shiny leaves—many of the groundcover types—are relatively immune to disease. In general, roses given a balanced program of fertilization supplemented with applications of potassium in higher doses than the other chemicals prove more resistant to disease.

There are two essential keys to growing lush, healthy plants. First, from the moment they are planted, they must be cared for properly, which includes furnishing them with all the elements necessary for their health. Second is disease prevention, which involves preventa-

*Opposite: symptoms of fungal diseases*
*a. Blackspot.*
*b. Powdery mildew.*
*c. Rust.*

tive treatments every 20 days from the beginning of spring on, especially in areas where certain types of infestations are common. It is a good idea to vary the kinds of products used. Two precautions: First, always rake away the dead leaves at the base of the plants, and burn them to keep the area around the roses clean; second, when spraying chemicals on roses, be sure to wet not only the leaves but also the lower areas of the plant as much as possible, including the ground at its base, which is where spores often take hold.

a

## Fungal Diseases
The fungal diseases of roses include blackspot (*Diplocarpon rosae*), powdery mildew (*Sphaerotheca pannosa* var. *rosae*), downy mildew (*Peronospora sparsa*) and rust (*Phragmidium mucronatum*). Less frequent are cankers that appear on canes (*Coniothyrium* sp. and *Cyptosporella* sp.), leaf spot (*Septoria*), botrytis blight (*Botrytis cinerea*) and anthracnose (*Sphaceloma rosarum*). There are also viral diseases, infections that spread through plant tissue, but these, fortunately, are not common. They include rose mosaics and crown gall (*Agrobacterium tumefaciens*). In such cases, all affected plant material must be removed and burned.

*Fungicides*
Many products are available for dealing with fungal infections, most of them mixtures of various active ingredients that form a broad spectrum for preventing and treating many different diseases. Some are more effective for specific types of infections. Almost all are systemic fungicides, which means that the chemicals enter the plant tissue and spread, so they act on the entire plant. Some mark leaves and flowers, so it is best to direct the spray upward from below, avoiding wetting the upper areas and sparing the flowers (see chart, pages 40–41).

b

## Insect Infestations
Various insects can threaten the beauty and health of roses. Some can do serious damage, but effective treatments are available for most of them. If you have only a few roses, you can use natural methods: removal by hand of beetles and slugs, preferably early in the morning; spraying with soapy water to discourage aphids; and spraying with mild organic mixtures that have a repellent action. If the plant in question is large and if the infestation has reached an advanced state, you may need to resort to a chemical agent. A large number of such products is available on the market, so you can easily choose ones that are less aggressive—in the sense of doing less harm to the plants as well as to

c

# DISEASES AND TREATMENTS

| DISEASE | Symptoms | Treatments |
|---------|----------|------------|
| ANTHRACNOSE | Gray spots on the surface of leaves, darkening of leaf margins, areas of dryness followed by leaf drop. | Triforine |
| BLACKSPOT | Round, fringed black spots on leaves; leaves later turn yellow and fall. Disease spreads rapidly. | Benomyl, theophanate-methyl, triforine, sulfur |
| BOTRYTIS BLIGHT | Leaves and young canes covered with gray spores; gray or black spots of decay on flower buds, which rot and drop off. | Sulfur; remove and destroy infected parts |
| CANKERS | Swellings form on canes, which turn brown and become brittle. | No chemical treatment; remove and destroy infected parts |
| CROWN GALL | Bacterial disease that causes rotting of plant parts and formation of irregular masses of swollen tissue (galls) at the base of stems and roots, especially at the crown, where the stems and roots meet. | No chemical treatment; if infestation is slight, destroy affected parts; if severe, destroy plant |
| DOWNY MILDEW | Irregular, angular purplish-black spots appear on leaves; gray mold may form on undersides of leaves, which turn yellow and fall. | No chemical treatment; remove and destroy infected leaves |
| LEAF SPOT | Many round or elongated spots, yellow or brown, appear on leaf surfaces and are followed by a tendency to dryness. | No chemical treatment; remove and destroy infected leaves |
| MOSAIC VIRUSES | Streaks or mottling appear on the leaves, spreading from the center outward. These viruses are deadly. | No chemical treatment; destroy infected plants |
| POWDERY MILDEW | Whitish powdery film appears on young leaves and spreads over shoots, deforming flowers and inhibiting growth. | Benomyl, triforine, sulfur |
| RUST | Dark spots appear on tops of leaves followed by rusty red powdery spots on undersides and on young stems. | Triforine, sulfur |

# INSECTS AND TREATMENTS

| INSECT | Description and symptoms | Treatments |
|---|---|---|
| APHIDS | Groups of tiny insects on undersides of leaves that produce a sticky "honeydew" which attracts ants. | Lady bugs, insecticidal soaps, pyrethrum, rotenone |
| LEAF-CUTTING BEES | Semicircular cuts, sharply made, along the margins of leaves. | No chemical treatment; destroy nests |
| LEAF-ROLLERS | Leaves roll up like cigarettes then become yellow and drop off. | Insecticidal soaps, pyrethrum, rotenone, carbaryl |
| MIDGES | Small yellow-brown flies that lay eggs in flowers and buds; plant parts wilt and turn black. | Pyrethroids, rotenone, acephate |
| MOTHS | Leaves thinned to the point of transparency or skeletonized. | Pyrethroids, acephate, rotenone |
| SCALE | Branches and canes covered with tiny white insects with hard shells that look like scales. | Dormant oil, rotenone |
| SLUGS | Slugs make holes in leaves or skeletonize them; they leave a silvery trail. | Pyrethroids, rotenone, acephate, carbaryl |
| SPIDER MITES | Minuscule spiders, some reddish, with delicate webs (best seen with a magnifying glass). Leaves become discolored and shiny. | Rotenone |
| THRIPS | Tiny winged insects, brown or yellow, that move rapidly; they leave silvery blotches or stripes on leaves and tips; buds and petals are deformed and discolored. | Pyrethrum, pyrethroids, rotenone, acephate |

## PREVENTIVE TREATMENTS

| | | |
|---|---|---|
| | Winter applications on bare branches and canes prevent scale and destroy fungal spores. | Mineral oils (white oil, paraffin oil) |
| | Preventive treatments during the winter against downy mildew, botrytis blight, crown gall, leaf spot and anthracnose. | Copper (Bordeaux mixture, copper sulfate) |
| | Blackspot, downy mildew, powdery mildew, rust and other leaf diseases. | Sulfur |

The most common insect pests
a. Aphids. b. Rose midges.
c. Scale. d. Spider mites. e. Rose
slugs. f. Leaf-cutting bees.
g. Gall wasps, larva and adult.
h. Inchworms. i. Thrips. j. Rose
chafers.

people and the environment. Some well-known products such as malathion are very effective against certain infestations but are also particularly aggressive. There are also insecticides such as pyrethrum, rotenone, sabadilla and insecticidal soaps that are considered organic because of their natural origin. One product will often prove effective against infestations of a variety of insect species. Among these, leaf-cutting bees are difficult to eliminate with pesticides if you do not destroy their nests at the same time.

The insects that most frequently attack roses are aphids, sometimes called plant lice (*Macrosiphum rosae* and other species); scale (*Aulacaspis rosae*); spider mites (*Tetranychus, Oligonychus, Panonychus*); rose slugs (*Cladius isomerus, Endelomyia aethiops*); leaf rollers (*Choristoneura rosaceana, Platynota* sp.), which make nests in which to lay eggs by rolling leaves; carpenter bees (*Cerantina* sp.), which bore holes in canes in which they lay their eggs; rose chafers (*Macrodactylus*), which feed on leaves and flowers; thrips (*Frankliniella*); and leaf-cutting bees (*Megachile* sp.). There is, in addition, a host of flies, moths and local pests, including insects that attack roots (see chart, pages 40–41).

PROPAGATION

Roses can be propagated in six ways: by cuttings, by grafting, by seed, by division, by layering and by meristematic cell division, an operation that requires, at the very least, a laboratory.

Cuttings and grafting are the methods most often used. Seeding is used only when one wants to obtain new varieties for hybridization; division is only for roses that naturally produce underground suckers or runners, such as the roses derived from *Rosa canina, gallica* and *rugosa* species; layering is good in a very few cases with roses—only in the types that easily form long roots on their branches such as *R. wichuraiana* and 'Max Graf.' Reproduction by cuttings is largely used by nonexperts, while grafting is used by rose breeders and nurseries to create plants for sale, an operation that requires skill and experience.

**Propagation by Cuttings**

Reproducing a rose with a cutting is not difficult and usually achieves good results, even if part of the cutting does not take root. Almost all roses can be propagated this way, although hybrid teas and floribundas may not grow fully and may have inadequate blooms.

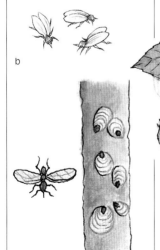

a

b

c

d

*Cuttings of Mature or Semimature Wood*

At the end of summer or in the fall at the end of the flowering season, select a healthy flowering stem from which you can cut sections of 6 to 8 inches (15–20 cm) with five or six buds. Using a sharp knife or a razor blade, make cuts at an angle above and beneath two buds (a, page 44), remove the thorns from the lower part and all the leaves except the last (b, page 44). Plant in a shady, protected area in soft soil with a high percentage of sand, burying two-thirds of the length of the stem and pressing the soil down firmly (c, page 44). You can cover the cutting with leaves or black polyethylene to keep it warm and reduce evaporation, or you can cover it with a bell jar or a cold frame. A common

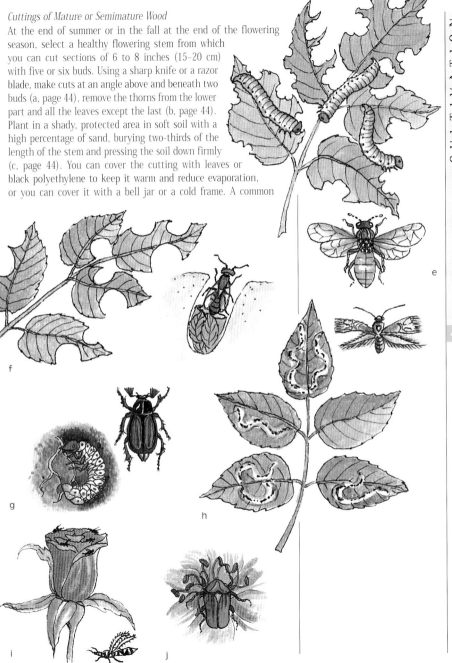

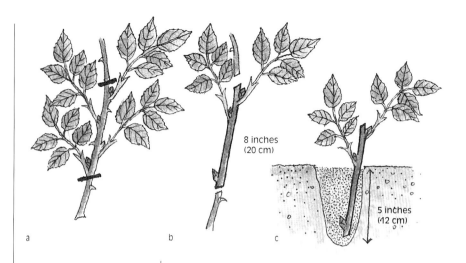

8 inches
(20 cm)

5 inches
(12 cm)

a                    b                    c

*a, b, c. Taking cuttings and
planting them.*

practice is to dip the base of the cuttings in rooting-hormone powder
(for cuttings taken from a mature bush) to favor the growth of roots.
Leave the cuttings undisturbed for six months; when they show signs
of good root growth, transplant them to containers. In general, this
will be the following spring; for some plants, such as antique roses, it
will be the following autumn.

*Cuttings of Young Wood*
In recent years, increasing use has been made of this method, especially with roses that have failed to give satisfactory results with cuttings from mature wood and with groundcover and patio roses.
Halfway through the spring or at the end of spring, choose a terminal section of young, green foliage. Cut stems no longer than an inch
and a quarter (3 cm) that have two buds; do not cut off the leaves.
Immerse them in a fungicidal solution to eliminate rot, dust the base
of each stem with a hormone powder suitable for immature wood, and
bury in sand. It is best to use covered trays heated from below. The
cuttings should not take long to root. Remove any leaves that fall.

**Propagation by Grafting**
The type of grafting most frequently used by rose breeders requires a
shoot with a bud from the plant you want to reproduce (called a bud
stick) and a rootstock, meaning a rosebush at least two years old. In
the past, the plant most commonly used as rootstock was *Rosa canina inermis*, but because of its tendency to send out suckers, it has
recently been replaced. Today, the most common rootstocks are
*R. corymbifera laxa* and *R. multiflora*. The season for grafting runs
from late spring to early summer, because good results are far more
likely if both the rootstock and the bud stick are full of lymph.

44

The essential factor in grafting is the cambium layer, the plant layer immediately below the bark that separates the bark from the woody part of the stem. The cambium layer is composed of growth cells (meristematic tissues) capable of regeneration. For the graft to be successful, the cambium layers of the two plants must be in contact. The bud is cut from a stem immediately after it has flowered. The necessary tools for the operation are a pruning knife, a strip of polyethylene and raffia for tying.

## Meristematic Propagation

This type of propagation has come into widespread use only in relatively recent years. It requires a chemical laboratory, since much of the operation takes place in test tubes, making use of the meristematic tissue of plants, meaning a small quantity of cells. There are enormous advantages to this method of propagation, since a single plant can be used to create an almost endless number of new plants. The method is particularly useful for miniature roses, which are for mass consumption, much like any of the other plants on grocery-store shelves; the method is still at the experimental stage for larger roses; for these, further guarantees of quality are needed in terms of growth, vigor, resistance and quality of bloom.

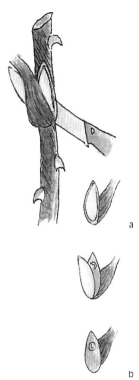

a

b

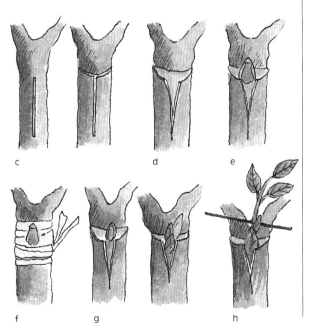

c    d    e

f    g    h

Bud grafting: a. Cut off a bud. b. Remove the wood to expose the cambium layer. c. Make a T-cut in the trunk of the rootstock. d. Bare the cambium layer of the rootstock using the point of a knife. e. Insert the bud. f. Wrap with a strip of polyethylene to prevent loss of moisture, but do not cover the bud; tie off with raffia. g. If the graft is successful, the bud will begin to sprout. h. In the fall or the next spring, cut off the vegetative part of the rootstock, and wait for the bud to continue growing. The next summer, the plant will be ready to produce its first flowers.

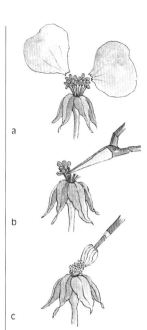

*Steps in hybridizing a rose:
a. Select the flower of the
mother plant, the one that will
produce the seeds. The bud
should be just open. Remove
the petals with a slight twist.
b. Using scissors or tweezers,
cut the filaments of the
stamens to prevent self-
pollination. c. After about a day,
when the stigma has become
sticky, indicating that it is
mature, brush it with pollen
from the father plant.*

a

b

c

## Hybridization

It is by hybridization that new roses are created. Aside from manual dexterity, the work of hybridization requires a broad knowledge of botany and genetics. Not all roses are compatible—the set of chromosomes for each class of roses differs from that of the others—and information based on the number of chromosomes is necessary before any decisions can be made about which plants to cross. This is clearly work for professionals. In addition to knowledge, it requires dedication, for the people who work in this field make hundreds upon hundreds of crosses each year to finally create only four or five roses with the qualities needed for the marketplace. And before those plants are ready for sale, another seven or eight years will go by.

The steps in the process are shown at left: a, b, c. When the procedure has been completed, the stem on which the operation has been performed is covered with a hood of paper to prevent contamination by pollen from other subjects and is labeled with the date and the names of the roses used in the operation. The pollen, taken from the father plant, can be preserved under refrigeration, between slides or in plastic containers for two or three weeks, until the mother plant is ready.

If the operation is successful, the fruit containing the seeds will be collected in the late autumn and kept in damp vermiculite or fine sand, labeled, as always, with the names of the parents and the date, at around 60 degrees F (16 degrees C). About two months later, the seed extracted from the rose hip is placed under refrigeration for 10 days to facilitate germination. Seeding is another operation that requires skill and precision. The seeds must be buried, ideally in a reasonably large box, at a depth of 5 inches (12 cm) in good compost that must not be allowed to dry out. The temperature must be maintained at a constant level at night, preferably with heating from the bottom. During the day, the box must receive abundant light.

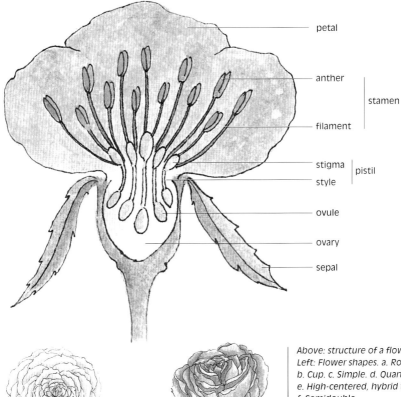

petal

anther

stamen

filament

stigma | pistil
style

ovule

ovary

sepal

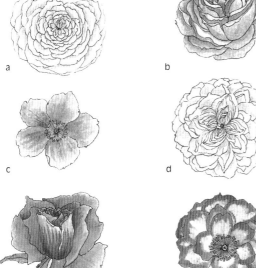

*Above: structure of a flower.*
*Left: Flower shapes. a. Rosette.*
*b. Cup. c. Simple. d. Quartered.*
*e. High-centered, hybrid tea.*
*f. Semidouble.*

a

b

c

d

e

f

*Cross section of a rose hip with seeds.*

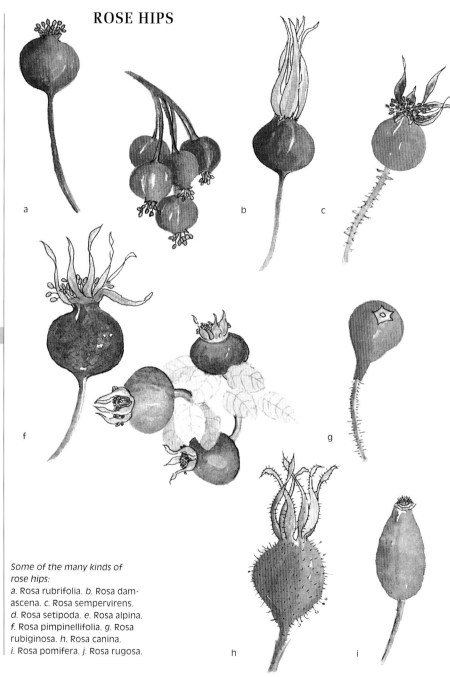

# ROSE HIPS

a

b

c

48

f

g

h

i

Some of the many kinds of
rose hips:
*a.* Rosa rubrifolia. *b.* Rosa damascena. *c.* Rosa sempervirens.
*d.* Rosa setipoda. *e.* Rosa alpina.
*f.* Rosa pimpinellifolia. *g.* Rosa
rubiginosa. *h.* Rosa canina.
*i.* Rosa pomifera. *j.* Rosa rugosa.

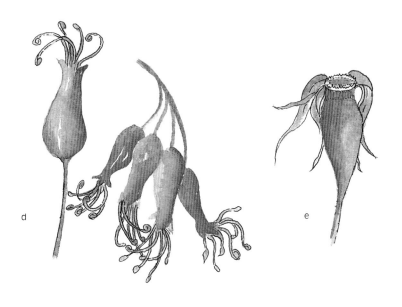

d

e

j

# CLIMBERS, RAMBLERS
## FOR WALLS, ARCHES, PILLARS

*R*oses are not climbing plants, having neither tendrils nor suckers for attaching themselves to things. But some roses do produce long runners, and in some cases, they are quite vigorous. Their correct scientific name could thus be sarmentose roses (from *sarmentum*, a Latin word for "runner"), but they are known simply as climbers and ramblers. The sarmentose roses we plant today are almost all modern roses and can only with difficulty be divided into classes, which is not the case, for example, with the modern shrub roses. Even so, within this large and varied group are two very precise categories with different characteristics and uses: climbers and ramblers.

Climbers are almost all roses with large, striking flowers; many are genetic mutations of hybrid teas or floribundas. Almost all are reflowering, have long, rigid but not numerous canes, a somewhat graceless growth habit and foliage that is sufficient but by no means dense. The qualities that make them useful are their decorative value, the visual power of their flowers, the great variety of available colors and their reflowering habit. These qualities enable them to perform key roles in the garden, scrambling around or over the front of a house, an arch, a pillar, a portico or an arbor. They can also be made to drape over wooden or ironwork structures—tripods or pyramids—that can be placed beside walkways or at the center of beds for height. You can see this

## TWO ROSES FOR LOVERS: 'MADAME GRÉGOIRE STAECHELIN' AND 'CUPID'

*'Madame Grégoire Staechelin,' created in Spain by Pietro Dot in 1927, enjoyed immediate fame and fortune but today has fallen into neglect, primarily because the public is attracted more to reflowering, which this rose does not do, than to other qualities. The delicate bright red buds open to large flowers that measure up to 5.5 inches (14 cm), are luminous, rippling and voluptuous, with a pale heart, darker undersides and petals that bend lazily in toward the bottom to reveal the stamens. The scent is delicate; the leaves are luxuriant and glossy. It flowers in June and produces apricot-colored hips in*

*the fall. A vigorous climber, it tends to become thin at the bottom, so it is best to direct the lower branches horizontally and prune the shrub severely to prevent it from growing too high.*

*'Cupid' (right) dates to 1915 and was created by B.R. Cant. It, too, flowers once, from May to June. This is its only drawback; all the rest is admirable. This rose enchants, moves, seduces. The appeal begins with its immense flowers— simple, fragile, delicate, diaphanous, they seem like shadows or ghosts of roses. Scented and paler than peach-pink, the petals fold in sinuous lines, slightly crinkled, toward the golden stamens at the center. It has been said that this*

*rose would merit a place in a garden even if it produced only a single flower each year. Graham Thomas suggests placing 'Cupid' near a shrub that it can climb over. Sometimes it has trouble flowering, and sometimes it produces a few flowers in the fall as it covers itself with orange hips.*

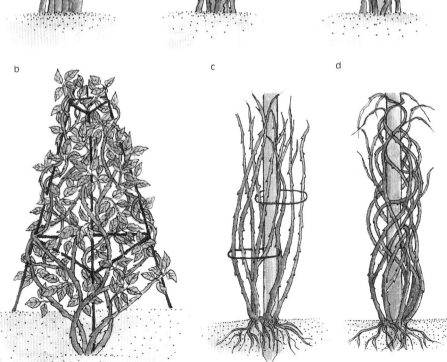

technique put to use in many famous rose gardens throughout the world, such as the Jardins de Bagatelle in Paris.

Various factors should be kept in mind when selecting one of these roses. Roses with semidouble and even single flowers are often looked upon as secondary to those with double blooms, which are far more striking, at times to the point of being excessive. But the single-flowered roses have led to a much-needed reevaluation and a renewed appreciation of simpler flowers, most of all those with solid colors, because precisely by being less aggressive, their beauty is more balanced and can be combined more easily with other elements in the garden.

Ramblers have come to enjoy great popularity in Great Britain, thanks to the work of such passionate gardeners as Gertrude Jekyll. Today, they are planted every bit as often as climbers. The two types have very different characteristics. Ramblers produce many ropelike canes that grow energetically in all directions, creating a soft, wonderfully fresh and colorful effect. They bear enormous cascades of small flowers in a single flowering each year. They can be invaluable in

**BANKSIAE ROSES** Most 19th-century gardens, especially those along the Mediterranean coast, had a pergola on which a Rosa banksiae triumphed. There were also unique specimens famous for their magnificence, such as the one still found in the gardens of the Alhambra, entwined around an ancient cypress, its branches reaching into the tree as far as 50 feet (15 meters) then falling back to drape across the tree's dark branches, cover-

ing them with its trembling yellow flowers. Tombstone, Arizona, boasts what has been declared the world's largest R. banksiae alba plena: The trunk of this "Tombstone Rose" measures 5 feet (1.5 m) in circumference, and its branches, supported by 54 pipes with wire cables, cover an area of 4,600 square feet (429 m²). One poetic soul compared it to a gigantic bank of snow shining in the sun. One can hope that wherever the

weather permits—banksiae are no fans of winter cold—at least one of the varieties is under cultivation somewhere.

The species Rosa banksiae normalis originated in the mountains of China. Its flowers are single, cream-colored and scented, but it is not in cultivation. The first variety to reach Europe, in 1807, was R. banksiae alba plena (or banksiae banksiae), renowned for its giant growth, since it reaches up to 50 feet (15 m) in height; it has double flowers, pale, with mixed-plant beds and are wonderful for covering bare corners and hiding sheds or dead trees. They can scramble over hedges, spill down rough embankments and create flowering garlands when draped over supports. They are unrivaled for softening overly rigid lines such as those of cement and steel structures, wires and fences and can be used to separate areas of the garden and bring an increased sense of spaciousness. They are ideal for covering gazebos, pavilions and bowers, those bits of domestic architecture so dear to the 19th century and once again back in style. Or they can scramble over and through the branches of trees. Even though the flowering does not repeat during the year, the spectacle can be truly extraordinary, at once dramatic and unforgettable.

Moderately cold-hardy, ramblers have long been popular in northern areas. Many people give them scarcely a second thought, mainly because most of them flower only once. Such doubters would be easily won over if they could have seen the glory of *Rosa banksiae* in the gardens of the 19th century. It is enough to plant just one to learn to love them; and if you can't do without a splash of powerful reflowering color, plant your rambler alongside a reflowering climber with big flowers. If that's not enough, a German hybridizer has recently put several reflowering ramblers on the market (see "Reflowering Ramblers," right).

## REFLOWERING RAMBLERS

*Toward the end of the 20th century, German hybridizer Karl Hetzel created a group of reflowering ramblers. With a height of 10 to 11.5 feet (3–3.5 m), they bear bunches of small flowers from the end of May to the end of autumn and are immune to disease. They include 'Super-Excelsa' (1996), with dark pink flowers (left); 'SuperDorothy' (1997), with pink flowers; 'SuperFairy' (1997), with very pale pink scented flowers; 'SuperElfin' (1997), with scarlet-orange flowers; and 'Super-Sparkle' (1997), with scarlet-crimson flowers.*

the scent of violets (page 54, top). The two varieties with butter-colored flowers are far more common. Of these, perhaps the best known is R. banksiae lutea, which produces surprising quantities of double flowers, small rosettes with fifty-odd petals, soft and gracious, not overly scented. The flowers of R. banksiae lutescens (page 54, bottom) are more modest—single and pale—but more fragrant. It arrived in Europe in 1870 and was cultivated for the first time at Villa Hambury, not far from Ventimiglia in Italy. The sweet flowering of banksiae roses takes place in April or May. Among their traits is the attractive rust-colored bark of the mature trunks, which peels off in a thin transparent film. All are completely thornless and very vigorous. They require no special treatment, although care should be taken when pruning, since they don't usually require it. And because the flowers open on the lateral branches that grew the preceding year, these must never be cut.

larger than the shrub's. At 4 feet (1.2 m) high, the shrub reflowers on new shoots that rise from the base throughout the season. The canes are thin, with few thorns, but they grow so densely, they can cover and hide the flowers. The bush is rather stingy with leaves. 'Cécile Brünner' is pretty when interwoven with the branches of an old tree. At times, its behavior may seem capricious, but this can be forgiven since it is typical of many Chinese roses.

**Origin:** a polyantha x 'Madame de Tartas' (some authorities give instead 'Souvenir d'un Ami').

## ALTERNATIVE SELECTIONS

For the shrub form, there is 'Bloomfield Abundance' (1), a rosebush often confused with 'Cécile Brünner,' although it is taller and lusher. It can be distinguished from 'Cécile Brünner' by its sepals, which are longer and more visible. A similar climber is 'Perle d'Or,' which has comparable characteristics but apricot flowers.

**Synonyms:** 'Sweetheart,' 'Mignon,' 'Madame Cécile Brünner'
**Height:** 13–26 feet (4–8 m)
**Flower size:** 1.2 inches (3 cm)
**Number of petals:** 20–40
(shrub form: Pernet-Ducher 1881; climbing form: Hosp 1894)

The universal word for this rose is "exquisite." Its most striking quality is the extreme delicacy of its flowers, which are pale coral-pink with darker shadows in the folds; because of the elongated, pointed buds, the flowers, when opening, have the perfection of a Chinese vase. This is an invaluable flower, mainly because it is so compact, a true miniature hybrid tea. Although the flowers are small, they grow in such profusion that they light up the entire plant. Flowering begins in June and lasts for weeks, and September brings a second but less copious display. The climbing form is so vigorous that its plum-colored canes can cover an entire wall. Its flowers and leaves are slightly

1

Climbers

# Clair Matin
*Modern Climber*

**Height:** 10–13 feet (3–4 m)
**Flower size:** 2–2.5 inches (5–6 cm)
**Number of petals:** 15
(Meilland 1960)

This is one of the best selections for those who love the so-called bunch roses. Winner of the prestigious Bagatelle prize, it has lost none of its appeal over the years. It continues to please because, as its name implies, it is as luminous as a clear morning. Guaranteed to succeed and easy to cultivate, it has lush, rigid, well-branching canes that produce two bursts of flowers in thick bunches. The flowers are semidouble and shaped like shallow cups; they are highlighted with orange when open-

ing, then turn pinker and paler. The fragrance is the delicate scent of a wild rose. Since both the first and fall flowerings are long and glorious, this rose can be placed on an important wall. It can also be made to grow as a free-standing shrub, without support, in which case, it will not grow beyond 6.5 feet (2 m). In humid, oppressive summer

heat, the plant may be attacked by powdery mildew, but it responds well to treatment.

It should be pruned like other modern climbers: Eliminate the old branches, shorten those that are too long, and leave only two or three buds on the side branches.

**Origin:** 'Fashion' x ('Independence' x 'Orange Triumph') x 'Phyllis Bide.'

### ALTERNATIVE SELECTION
'Bantry Bay' (1), a rose created by McGredy in 1967 and another prizewinner, has semidouble flowers larger than those of 'Clair Matin'; they are pink with paler shadings and a sweet scent of apples. Flowering is continuous.

Climbers

flowering, once in June and again in September, with an occasional bloom between the two. The stems are rigid and strong, and the bush is well branched and protected by large red thorns. It is well covered with foliage all the way to its base, something that cannot be said of all climbers. Its resistance to disease and cold is excellent.

Lacking sufficient vigor to cover an entire wall, 'Compassion' is best when wrapped around a pillar, used to cover a support or grown to frame an entryway. It is one of the parents of two magnificent roses, 'Paul Shirville' and 'Rosemary Harkness.'

**Origin:** 'White Cockade' x 'Prima Ballerina.'

### ALTERNATIVE SELECTIONS

Several climbing hybrid teas boast beautiful color shadings that run from apricot to coral and peach. 'Breath of Life', also by Harkness (1980), is pink with a decided apricot tone and a winner of awards in Germany and Japan. There is also a shrub form.

'Comtesse Vandal' is another hybrid tea, a vintage one. Created in both bush and climbing forms and introduced by the famous American company Jackson & Perkins, it is an elegant rose, silvery pink with orange shadings, although its scent is weak.

A rose that merits rediscovery and is worth seeking out is 'Souvenir de George Pernet', created by the great hybridizer Pernet-Ducher and awarded a Bagatelle in 1921; the flower has a magnificent form, and its pink coloring bears salmon highlights.

**Height:** 11.5 feet (3.5 m)
**Flower size:** 4 inches (10 cm)
**Number of petals:** 35–40
(Harkness 1973)

One of the nicest creations of the English hybridizer Harkness, and justly famous, this rose has won many medals, including two for its intensely sweet scent. Often requested and often culti-vated, it is a favorite in both American and European gardens. The form of the flowers is pretty, not overly full, and the coloring is very delicate—apricot-pink with orange highlights, which contrasts beautifully with the dark semiglossy leaves. The sheer abundance of its flowers, solitary and in small groups, is wonderful, as is its excellent

# Constance Spry
English Rose

4 ⬭ ◎ ✕ ⠿

**Height:** 6.5–13 feet (2–4 m)
**Flower size:** 4–5 inches
(10–12 cm)
**Number of petals:** 45–55
(Austin, presented by Thomas
and introduced in 1961 by
Sunningdale Nurseries)

This was one of the first creations of English hybridizer
David Austin, and it was the
success of this rose that led to
the founding of the empire of
English roses. Obtained by
crossing the splendid antique
rose 'Belle Isis' with an interesting floribunda, 'Dainty Maid,'
'Constance Spry' does not
resemble either of them. Its
sumptuous flowers, as large as a
peony's, are cupped, globular
and composed of silky petals

that reflex at maturity. The flowers are sweetly pink with that
particular intense scent known
as myrrh. A large bush with a
wide habit and a strong constitution, when placed against a
wall or trellis, it will transform
itself into a climber and display
the full opulence of its blooms.
Such is its beauty that one over-
looks the fact that it flowers

only once, early in the summer.
It should not be placed in tight
corners, where it would be wast-
ed, but given as much space as it
needs.

**Origin:** 'Belle Isis' x 'Dainty
Maid.'

### ALTERNATIVE SELECTION
Large, spherical flowers with the
same opulence and antiquated
grace as those of 'Constance Spry,'
although slightly smaller and of a
different color, can be found in
'Pierre de Ronsad' syn. 'Eden Rose
88' (1), by Meilland. The 4-inch
(10 cm) flowers are milk-white
edged with an intense pink. This
rose has the fineness of porcelain
and a subtle scent. Long-flowering,
it also repeats a few blooms. It
grows to 6.5 to 10 feet (2-3 m).

# Dortmund
## Hybrid Kordesii

5

**Height:** 10 feet (3 m)
**Flower size:** 4 inches (10 cm)
**Number of petals:** 5
(Kordes 1955)

Beginning with *Rosa* x *kordesii*, a hybrid that originated with *R. rugosa*, the German breeder Kordes, always in search of the strong, cold-resistant roses suited to his market, created a series of climbers of unquestionable virtue: hardy, disease resistant, dependably reflowering and beautifully branched.

'Dortmund' was one of the first and has made a place for itself in our gardens. It offers great vigor, long branches that wander energetically, healthy, glossy foliage and well-formed red flowers with white eyes at the center of which the stamens add a dollop of gold. The scent is slight. This strong plant presents no problems and will prosper even without much sun. It will repeat bloom, especially if care is taken to deadhead the spent flowers. Flowers left on in the fall, however, will become large, decorative hips, pretty enough to bring indoors. Those looking for a climber with bright red flowers would do well to choose a rose with single flowers because of the aggressiveness of the color.

**Origin:** a sport x *Rosa* x *kordesii*.

### ALTERNATIVE SELECTIONS
Characteristics very similar to those of 'Dortmund' can be found in 'Altissimo', a French rose from 1966 signed by Delbard-Chabert. Its single flowers are even larger and have seven petals of a brilliant blood-red with prominent yellow stamens. Suitable for a column or arch, provided it doesn't need to grow higher than 6.5 feet (2 m), it flowers continuously from June on, the flowers spread along the branches.

Another pretty rose by Kordes (1952), which originated from *Rosa gallica*, is 'Scharlachglut' syn. 'Scarlet Glow' (1). It has large flowers of a splendid scarlet, the stamens providing a touch of yellow at the center. The leaves are opaque. The plant grows up to 6.5 feet (2 m) high. It flowers once, and in the fall, it is covered with red hips.

1

Climbers

# Étoile de Hollande
*Climbing Hybrid Tea*

**Origin:** 'General MacArthur' x 'Hadley.'

## ALTERNATIVE SELECTIONS

An equally good choice is 'Ena Harkness,' one of the most popular roses in English gardens in the 1950s. It has retained much of its popularity even when measured against more vigorous roses. The beauty of the flowers, the richness of the crimson color with just a touch of scarlet, the intensity of the fragrance and the outstanding and long—although not repeated—flowering that begins in May are its great qualities. It does best in rich soil.

No less famous is 'Crimson Glory' (1), known throughout the world; it is the mother of 'Ena Harkness.' Its 30-petaled flowers take on purple shadings. The spectacular flowering will fill an entire garden with an

**Height:** 6.5–13 feet (2–4 m)
**Flower size:** 3.5 inches (9 cm)
**Number of petals:** 40
(shrub form: Verschuren 1919; climbing form: Leenders 1931)

Red roses—the intense red once found on theater seats—that also have the popular flower shapes of hybrid teas have always been favorites in gardens. They also happen to be the most fragrant roses. 'Étoile de Hollande' is a vintage hybrid tea that has enjoyed great success. Much loved in the period between the two world wars, it has never been cast aside. It owes its enduring popularity to the intense crimson of its flowers, its exceptional fragrance and the generosity of its flower-ing. Some people claim they have seen it in flower for 135 consecutive days; indeed, it often produces a few flowers in late autumn. The flowers are not of the highest quality, but they are very effective. The more demanding say that this rose has two defects: First, its flowers tend to fold back onto the pedicels, a serious defect in a shrub but almost a vice in a climber, which is seen from below; second, its color tends toward purple with age. One might argue that it is fascinating to see such different shadings on the same plant. The leaves are dark and opaque; the young shoots have an attractive plum tint. It does best in a protected position in a temperate climate.

1

intoxicating, spicy scent. A few flowers will sometimes appear in the fall.

Yet another red rose is 'Sympathie' (Kordes 1964), which has prettily shaped dark red flowers tending to scarlet; they are scented and appear in abundant quantities throughout the entire season.

19th century and its continued success are merited. It is a rose found in any respectable garden. It flowers early and continues tirelessly; it will tolerate some frost, but it does not like humidity. It is subject to powdery mildew and blackspot but no more so than many others. This plant is so vigorous that at times one doesn't know what to do with it. Since it tends to be a little bare at the bottom, like most antique and modern climbers, why not plant it behind a rose with a low habit that is full of branches and flowers of a pleasing shade such as 'Crystal Palace' or 'Sussex'?

**Origin:** a tea rose x 'Souvenir de la Malmaison.'

### ALTERNATIVE SELECTIONS

A climber of the Noisette group, 'Desprez à Fleurs Jaunes' flowers and reflowers with much zeal. The flowers are pretty but not as glorious as those of 'Gloire de Dijon'; smaller and a warm yellow with peach tones, they open flat and are scented.

'Madame Jules Gravereux' is another pretty tea rose, from 1901, also yellow and peach, with high, double, slightly scented flowers. Up to 10 feet (3 m), tall; it reflowers.

'Paul Lédé', the climbing form of a famous rose from early in the 20th century, is resistant to cold and has good reflowering. The flowers are semidouble, big and soft, with the scent of tea. The color is a soft yellow with pink tints at the center.

**Height:** 13 feet (4 m)
**Flower size:** 4 inches (10 cm)
**Number of petals:** 45–55
(Jacotot 1853)

Because of its mixed characteristics, this is classified as both a tea and a Noisette, but either way, it merits the adjective glorious. Glorious are its large, spherical flowers, at first cupped, then flat and quartered when they open; they carry a strong scent of tea. The color could be described as ocher-pink-gold or cream-apricot-orange; it is changeable and hard to define because it is so shaded and sensual. When grown against an old brick wall, this rose tends to take on almost gilt shadings. Thus both the furor it awakened in the

62

Climbers

# Golden Showers
*Modern Climber*

little sun, and it flowers continuously from June to October. It is well suited to small gardens because it is short and easy to contain; it tends to form a shrub before deciding to climb.

**Origin:** 'Charlotte Armstrong' x 'Captain Thomas.'

### ALTERNATIVE SELECTIONS
Presented by Kordes in 1984 and listed in the Barni catalog, 'Golden Olympus' is a pretty climber that grows to only about 6.5 feet (2 m). It has large flowers of a pleasing shape with ruffled petals, gold with coppery shadings, that hold up to rain. Reflowering and robust, its foliage is abundant. It is suitable for cold climates.

Despite its name, 'Easlea's Golden Rambler' is more of a climber, as indicted by its thick, rigid canes and the width and shape of its flowers. Its 35-petaled flowers are 4 inches (10 cm) in diameter, gilt yellow and very fragrant. Competition judges find favor with it and have awarded it two important prizes, but so far, it has won little popularity, perhaps because it flowers only once. And yet it is a fine rose, dependable and without defects.

**Height:** 6.5–10 feet (2–3 m)
**Flower size:** 4 inches (10 cm)
**Number of petals:** 25–30
(Lammerts 1956)

This is doubtless the most popular yellow climber in both North America and Europe. The two medals it was awarded in the United States helped call attention to it. The elegant, elongated buds open into large flowers of a daffodil yellow that later takes on creamy shadings; the blossoms are at first high-centered, then the petals spread and become ruffled. They are romantic flowers and beautiful in a vase, especially when accompanied by the shiny leaves. Easy to grow, this rose will tolerate a position against a wall in

# Kathleen Harrop
*Bourbon*

semidouble to double scented flowers and pale, broad leaves. For an arrangement of great delicacy, plant sage or 'Hidcote' or 'Munstead' lavender at its feet.

**Origin:** a sport of 'Zéphirine Drouhin.'

### ALTERNATIVE SELECTIONS

Another unjustly neglected Bourbon is 'Souvenir de St. Anne's,' a sport of the famous 'Souvenir de la Malmaison' that was found in a garden near Dublin and introduced by Graham Thomas. At 6 feet (1.8 m) in height, it has equally good qualities, including charming semidouble flowers, very pale, slightly shaded pink; a strong fragrance; and the delicate symmetrical shape of a camellia. Excellent flowering.

For a more aggressive flower, why not simply turn to the parent of 'Kathleen Harrop,' 'Zéphirine Drouhin' (1)?

**Height:** 8 feet (2.5 m)
**Flower size:** 4 inches (10 cm), many doubles
(Dickson 1919)

Some people think this rose has been held back by its name, but if anything is getting in its way, it is the fame of 'Zéphirine Drouhin,' the rose of which it is a sport discovered by Dickson & Sons of Northern Ireland. It deserves greater attention, for it is decidedly superior given the more orderly shape of its flowers and their sweet coral-pink color. The fact that it is totally without thorns makes it ideal for use on a terrace, or in a highly trafficked area or in a place where children play. It flowers from mid-June to winter and has

1

# Ophelia
## Climbing Hybrid Tea

er tones at the center that give it depth. The flowers of 'Lady Sylvia,' which have a very intense fragrance, may well be the prettiest of the three. The flowers contrast nicely with sharply defined, elegant gray-green leaves. Flowering usually begins at the end of June, repeats with regularity and is spectacular in the fall. Vigorous climbers, these roses tolerate difficult conditions; the only attention they need is pruning with a light hand so as not to reduce flowering. These are perfect roses for vases: 'Lady Sylvia' is one of the most widely cultivated for cut flowers.

**Height:** 13 feet (4 m)
**Flower size:** 3 inches (8 cm)
**Number of petals:** 28
(shrub form: Paul 1912;
climber: Dickson 1920)

'Ophelia,' its genetic mutation 'Madame Butterfly' and 'Lady Sylvia,' a sport of 'Madame Butterfly,' are closely related and very similar roses. All three

boast the same valuable characteristic: the exquisite, perfect shape of their flowers. And all three merit a place in a garden. All three are of delicate color: 'Ophelia' is a very pale pink, almost white; 'Madame Butterfly' is a slightly darker pink; 'Lady Sylvia' is almost a flesh-pink touched with apricot and dark-

# Madame Alfred Carrière
Noisette

form and become disheveled. The color is creamy white with a touch of pink. The scent is slight and of tea but of high quality. The plant has an upright habit; its canes have few thorns, tend to bend and maintain a pale green color; the leaves are semiglossy. Its virtues are many, although it does have a propensity to disease. It must be pruned to maintain its shape. It is valued because it is useful in difficult spots such as north-facing walls, but it is not a rose anyone will go wild over. Even so, a very old specimen such as the one on the wall of a cottage at Sissinghurst is truly spectacular in full bloom—a heavy blanket of soft snow.

### ALTERNATIVE SELECTION

Although a reasonably recent creation, being one of the group of *Rosa* x *kordesii* hybrids, 'Ilse Krohn Superior' (Kordes 1964) has pretty flowers of an antique shape, large and full, strongly scented and with no fear of rain. It is an excellent choice for a white rose about 10 feet (3 m) tall.

**Height:** 15 feet (4.5 m)
**Flower size:** 2.5–3 inches (7–8 cm)
**Number of petals:** 35
(Schwartz 1879)

One of the antique climbers most often met in gardens and, at least in Great Britain, one of the most popular is 'Madame Alfred Carrière.' A pretty rose that can be placed anywhere, it is easy to accompany, undemanding and in continuous flower from mid-June on. It prefers a sheltered position and does not like a cold climate. The flowers grow in clusters and are of the hybrid tea type, with equal-sized petals. They bring gardenias to mind as they open, but after that, they lose their

## *Meg*
*Climbing Hybrid Tea*

stupendous, with vibrant, undulating petals that seem to move as though in a slight breeze. The flowering is pretty and long and includes a few late blooms; in some gardens, it reflowers. Because of its vigor and rigid canes that hold themselves up well, it is suitable for growing alone in a corner with a green backdrop; its flowers rise from long, arching canes and offer themselves to examination while spreading their warm light. If it is to grow against a wall or pillar, it must be trained and tied into position.

**Origin:** 'Paul's Lemon Pillar' x 'Madame Butterfly.'

### ALTERNATIVE SELECTION

'Summer Wine' (1), a climber created by Kordes in 1984, has large, scented flowers with five petals, pink with warmer shadings and illuminated by coppery stamens. The leaves are large and semiglossy. A vigorous plant, it produces a profusion of flowers that come into bloom over a long period. It is spectacular when its branches wrap around a tree's and the bright flowers glow coral in the mixed foliage.

**Height:** 8 feet (2.5 m)
**Flower size:** 5–5.5 inches (12–14 cm)
**Number of petals:** 10
(Gosset 1954)

This could be called the twin to 'Compassion' but with flowers just barely semidouble, pink with apricot centers, large and

1

# *Mermaid*
*Hybrid Bracteata*

leaves always has something to show off. It is disease resistant and does not require pruning. It can be pruned if you need to restrain it, but it's better to let it grow at will, running over hedges, stretching across the ground or covering a bower. If you're after a true forest of roses, plant it with *R. bracteata*, and the area will become as wild and overgrown as a tropical forest.

**Origin:** *Rosa bracteata* x a yellow tea rose with double flowers.

### ALTERNATIVE SELECTIONS
Two interesting yellow roses that can take the place of 'Mermaid' in colder climates are 'Rêve d'Or' and 'Lawrence Johnston' syn. 'Hidcote Yellow'. These are nearly twins, since both were born of the same cross of *Rosa foetida persiana* offspring, to which they owe their luminous yellow. The first has single flowers with prominent stamens and is slightly less vigorous; the second has large, scented, semidouble flowers that open to cups. The flowering is more spectacular than that of 'Mermaid', since the flowers open at the same time instead of a few at a time. Occasionally there is a second flowering.

**Height:** 26 feet (8 m)
**Flower size:** 4–6 inches (10–15 cm)
**Number of petals:** 5
(Paul 1918)

The sole descendant of *Rosa bracteata* (1), a giant Chinese of exceptional beauty, 'Mermaid' won a gold medal from the Royal National Rose Society. It can be grown wherever there is enough space and the climate permits, for does not tolerate frost. The ideal climate is temperate, but it can be grown in far cooler areas if kept out of the wind, in which case, it can even face north. Even if the cold of winter massacres it, it can easily be brought back from the roots. Like *R. bracteata*, it is irrepress-

ible, slow to get established but then unstoppable. The dark canes are armed with deadly thorns; the elegant, large, single flowers open to form a yellow cup that turns to cream, showing highly visible amber stamens. A few flowers bloom at a time throughout the entire season, so the magnificent coat of dark, semiglossy, semievergreen

# New Dawn
*Hybrid Wichuraiana*

14 Ⓠ ◎ ⓠ ⁚⁚⁚

Boerner in 1951. It is a pretty coral pink, but the flowers are somewhat pudgy and less than graceful. 'Parade', also from Boerner (1953), has fully double flowers, between cherry and crimson in color. 'Pink Perpétue' (1) was developed by Gregory in Great Britain in 1965. A hardy climber of moderate size, it has enjoyed a modicum of success, although the double flowers have a gaudy color that is difficult to combine with others. But its flowering is excellent, even in the autumn. A pretty, more luminous pink is that of 'Morning Jewel', created in Scotland in 1969 and, according to some, the preferable variety, with semidouble flowers of pleasing fragrance; reflowering is not exceptional. The most recent gift from 'New Dawn' arrived in 1998. Called 'Penny Lane', it was declared rose of the year, the first time that distinction was accorded a climber. It has the pretty flowers of 'New Dawn', is of antique form, and its color varies from champagne to coral; it offers abundant flowering and very good reflowering.

**Height:** 10–13 feet (3–4 m)
**Flower size:** 3–3.5 inches (8–9 cm)
**Number of petals:** 40
(Dreer, Somerset Rose Nursery 1930)

So unusual was this rose when it initially appeared that it was the first to be granted a U.S. patent and be written up in official registers with its name, presenter, origin and characteristics. It may well be the most frequently planted rose in the gardens of the world, yet it is so exquisite that its ubiquity has not made it commonplace. It is a delight because of its fragrant flowers, just the right size, so delicate and pretty in their appearance and shape, so pure in color, a pale pink with pearly reflections. It resists cold, wind and mistreatment with its strong branches and lustrous, abundant leaves. 'New Dawn' never disappoints. The first flowering is good, and a second occurs in the fall. It can be pruned to grow as a free-standing shrub or made into a hedge. The delicate pink of 'New Dawn' is pretty when matched with the violet of a *Maurandia* or a clematis.

   **Origin:** a sport of 'Dr. Van Fleet.'

## THE DESCENDANTS OF 'NEW DAWN'

'New Dawn' was the first of a group of roses that is worth mentioning, even they don't all hold the same fascination. The first of these, 'Coral Dawn', was developed in America by

1

# Peace
*Climbing Hybrid Tea*

15

the end of World War II, a symbol of peace among nations, and between 1945 and 1965, it won the most prestigious rose competitions. Although it was born a shrub, we prefer it as a climber, particularly once it has reached full growth. This rose is the result of a great many crossings and pleases everyone with its immense, lush, creamy yellow flowers (tending to yellower shades in colder climates) edged in pink; they are high-centered and open in a more or less orderly fashion. The flowering comes late but is excellent throughout the season; the foliage is ample and shiny, and the canes have very few thorns. This is a rose with a robust constitution. In fact, it is difficult to find anything bad to say about it, except perhaps that its scent is weak.

**Origin:** ('George Dickson' x 'Souvenir de Claudius Pernet') x ('Joanna Hill' x 'Chas. P. Kilham') x 'Margaret McGredy.'

### ALTERNATIVE SELECTION
'Handel' (1) is another famous rose appreciated for the decorative value of its flowers, which are cream colored with a deep pink border, beautifully shaped and semidouble. The leaves are tinted bronze. Flowering is very long. Care must be taken to prevent attacks of powdery mildew and blackspot.

**Height:** 10 feet (3 m)
**Flower size:** 6 inches (15 cm)
**Number of petals:** 40–45
(shrub form: F. Meilland 1945; climber: Brandy 1950)

The most famous rose in the world, 'Peace' is known as 'Madame Antoine Meilland' in France, 'Gloria Dei' in Germany and 'Gioia' in Italy. It arrived at

70

# Polka 91
*Modern Climber*

16

## ALTERNATIVE SELECTIONS

'Schoolgirl', often overlooked, has flowers of the typical hybrid tea form, between apricot and orange; the leaves are broad and dark.

'Leander' (1) by Austin, is a shrub rose, but given its propensity to form long, robust branches, it is best used as a climber. On a support or near a tree, it reaches up to 10 feet (3 m). The color is a splendid brilliant apricot of varying shades, the shape of the flower is an enchantingly perfect rosette, and the scent—of fruit and apples—is delicious. Robust and healthy, it has a single luxuriant flowering that it occasionally repeats.

A rose with a less intense apricot color is 'Royal Sunset'. As is the case with similarly named roses, the word "sunset" refers to the warm tones of its flowers. It has many virtues and just one drawback: It cannot abide overly cold climates (even when protected during winter). It won a gold medal at Portland for its enormous, enchanting, cup-shaped flowers, which have only 20 petals and are very graceful. The fragrance is rich.

**Height:** 6.5–10 feet (2–3 m)
**Flower size:** 4.5 inches (11 cm)
**Number of petals:** 45
(Meilland 1991)

This interesting climber, eminently suited to framing a doorway or covering a pillar, is valuable because of the relative rarity of its coloring, which is reminiscent of mandarin oranges. With their fruity scent, the many flowers bring delight to any garden, standing out clearly against the dense, dark green leaves. As a climber, it is highly resistant to disease and cold, solid and easy to grow. The flowering is excellent. For a pretty combination, grow a low-habit bushy rose at its feet; striking choices would be 'Sunset Boulevard' and 'Southampton'; a more delicate arrangement could be achieved with 'Grüss an Aachen.' Even a groundcover rose such as 'Sussex,' with its refined, pale colors, would to set off 'Polka 91' beautifully.

1

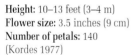

**Height:** 10–13 feet (3–4 m)
**Flower size:** 3.5 inches (9 cm)
**Number of petals:** 140
(Kordes 1977)

The huge number of petals on the flowers of this rose—a big favorite in the United States and Germany—give an astonishingly dense appearance. So tightly are the petals packed one against another that there seems to be no room for air (on rare occasions, this rose will produce less densely packed flowers). Even the buds are ponderous at first and then flatten. On top of that, the flowers are large and arranged in bunches, so at the moment of flowering, one sees only the intense pink, which eventually becomes lighter with silvery overtones. In full bloom, this rose in an impressive spectacle that is most pleasing to those who are drawn more to flamboyance than to delicacy. This is a hardy plant, heedless of frost and other inclement weather, nicely reflowering, and it has pliable canes and copious leaves, ample and light green. Its fragrance is reminiscent of green apples.

## ALTERNATIVE SELECTIONS

The flowers of 'Rosarium Uetersen' resemble those of a celebrated rose from the late 19th century, the Bourbon 'Madame Isaac Pereire' (1). It has the same almost strident color, a crimson that tends toward magenta, and similar flowers—large, measuring more than 4 inches (10 cm)—and although the flowers have no more than 60 petals, they seem very double. The rose bears the pompous name of the wife of a rich Paris financier—and it has plenty of pomp but no real elegance. The flowers are sometimes orderly, deeply cupped and quartered; at other times, they are looser. Its scent is very intense. The shrub is almost frighteningly vigorous and is best treated as a climber; it will easily cover more than 10 feet (3 m). The flowering is abundant from mid-June on. The first blooms often open imperfectly and are poorly formed, but the next flowers will be fine, and the autumn flowering is the prettiest of all.

1

Climbers

# Sombreuil
*Noisette or Tea*

18

**Height:** 10–13 feet (3–4 m)
**Flower size:** 4 inches (10 cm)
**Number of petals:** about 100
(Robert 1850)

It seems truly incredible, but the most beautiful climbers are to be found among the antique roses. The origin of 'Sombreuil' is uncertain, but its traits are clearly those of a Noisette or a tea. Precisely why it is planted less often than others from those two classes is not clear, given its refined, elegant nature; perhaps it is held back by its one known defect—it needs a warm, well-protected spot. In other positions, it suffers, its flowering becoming less satisfactory. Even so, it is less delicate than others of its category in terms of winter temperatures, is vigorous and of excellent growth, healthy, with a sweet scent and recurrent blooms. Its true charm is the shape of its flowers: quartered and flat, composed of numerous petals packed in one against another to form perfectly symmetrical rosettes. The color is creamy white with a touch of pink in the center that later gives way to overall white. The flowers are like small works of art made of tissue paper. It deserves a place in a garden, at least where its needs can be met, perhaps against an old brick wall or against one of pink plaster for the contrast. Given such an opportunity, it will give the best of itself.

**Origin:** a sport of 'Gigantesque.'

## ALTERNATIVE SELECTIONS

Roses comparable to 'Sombreuil' can be found among the albas, roses that boast all the characteristics of refinement, freshness and elegance. 'Madame Plantier' (1) and 'Madame Legras de Saint Germain' are sometimes classified among the albas and sometimes among the Noisettes, which explains their affinity with 'Sombreuil.' Both can be advantageously planted as climbers: 'Madame Plantier' easily reaches 10 feet (3 m), and 'Madame Legras de Saint Germain' usually grows to 6.5 feet (2 m) but will easily reach twice that when placed against a wall. The former has rather small flowers shaped like pompoms in a pale cream color that later becomes pure white with a green button eye in the center. The scent is sweet, the leaves glaucous green. So striking is this rose that it is worth a trip to Sissinghurst Castle to see examples growing around the trunks of ancient apple trees. 'Madame Legras de Saint Germain' is very similar but with more delicious flowers, more scented, in thick bunches. Both tolerate shady sites and have a single rich flowering in the summer.

1

**Height:** 10 feet (3 m)
**Flower size:** 4 inches (10 cm)
**Number of petals:** 65–75
(Béluze 1843)

Dedicated to the memory of Empress Josephine and to her famous rose garden, this rose has never been cast aside, never fallen out of favor in gardens, whether as a climber or a bush. Finding a more seductive rose would not be easy because of its subtle scent, with a touch of spice, and because of its color, a pale pink that later takes on ashy shadings and even flesh tones, according to the age of the flower. And then there is the admirable shape of the flowers, rosettes that are flat and quartered, but naturally so, without geometric rigidity. Flowers with very short stems appear on the ends of canes and also, abundantly, along the canes. The branches are not overly thorny and the leaves not particularly abundant. Many things have been said about its flowering: that the shrub form is more reflowering, that the climber repeats only in good years. We have seen many specimens of this rose in many gardens, always in flower except in a warm August. In temperate climates, it may flower at Christmas and produce a few blooms in February, but cold would not permit such flowers to open. What is certain is that if the temperature is not sufficiently high, the flowers fail to open. In such situations, the rose can take on a less than pleasant appearance. All that is needed is patience, for as the air warms, the flowers will open perfectly; the autumn flowering is regal. There is also a trick, suggested by an English rose gardener, to help the flowers open in a difficult spring: Give the buds a gentle squeeze with your fingers just as they are about to open.

No big fan of rain or humidity, this rose prefers to grow in a serene climate against a sheltered wall in a protected site and in well-drained soil. Such are the requirements for getting the best out of this rose, but it will be even more striking if placed alongside 'Gloire de Dijon,' with its more shaded and warmer tones.

**Origin:** 'Madame Desprez' x a tea rose.

### ALTERNATIVE SELECTION

Another seductive rose is the tea rose *Rosa devoniensis*, also called 'Rosa Magnolia' because of the sweet flesh tones of its petals. Highly refined, this rose is also somewhat delicate, so it is best suited to a temperate climate or a well-protected spot in full sun. Its branches are mahogany-colored, and the flowers are a magnificent cream with pink shadings and an edging of apricot. They are large and double and repeat throughout the season. This rose was much cultivated in English gardens in India and is ideal for a veranda.

# Souvenir du Dr. Jamain
*Hybrid Perpetual*

**Height:** 10 feet (3 m)
**Flower size:** 3 inches (8 cm)
**Number of petals:** 20–25
(Lacharme 1865)

Red is a much-loved color, the color of ardent passion, and the roses of myth, legend and literature are most often red. Many people find that red inspires the deepest emotions. The prettiest red among roses is neither vermilion nor scarlet but a deep red with shadowy folds and velvety reflections. 'Souvenir du Dr. Jamain' boasts a special red, a plum shade suffused with intense crimson. Some say it is the color of port wine; others say burgundy. The color later turns to purple, which should be kept out of direct sunlight, so it is best to grow this plant in a shady area of the garden, perhaps at the foot of a large leafy tree. The flowers open to form cups illuminated at the center by stamens from mid- to late June. The reflowering is good. Autumn brings orange hips. The leaves are dark and the branches slightly thorny. By nature, 'Souvenir du Dr. Jamain' is a large bush, but because it produces long, disorderly branches, it is best to use it against a wall or lean it on a support to help it behave like a climber.

**Origin:** 'Charles Lefèbvre' x an unknown rose (according to some experts 'Général Jacqueminot' x 'Charles Lefèbvre').

**ALTERNATIVE SELECTION**
In terms of color, few climbers can bear comparison with 'Souvenir du Dr. Jamain.' 'Guinée' (Mallerin 1938) is one of those few—a velvety dark crimson rose with double flowers that give a glimpse of the stamens and are strongly scented. A wonderful, luxuriant rose, it climbs up to 13 feet (4 m) and sometimes flowers a second time.

**Height:** 10 feet (3 m)
**Flower size:** 3 inches (8 cm)
**Number of petals:** 30
(Kordes 1995)

Red roses are always in demand because they add such pleasure to a garden, so the selection is reasonably broad. The most popular are those with flowers in bunches because they are less pretentious and more natural and easygoing. Among the most famous and widely used of these is 'Tradition 95' (the improved form of 'Tradition'), which is a brilliant blood-red that sun, rain and age do not fade. The medium-size flowers are grouped in large bunches, but like all roses of this type, they offer very little scent. The shape of the flower is of a better quality than usual. The leaves are shiny and dark. The plant is well branched, robust and of medium habit; it has pretty repeat blooms.

## ALTERNATIVE SELECTIONS

'Dublin Bay' is a possible choice but has the drawback of being hard to find. The climbing form, created in New Zealand by McGredy, has the

1

same characteristics as 'Tradition 95' but grows to just over 6.5 feet (2 m).

Among the *kordesii* hybrids is 'Parkdirektor Riggers' (1), popular despite (or perhaps because of) its odd name. This grows to 13 feet (4 m) and has semidouble flowers of a velvety blood-red with a touch of crimson. They grow in bunches that are sometimes composed of as many as 50 flowers. It reflowers abundantly. The scent is weak, and the plant is susceptible to blackspot.

Another rose with red flowers that grow in bunches is 'Danse du Feu', which has enjoyed popularity since 1953, when it was created in France by Mallerin. It is fire-red, but the color does not endure; it flowers well in summer and fall, producing medium-size, 32-petaled flowers and a great abundance of leafy branches. It easily reaches a height of 16.5 feet (5 m).

**Height:** 6.5–10 feet (2–3 m)
**Flower size:** 4 inches (10 cm)
**Number of petals:** more than 50
(Barni 1996)

'White Rock' and 'Swan Lake' are both climbing roses known for their pretty flowers and evocative names. 'Swan Lake' has prettily shaped flowers, high at the center, that are pure white with a touch of pink in the middle and grow in bunches. It is generous with its flowers and its reflowering. Nor does it fear rain, something that can't be said of many roses, which are often reduced to torn rags by a good downpour.

'White Rock' is an excellent vigorous climber created by Barni. It has abundant, shiny branches. Reflowering is good; resistance to disease is good. Most pleasing of all are its flowers, with their silky, ruffled petals, pretty without putting on airs.

**ALTERNATIVE SELECTIONS**
Other pure white roses with flowers typical of hybrid teas are 'White Cockade', 8 feet (2.5 m) high, and 'Mrs. Herbert Stevens', a cold-resistant tea that is white with green shadings.

Always beautiful is the climbing form of 'Iceberg' (1), a mutation of the famous floribunda with all of its valuable traits, including that of always being in flower except for a few brief pauses; it is the first and last rose to bloom in the garden. Only rarely will it grow very tall, however, tending to behave more like a tall bush full of branches.

# Albéric Barbier
*Hybrid Wichuraiana*

23

that needs covering up. It is also good when allowed to run up and climb over and around the branches of a big tree.

**Origin:** *Rosa wichuraiana* x 'Shirley Hibberd.'

### ALTERNATIVE SELECTIONS

*Rosa* x *fortuniana* (1) has beautiful ivory-white flowers with the scent of violets. The flowers are large for a rambler, almost 3 inches (7 cm), and the petals are nicely arranged around a button eye. It was imported from China in the 19th century by the plant hunter Robert Fortune. Without doubt, it is a hybrid of *R. banksiae*, which explains its preference for temperate climates and its thornless canes, which at maturity become rusty and peel. Its single flowering is enchanting, and its dark leaves are beautiful.

Another variety from *Rosa wichuraiana* is 'Gardenia,' with yellow buds and very double cream-to-yellow, scented flowers. A long flowering begins in mid-June and is followed by a few occasional blooms in fall. It has copious leaves, shiny and hardy, and reaches a height of 20 feet (6 m).

**Height:** 20–23 feet (6–7 m)
**Flower size:** 2.5–3 inches (6–8 cm)
**Number of petals:** 45–55 (Barbier 1900)

The early years of the 20th century were very active for the Barbier brothers at the family firm in Orléans, where they used *Rosa wichuraiana* in particular. The first and most popular of their ramblers is 'Albéric Barbier.' The branches of this very hardy, vigorous plant will cover many feet wherever they find room to climb or spread, creating a little forest of shiny leaves. And once a year, as soon as spring weather has truly arrived, this rose covers itself first in small bright yellow buds and then in flowers, large for a rambler, that are white with lemony centers and densely packed with thin petals. Later, they become a little less orderly. The flowering, abundant and beautiful, lasts for three weeks; an occasional flower appears in autumn. This is the perfect rambler for an arbor or a place in the garden

1

78

Ramblers

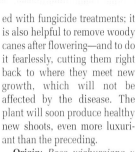

**Height:** 15 feet (4.5 m)
**Flower size:** 4 inches (10 cm)
**Number of petals:** 30–40
(Barbier 1921)

Usually considered a twin of 'Albéric Barbier,' 'Albertine' is well known and well loved. Its appealing characteristics include its flowers, which are of the typical hybrid tea shape in a warm rose color so coppery that some call it lobster; its excellent scent, which fills the garden; its great vigor; and the generosity of its flowering, which is usually early. Its flowers, which lose their shape as soon as they are fully open, come in small bunches. The branches, a little too rigid for a good rambler, should be firmly attached to a trellis or grate or made to grow on a pergola rather than on a wall (a wall limits air circulation, which increases the chances of this plant developing powdery mildew). Given its lack of flexibility, it is not the best plant for the foot of a tree. In gardens in England, one often sees the beautiful sight of an 'Albertine' trained to creep across a boundary hedge.

Powdery mildew usually attacks 'Albertine' after it flowers, so its blooms are not affected. The disease can be prevented with fungicide treatments; it is also helpful to remove woody canes after flowering—and to do it fearlessly, cutting them right back to where they meet new growth, which will not be affected by the disease. The plant will soon produce healthy new shoots, even more luxuriant than the preceding.

**Origin:** *Rosa wichuraiana* x 'Mrs. Arthur Robert Waddell.'

### ALTERNATIVE SELECTIONS

The many offspring of *Rosa wichuraiana* include 'Alida Lovett,' developed in America and widely planted in the United States. It has elegant bright orange buds and beautiful large flowers, shell-pink on a base of saffron yellow and flat when open. They grow in bunches. The plant has few thorns, and the shiny dark leaves contrast nicely with the sweet color of the flowers.

There is also 'François Juranville,' yet another rambler made by the Barbier brothers when they were experimenting with *Rosa wichuraiana*. So similar is this rose to 'Albertine' that the two are often confused. This rose has strongly scented double flowers, pink with salmon shading, made up of narrow petals around a button eye. It grows rapidly, easily scrambling over structures and supports. It is hardy and disease resistant. It will grow to around 26 feet (8 m).

## *Bobbie James*
*Hybrid Multiflora*

⚓ ◉ ✕ ⚏

are strongly scented. The height is 26 feet (8 m).

'Francis E. Lester' (1), a far more tranquil rambler, is happy to stop growing at 16.5 feet (5 m). It is descended from a hybrid musk, an unusual origin that explains why it is different. Different most of all in terms of its flowers, whose rounded petals resemble small buttons; the overall effect is reminiscent of apple blossoms. Each petal is marked with a pink thumbprint. The flowering is marvelous, as is the scent of oranges and bananas. In the fall, the plant is decorated with small, pleasing hips, and a few late flowers may also put in an appearance. The leaves are elegantly shaped and have delicate, pointed leaflets.

A rambler of similar size is 'Seagull', well known and highly valued for its terrific flowering of small white flowers with yellow centers. It forms a pale cloud floating on green.

**Height:** 26 feet (8 m)
**Flower size:** 2 inches (5 cm)
**Number of petals:** 7–9
(Sunningdale Nurseries 1961)

Plenty of ramblers have white flowers, but very few are as exuberant as 'Bobbie James.' If you aren't prepared for it, this rose's rapid growth may seem excessive; its placement requires planning because it will quickly scramble over anything and everything in its path. On the other hand, its dense foliage can be put to advantage if you want to turn a large sunny spot into a shady one; just remember to give it a support that is large enough and strong enough to take its weight. You can also use it to blanket a corner you'd like to make green. This is a pretty rambler with a scent that fills the air and can be picked up from a good distance. The flowers are cupped, hardly more than single and grow in large bunches; the flowering is overwhelming. The leaves are a shiny light green; the canes are robust, grow with surprising speed and can become surprisingly thick. In the fall, this rose produces abundant small hips as decorative as the flowers.

### ALTERNATIVE SELECTIONS
Another good rambler is 'Wedding Day', a hybrid of *Rosa longicuspis* var. *sinowilsonii*, luxuriant and thorny. The buds are apricot and the flowers single with wedge-shaped petals of creamy yellow that shade into white and then turn pink at the end. They

Ramblers

# Crimson Shower
*Hybrid Wichuraiana*

26

81

**Height:** 11.5 feet (3.5 m)
**Flower size:** 1.2 inches (3 cm)
**Number of petals:** 20–40
(Harkness 1951)

Since they are descendants of pale roses, ramblers almost always have light-colored flowers; red is not common. But crimson tending to purple is the color of 'Crimson Shower,' which descends from a favorite rose in the gardens of the past— 'Excelsa,' a sister of the even more popular 'Dorothy Perkins.' Both of those roses have been left behind today, too easily prey to powdery mildew. 'Crimson Shower' is far more resistant to disease and also produces pleasing double flowers in large bunches that bend forward in cascades. The flowering begins late, in July, when most other ramblers are spent, and continues up to September. The leaves are small and very shiny, the canes are flexible and almost without thorns. The tree form is very pleasant; the plant can also be grown on a tripod or other similar support.

**Origin:** a sport of 'Excelsa.'

### ALTERNATIVE SELECTIONS

'Crimson Rambler', vigorous and highly floriferous, with crimson semidouble flowers, is little appreciated today because, like 'Excelsa', it is prey to powdery mildew.

Another rambler long forgotten but, in this case, without good reason is 'Russelliana' (syns. 'Russell's Cottage Rose', 'Old Spanish Rose', 'Souvenir de la Bataille de Marengo'), a hybrid multiflora that was planted in the gardens of the 1840s and dearly loved: Many English cottages and country homes still boast ancient examples. It has pretty flowers, small and very double, highly scented and between cherry and purple in color; they grow in dense bunches. The branches are covered with tiny prickles. Height is about 20 feet (6 m).

Another rambler with red flowers is 'Alexander Girault', the color of which is difficult to describe: strawberry with coppery and pinkish shadings touched by yellow with a white center. Even the shape of the flowers is odd; they have narrow, pointed petals that wrap around themselves. Some like it, some don't, but the effect is always striking. It has an intensely fruity fragrance.

Among the more recent reflowering ramblers is 'Super Elfin', a small plant with scarlet flowers.

# Félicité et Perpétue
## Hybrid Sempervirens

27

**Height:** 20 feet (6 m)
**Flower size:** 2 inches (5 cm)
**Number of petals:** 65
(Jacques 1827)

One of the oldest ramblers, this was created by the director of the gardens of Louis-Philippe, duc d'Orléans and later king of France, in Neuilly and dedicated to his two daughters. Enchanting because of its rosette-shaped flowers, perfectly symmetrical and so precise they seem to have been trimmed with scissors; they are white with a touch of pink, which is visible in the bud. The fragrance is light, of primroses. The foliage is dense, dark green, shiny and semievergreen; the canes are thin and very flexible and have few thorns. You

can create a surprising effect by wrapping the canes around three poles arranged in a pyramid, which will give the plant the vertical structure that best shows off its abundant flowers, soft as a fall of new snow. Generally hardy and easy to grow, it requires no pruning but can be rejuvenated every two or three years by detaching it from the support and cutting away the deadwood—a large-scale undertaking but well worth the effort.

## ALTERNATIVE SELECTIONS
'Baltimore Belle', another antique

rambler, is gracious and elegant. Beloved by 19th-century Americans, it produces cascades of pretty rosette-shaped double flowers with a tidy form in a very alluring pink that turns to cream. Flowering is late. Height is 13 feet (4 m). This rose has become easier to find since its inclusion in the David Austin catalog.

'Sanders White', another *Rosa wichuraiana* hybrid, dates to 1912, but time has done nothing to diminish its popularity. This rambler will climb up trees and over arbors and arches and can be used as a groundcover. It can also be grafted to create a tree rose; as such, it will form a small umbrella of flowers and leaves. The white flowers are very regular, packed with petals and have visible stamens. They grow in large, cascading bunches and have a marvelous scent. Flowering is late, at the end of July. The plant has dark leaves and flexible canes.

82

Ramblers

# Ghislaine de Féligonde
*Hybrid Multiflora*

every point of view. You can grow it as a large shrub by leaving it be or make it into a rambler by fixing it to a support. In any situation in the garden, one can admire the pretty, drooping branches, which have so few thorns as to be almost bare. The leaves, healthy and shiny, grow densely. The large bunches of small, attractive flowers, apricot edged with pink, have a nice fragrance.

**Origin:** 'Goldfinch' x an unknown rose.

### ALTERNATIVE SELECTIONS

'Goldfinch' (1) has similar characteristics: flexible canes without thorns and the same height—it is a rambler but not overly vigorous. But its flowers are a mixture of yellows, "a plate of scrambled eggs," in the words of the great gardener and writer Vita Sackville-West. Her description is perfect as long as it is not taken negatively; the bright yellow buds and the primrose-yellow flowers opening to amber anthers, at maturity a pale cream, are truly delicious to look at. And fragrant.

'Lykkefund,' a very vigorous rambler derived from *Rosa helenae*, has strong canes, almost without thorns, and can reach 26 feet (8 m). It bears immense bunches of creamy yellow flowers with a hint of pink; they are semidouble, of medium size and strongly scented.

Yet a another selection is 'Adélaide d'Orléans,' one of the most elegant ramblers, with pretty flowers, creamy pink and semidouble. Height is 10 feet (3 m).

**83**

**Height:** 8 feet (2.5 m)
**Flower size:** 1.5 inches (4 cm)
**Number of petals:** 20–40
(Turbat 1916)

This rose bears an awkward name that might be better suited to the heroine of a chivalric romance. While indeed romantic, this is a nicely behaved and gracious rose, very appealing from

Ramblers

# Kew Rambler
*Hybrid Soulieana*

**Height:** 18 feet (5.5 m)
**Flower size:** 1.2 inches (3 cm)
**Number of petals:** 5
(found in the Royal Botanic
Gardens at Kew and introduced
in 1912)

The small, copious, gray-green
leaves that bespeak the species
from which this rose comes are
the perfect backdrop to its
dense bouquetlike bunches of
pink flowers illuminated at the
center by shining stamens. The
rose is as delightful as a wild
rose found in a thicket. This is a
fine rambler near water, on an
arbor or winding around a tree.
There is only one flowering, but
it is long, beginning in the middle of May; the fall brings tiny
orange hips that create a picture

every bit as pretty as the flowers.

**Origin:** *Rosa soulieana* x
'Hiawatha.'

## ALTERNATIVE SELECTIONS
'Blush Rambler' (1), with pale pink
semidouble flowers, is from *Rosa
multiflora*. Very popular in the opening decades of the 20th century, it
was the preferred ornament for hundreds of English cottages. It merits

1

more attention because of its tri-
umphant flowering; the sweetly colored flowers turn outward to form
scented cascades.

Also pink but with double flowers
is 'Champneys' Pink Cluster', the rose
that gave birth to the Noisettes. It
has 2-inch (5 cm) flowers with 24
petals that grow in large bunches.
The flowering is very long, repeated,
splendid, and highly scented. A highly recommended rose, but not one
for overly cold climates.

For cold resistance, there is 'Débutante', which has double flowers in
rather small rosettes despite the
plant's derivation from a *Rosa wichuraiana* and the pretty 'Baroness
Rothschild', from which it gets its
lovely color. Perfumed, it produces a
few flowers even after summer's end.

Another pink rambler with double
flowers is 'Apple Blossoms', relatively
unknown but worth more attention.

Ramblers

# Léontine Gervais
*Hybrid Wichuraiana*

30

**Height:** 20–26 feet (6–8 m)
**Flower size:** 3.5 inches (9 cm)
**Number of petals:** 20–40
(Barbier 1903)

Another pleasant creation by Barbier, this rose is of particular interest because of the lovely color of its flowers—salmon to yellow with orange highlights. Some call the color copper. This special coloring brings a pleasing light into the garden and is truly splendid at sunset, set off by the dark, shiny foliage. A word of praise also goes to the shape of its flowers, which have large, wavy petals that fold and unfold with great softness.

**Origin:** *Rosa wichuraiana* x 'Souvenir de Cathérine Guillot.'

## ALTERNATIVE SELECTIONS

Barbier and *Rosa wichuraiana* were also responsible for 'Auguste Gervais', which has semidouble 3-to-4-inch (8–10 cm) flowers and yellow-salmon-copper coloring that gives way to cream. The flowers come in large bunches and are highly scented. The plant's dense foliage is composed of small, dark, shiny leaves; its height is 11.5 feet (3.5 m).

'Paul Transon' is another rambler with an interesting, indefinable color—salmon pink on a cream ground accented with coppery lights. The flowers are small, only 2.5 inches (6 cm), single and have a less pleasing shape than the above; they are double and open flat and have slightly disorderly petals. The branches are copper, and the light green leaves have coppery overtones. Flowering begins in mid-June. Two virtues: the scent of apples and the ability to reflower in the autumn if planted in a warm, protected site.

'Aviateur Blériot', a hybrid wichuraiana, but not one signed by Barbier, is another rambler of ancient date. While little known, it has not fallen into oblivion. Vigorous, a little rigid and almost without thorns, it has strong, smooth leaves and large bunches of scented flowers in a yellow-orange that fades to cream.

dously hardy, as are all the roses from the Kordes company. Ideal in a shady spot, to train up a pillar, run along the ground or simply plant as a large shrub.

**Origin:** *Rosa* x *kordesii* x 'Golden Glow.'

### ALTERNATIVE SELECTION

'Alister Stella Gray' syn. 'Golden Rambler' (1) is, like all the Noisettes, valued for its continuous flowering, which has only a very brief interruption. The last bunches, very large, come in the autumn on that year's canes. The buds are egg-colored, and the flowers are quartered, 2.5 inches (6 cm) in diameter and an intense yellow that pales to cream; the petals are reflexed and the scent is a strong musk. This is a vigorous shrub that can be treated as just that in a spacious corner, or to take advantage of its long canes, it can be set against a support or trained over an arch or pillar, in which case it can reach up to 13 feet (4 m). It has large, dark leaves and few thorns. When pruning, do not cut back the length of the branches; eliminate old wood from the bottom instead.

**Height:** 10 feet (3 m)
**Flower size:** 3 inches (7.5 cm)
**Number of petals:** 24–30
(Kordes 1954)

A rare yellow-flowered offspring of *Rosa* x *kordesii*, 'Leverkusen' is valued for its long summer flowering, which repeats later although less abundantly. The lemon-yellow flowers, which have a pleasant fruity fragrance, are high-centered at the beginning and later form rosettes with many thin petals in the form of a small pad at the center while the exterior petals spread out and ripple. Also splendid are the leaves, shiny and bright, with closely spaced leaflets. The plant is robust, resistant to cold and tremen-

1

Ramblers

be appreciated even from a distance. Resistant to cold and immune to disease.

**Origin:** *Rosa wichuraiana* x 'Champion of the World.'

### ALTERNATIVE SELECTIONS

'Gerbe Rose', like 'Débutante', came into being through the cross of a *Rosa wichuraiana* with the pretty 'Baroness Rothschild'. It inherited from the latter not only its pink color but also the rather large double flowers, flat once they fully open, with a slight sweet scent. The leaves are large and shiny, the flowering is quite long, and occasionally, a few flowers appear later. Not overly vigorous, it stops growing at 10 feet (3 m).

'Madame Sancy de Parabère' is a climber from the small group of so-called Boursault roses, of which little is ever said. Its deep pink flowers open to form large 5-inch (12 cm) rosettes at the center of which numerous small petals are packed symmetrically. Height is 15 feet (4.5 m); the foliage is well colored, thick and without thorns. Flowering is early and generous, and the fact that it happens only once a year should not prevent anyone from choosing this very interesting and overlooked rose, which can be used in place of any rambler.

**Height:** 20 feet (6 m)
**Flower size:** 3–3.5 inches (8–9 cm)
**Number of petals:** 45–55
(Manda 1898)

A well-named rose, this plant dominates May with the heady scent of its blooms. The bright pink flowers are cup-shaped and have a central button eye that recalls the sweet roses of the past; the flowers later assume a mauve tone and tend to lose their form. The intense fruity scent, reminiscent of green apples, fills the air. When climbing a tree, this rose gracefully wraps its supple canes around branches, elegantly displaying its flowers against the shiny foliage, an effect that can

# Paul's Himalayan Musk
## Hybrid Musk

**33** ⚓ ◎ ✕ ⠿

**Height:** 20–26 feet (6–8 m)
**Flower size:** 1 inch (2.5 cm), double
(introduced by Paul)

This is an ambiguous name for a rose whose origins are unknown but which shares some characteristics of *Rosa multiflora*, *sempervirens* and *moschata*; its downward-turning gray-green leaves are inherited from the *moschata*. Ramblers are always plants of great grace, but this is the most graceful of all because of the soft bearing of its thin, flexible canes, which produce large bunches of well-spaced flowers, dense rosettes of a sweet lilac-pink scented of musk. They have the appearance of great buoyancy. This is a strong climber, good for any site where there is enough space for it. The stupendous flowering begins at the end of June.

### ALTERNATIVE SELECTIONS
'Princess of Nassau' (1) (also called 'Princesse de Nassau' and attributed to Laffay) is a rarely grown rambler that merits more attention, not only because of the grace of its pink buds that look as though they're made of silk and its white flowers with gold stamens but because of its reflowering; it produces a series of delicate bunches of flowers over a very long period. It is not the best choice, however, if you're looking for an overwhelmingly spectacular flowering.

Two vigorous subspecies of *Rosa multiflora* also merit greater attention. *R. multiflora carnea*, originally from China, has very double flowers with regular rounded petals that form small, pale pink cupolas; *R. multiflora platyphylla* is even more striking with its larger flowers. This flower was loved by the Victorians, who called it the 'Seven Sisters Rose' because its flowers have seven different shades: dark pink, light pink, crimson, cherry, mauve, lilac and purple.

# *Rosa filipes* 'Kiftsgate'
*Hybrid Filipes*

34

and 50 feet (15 m) wide that bears immense bunches of flowers in just one of which the owner counted 428 flowers. The small, creamy white scented flowers give way to tiny orange hips. The effect is spectacular near a pond or lake, because the water reflects the flowering branches. This is a useful rambler because of its vigor, simple grace and sweet beauty rather like that of a flowering fruit tree.

### ALTERNATIVE SELECTION
'Brenda Colvin' (1), which began with a sport of 'Kiftsgate', displays the same vigor—stretching up to nearly 33 feet (10 m)—and the same profusion of flowers, which are about 1.5 inches (4 cm) in diameter and a lovely delicate pink. The fragrance is intense. It is pretty when framing a large window or running along a low wall; like 'Kiftsgate', it is ideal on the bank of a pond, particularly when woven into and supported by shrubbery.

89

**Height:** 26 feet (8 m)
**Flower size:** 1.2 inches (3 cm)
**Number of petals:** 5
(China 1908)

This is a Chinese rose with the same explosive growth of 'Bobbie James.' Perhaps even more so, since the garden from which it takes its name has a famous specimen 65.5 feet (20 m) high

1

# The Garland
*Hybrid Musk*

35

and small, dark leaves. The autumn brings a crop of beautiful tiny oval hips. This rose is sometimes classified among the hybrid multifloras. It is a perfect rambler to place behind a border of antique roses.

**Origin:** *Rosa moschata* x *Rosa multiflora.*

### ALTERNATIVE SELECTIONS
Another rose with semidouble flowers, white with a pretty tuft of yellow stamens in the middle, is 'Rambling Rector', which has all the best qualities of the category: luxuriant growth; glorious flowering with semidouble cream flowers that have been compared to a waterfall, the apparently infinite number of flowers like drops of water; resistance to disease; and even decorative hips in autumn. It will grow up to 20 feet (6 m). Because of the weight of its branches, it should be given a structure capable of supporting it: If trained to a tree, it must be a big one; if made to cover a shed, the shed's walls must be solid. Nothing will diminish its power.

Yet another rambler, this one sadly overlooked, is an Italian variety called 'Purezza', which won a gold medal in Rome in 1960 and was created by Mansuino. It is offered by the Barni company. It bears bunches of large very double white flowers. The flowering is not long, but the plant reflowers in the autumn. It is a descendent of a *Rosa banksiae* and is thornless.

**Height:** 16.5 feet (5 m)
**Flower size:** 1.5 inches (4 cm)
**Number of petals:** 12–14
(Wells 1835)

"It is well worth getting up at 4 a.m. on a mid-June morning to see the tender loveliness of the newly opening buds; for beautiful though they are at noon, they are better still when just awakening after the refreshing influence of the short summer night." So wrote Gertrude Jekyll, writer and passionate lover of roses. This wonderful rambler has inherited the best of its parents: creamy white flowers touched with pink, their petals folding out like daisies' and joined in tight, erect bunches; a scent that delights the air;

Ramblers

90

# Veilchenblau
*Hybrid Multiflora*

**Height:** 15 feet (4.5 m)
**Flower size:** 1.2–1.5 inches (3–4 cm)
**Number of petals:** 10–20 (Schmidt 1909)

This is also called 'The Blue Rose,' although its flowers are really an unusual and surprising shade of bluish violet with flashes of white and illuminated by yellow stamens. As they age, the flowers darken to lilac with gray and blue tones. The coloring is worth protecting, so it is best not to plant this rambler in full sun. The minuscule flowers are semi-double, cup-shaped and scented; the branches are almost thornless; the leaves are broad, pointed, shiny and apple-scented. A glorious effect can be achieved by using 'Veilchenblau' on a pergola or fence accompanied by a pale-flowered rambler such as 'The Garland' or 'Purezza.' Or it can be combined with a rose such as 'Débutante.' Attacks of powdery mildew are not serious and can be prevented with proper treatment.

**Origin:** 'Crimson Rambler' x 'Erinnerung an Brod.'

ALTERNATIVE SELECTIONS
Three other ramblers, all descendants of the multifloras, boast exceptional colors: 'Rose Marie Viaud,' which is scentless; 'Violette,' which has small flowers of a darker purple-violet with a touch of yellow at the base of the petals and a slight fruity scent; and 'Bleu Magenta' (1), which is between violet and cherry in color and produces small double flowers in dense bunches.

# ROSES IN BEDS

**M**uch as a flowerbed is an island within a garden, a rose garden is one or more large beds of roses arranged according to some design. Every garden should have its section of roses, even if very small; even English gardens, often considered kingdoms of unbridled naturalness, usually include a more formal area where roses are planted in an orderly and symmetrical way.

Such beds are reserved for the most "important" shrub roses, the reigning nobility of the garden. These are plants to be studied one by one in order to fully appreciate the geometry of their forms, to enjoy their colors and to take in their subtle fragrances. They are proud and erect, and any that demonstrate a tendency to untidiness will be put back in order by drastic pruning at the end of winter, when every bush is cut back to the same level. These are plants with copious, long-flowering, showy flowers that make the rose bed the center of attention. The plants in such beds are usually about 4 feet (1.2 m) high, but they will need to be a little taller if the bed is surrounded by a hedge 24 to 32 inches (60–80 cm) high so that they can be seen.

Most of the roses in such beds are either hybrid teas or English roses. The hybrid teas are familiar to almost everyone, even people without gardens, since they are the classic florist's roses, with long

## BICOLOR ROSES

Bicolor roses can be quite striking but must be used with care to avoid gaudy effects. Almost all of them are hybrid teas. The best known include:

**'Alleluia,'** purple with silver reverse

**'Cleopatra,'** wine red with gold reverse

**'Colombina,'** yellow edged with pink

**'Contesa de Sastago,'** coral-pink with gold reverse; this rose was famous in the 1930s

**'Double Delight,'** creamy yellow edged with crimson

**'Kordes Perfecta,'** cream, edged and suffused with crimson

**'Kronenbourg,'** plum with straw reverse

**'Joseph's Coat'** (above left), yellow that fades to red

**'Piccadilly,'** scarlet with gold reverse

**'Shot Silk,'** cherry with deep yellow reverse

**'Tequila Sunrise,'** yellow edged in scarlet

Two interesting bicolor

floribundas are 'Suni' (Barni 1993)—awarded in Genoa for its unfailing blooms, given a recommendation at Glasgow and awarded a Gold Rose in Geneva—with large double scarlet flowers with a silvery cream reverse; and 'Tempi Moderni' (Barni 1996), flaming gold, orange and vermilion (above right).

There is also a bicolor pink rose created by David Austin, 'Pat Austin,' which is quite vivid, its petals a shiny copper on the inside, pale yellow-copper on the reverse.

## TREE ROSES

*Known as tree roses, or standards, in English,* rosiers tiges *in French,* Stammrosen *in German and* rose ad alberello *in Italian, these are a sophisticated invention of humans. They are roses grafted onto a rootstock so as to form a large clump of foliage atop a thin, bare trunk; whether the clump of foliage will droop and by how much depend on the type of rose. This form, even though very unnatural, is a wonderful addition to a formal garden because along with roses trained on supports, it supplies the important dimension of height. A single tree rose at the center of a bed—or two, if the bed is rectangular or oval— breaks up the monotony. Such roses are also useful to add a point of interest where the garden needs it: flanking a gate at the end of a path, alongside a niche in a wall or in the center of a vegetable or herb garden as a focal point.*

*Many kinds of rose are offered as standards. Among them are hybrid teas ('Antico Amore,' 'Ingrid Bergman,' 'Magia Nera,' 'Peace,' 'Royal William') and floribundas ('Friesia,' 'Iceberg,' 'Margaret Merril,' 'Rita Levi Montalcini'). Austin offers standard versions of many English roses. Even so, many other kinds of roses make prettier standards because the difference between the size of the rose and the thinness of the trunk is less marked, so the plant looks less disproportionate. Many patio, groundcover and even rambler roses make pretty standards. With their small, graceful blooms, they give the form a gentle appearance not unlike that of little fruit trees. Good choices are 'Festival,' 'Crystal Palace,' 'Sweet Dreams,' 'Gwent,' 'Nozomi,' 'Ballerina,' 'Lavender Dream,' 'Centenaire de Lourdes,' 'Sea Foam,' 'Surrey,' 'The Fairy' and 'Venere' (below). Standards created with ramblers have branches with an even greater weeping effect; good choices are 'Albéric Barbier,' 'Canary Bird,' 'Crimson Shower' and 'Castore.'*

95

stems and the typical high-centered blossoms that form a cone, superb in size and color. The bush they grow on, however, is often unsatisfactory—rigid, twiggy and ungainly. In truth, hybrid teas are pretty only in bud or just open or else in a vase. These roses came into being near the end of the 19th century and became the queens of rose competitions. Hybridizers turned them out in the tens, hundreds and thousands, even though the most recent arrivals almost inevitably obscured the fame of the previous year's cultivars; many were lost along the way.

## ALMOST-BLUE ROSES

Lilac, magenta and lavender are shades that often awaken perplexity but, in the end, succeed in enrapturing. A special effect can be achieved by dedicating a small part of a garden to roses in these shades. Here is a short list of the roses whose color contains the most blue:

**'Blue Moon'** (Tantau 1964), hybrid tea, silver lilac

**'Blue Nile'** (Delbard 1981), hybrid tea, lavender

**'Blue Parfum'** (Tantau 1978), hybrid tea, mauve

**'Blue River'** (Kordes 1984), hybrid tea, lilac with darker shadows

**'Charles de Gaulle'** (Meilland 1975), hybrid tea, mauve, strongly scented (left)

**'Charles Rennie Mackintosh'** (Austin 1988), English rose, magenta to lilac, very floriferous; its flowers are not large but of a graceful shape and so numerous that they hide the leaves (far left)

**'Lagoon'** (Harkness 1973), floribunda, lilac

**'Lake Como'** (Harkness 1968), floribunda, lilac

**'Lavender Pinocchio'** (Boerner 1948), floribunda, pink-lavender.

The other class is English roses, signed by a single maker, David Austin. Beginning in the 1970s, these roses more or less took over the world: highly scented and offering enchanting blossoms in every color one could want as well as leafy shrubs with attractive shapes. The fruit of an ingenious intuition, they result from crossings between an antique rose and a modern, and they display the best qualities of both.

*'Alba Meillandécor.'*

Antique roses are also good choices for beds. It's best to seek out the more compact forms, those of medium size and especially those that reflower, since bare patches are not wanted in such an important area of the garden.

You can create a bed with only one variety. The effect may be striking, but it could also be monotonous. Each gardener must make his or her own decisions about which roses to plant together. Two rules dictated by experience are to form groups of roses that share some characteristics, including height, and never to mix different types: Keep English roses in one place, hybrid teas in another and antiques on their own. As for color, mixing and matching is an art that requires skill: Red can be tempered with white, for example, but a red that tends toward scarlet should not be planted near a purplish one; yellow can be set off with pastels or white; graduating nuances of a single color produces a refined effect.

Yet another class of roses, the floribundas, can be used in beds. They are very orderly, very floriferous and very everblooming. On paper, they are often considered to be of lower quality and relegated to mass plantings. Although this type of planting can be very effective, using floribundas only in this way would be to seriously undervalue them. They bear bunches of very small flowers that are perhaps less refined than those of some other roses, but it is precisely their lack of pretense that makes them so alluring. Their beauty is simple and always graceful. And they are almost always highly resistant to disease. They can be used to form those ever popular strips of color—as often seen in flowerbeds in public parks or at big luxury hotels—or to bring a spot of brightness to a garden. But they also have a use in beds. It is best to alternate colors and pay close attention to balance. Using them alone as specimen plants is probably not a good idea; instead, arrange them in small groups of the same variety, perhaps in groups of three.

Hybrid teas, English roses and floribundas do not necessarily end the list of roses for beds, even though they are the classic roses for this purpose. Nothing and no one prohibits you from putting other types of roses in a bed. An unexpected choice can give an interesting effect. In a small bed without a border or only a very low wall or dwarf plants surrounding it, groundcover roses can be pleasing, provided the type chosen is compact and has an orderly growth habit. Particularly adapted are 'White Flower Carpet,' 'Snow Ballet' and 'Alba Meillandécor' for white; 'Norfolk' and 'Gwent' for yellow; 'The Fairy,' 'Queen Mother' and 'Surrey' for pink; and 'Elegant Pearl' for cream. Patio roses, which are really small polyanthas, can also be used in beds. As these roses tend to have modest-size flowers, it is probably best to use them to create an area of a single color or to mix only two blending colors such as white and yellow to avoid jarring contrasts.

## FOR THOSE WHO FEAR THORNS

*Hybridizer Harvey Davidson is responsible for a small group of hybrid teas that are very pleasing to those who dislike thorns. These totally thornless roses include 'Smooth Angel,' apricot (below left); 'Smooth Lady,' pink (below right); 'Smooth Prince,' red; 'Smooth Satin,' peach-pink; and 'Smooth Velvet,' dark red.*

the weight of the flowers, which follow one another with regularity. The leaves are large and shiny. This is a big plant that will grow even larger and become quite decorative if trained onto a trellis. In a bed, it should be accompanied by others of the same vigor.

**Origin:** 'Yellow Cushion' x 'Aloha.'

### ALTERNATIVE SELECTION

'Charles Austin' (1), an older English rose (1973), lacks the indefinable shadings of 'Abraham Darby' but is of a luminous warm color between yellow and apricot. Its flowers maintain their shape from the moment they open until the end. This large shrub will grow even larger than its usual 5 feet (1.5 m) if trained onto a tree. For good flowering, it must be pruned drastically.

**Height:** 4–5 feet (1.2–1.5 m)
**Flower size:** 5.5 inches (14 cm)
**Number of petals:** 55
(Austin 1985)

Sumptuous and opulent are words often used to describe the flowers of English roses, and such are the flowers of 'Abraham Darby.' They are majestic, deeply cupped, richly double and of a surprising apricot with darker tones and almost fiery lights at the center; they are shaded with pink toward the edges. Their intense fragrance is fruity. Once they are completely open, however, the flowers do not maintain their impeccable shape. The large shrub, with a rounded form, has energetic canes that tend to bend under

1

The Great Stars

# *Anna Pavlova*
Hybrid Tea

'Royal Highness' is another rose reminiscent of transparent porcelain, with large, perfect 40-petaled flowers in flesh-pink on tall stems. A competition rose and a rose to use as a cut flower, it has certain disadvantages in the garden: It does not like rain, which destroys its flowers, and it can fall victim to powdery mildew, neither of which has prevented it from winning two gold medals.

'Beatrice' (1), created by Barni in 1995, is a pretty Italian rose that competes with the two preceding roses in terms of delicacy, the pretty form of its flowers and its sweet color. It is pale pink washed in cream with darker shadows. A descendant of 'Asso di Cuori' and 'Donna Marella Agnelli', its flowers are 3 to 4 inches (8–10 cm) in diameter and have 30 to 35 petals.

**Height:** 4 feet (1.2 m)
**Flower size:** large, very double
(Beales 1981)

The creator of this rose has misplaced its pedigree, a fact that in no way diminishes its beauty. That beauty results in part from very double flowers in the form of rounded cups with soft, slightly ruffled petals. The color is a very pale pink accented by a few darker shadows. The scent is intense and the flowering continuous. It will grow best if located in a warm, sunny spot.

The creator advises against pruning beyond the simplest, minimal cleaning.

## ALTERNATIVE SELECTIONS
To find equally delicate roses, we must turn to two hybrid teas, both of them at the top of any list of successful roses. 'Savoy Hotel' (1989) was awarded two prizes in Ireland, and its perfect shape has attracted much attention in contests and led to it being declared one of the best roses as a cut flower. It has very large double flowers, very pale pink but more intense in the folds. The stems are short, and it has little scent. The height is 3 feet (90 cm).

1

# Antico Amore
*Hybrid Tea*

39

**Height:** 32 inches (80 cm)
**Flower size:** 4–5 inches (10–12 cm)
**Number of petals:** more than 40
(Barni 1988)

The list of roses in shades of coral, salmon and apricot is quite long, but it's a pleasing range of colors that create light and harmonize with the green background of the garden. This member of the group, 'Antico Amore,' is an Italian rose, a magnificent example with a flower shape that finds nothing to envy in an antique rose. Created by Barni in 1988 and offered in the Barni catalog, 'Antico Amore' can be seen in Rome's Roseto (rose garden). The color is a delicate flesh-pink shaded with peach; like the "old love" of its name, it comes with a seductive fragrance.

## ALTERNATIVE SELECTIONS

The outstanding qualities of 'Paul Shirville' (1) are a pleasing shade of salmon on a peach base and an intense, sweet fragrance. It has other attractive characteristics, such as the elegance of the classic shape of its blooms and excellent flowering all season. The shrub is open but well dressed in abundant dark leaves; it has large, dark red thorns of the same color as the young buds.

'Blessings' flowers profusely, and the blooms, a pretty coral-pink, maintain their beauty whatever the weather.

'Apricot Silk,' as indicated by its name, is an unusual apricot color with an orange reverse; it would be far more popular if it were easier to find.

'Alpine Sunset,' a rose created in Great Britain, has very large flowers—6.25 inches (16 cm) in diameter—in a creamy color drenched in peach and is highly scented.

'Silver Jubilee,' winner of four awards, including two gold medals, is a hybrid tea by Cocker. The large flowers are well designed and have elegant, elongated petals of a deep salmon with copper shading. It is not to be confused with the American 'Diamond Jubilee,' an equally famous rose with far paler tones—a creamy ocher with slight orange shadings.

'Tiffany,' a superb rose created in California in 1954, falls in the group between peach, yellow and salmon.

'Michele Meilland' is pinker with a wash of orange-yellow, very pretty and delicate. Created in 1945, it won a gold medal at Bagatelle. An ageing celebrity, it is holding its own.

1

# Baroness Rothschild
*Hybrid Perpetual*

**Synonym:** 'Baronne Adolphe de Rothschild'
**Height:** 4–5 feet (1.2–1.5 m)
**Flower size:** 5.5 inches (14 cm)
**Number of petals:** 40
(Pernet Père 1868)

The qualities of this famous antique rose are still greatly appreciated—as a flowering shrub, it is a joy to behold. Upright and well branched, with smooth canes and semiglossy, gray-green leaves, it has full, pale pink flowers with a darker center in a truly impeccable shape. The tips of the petals reflex. It gives a rich flowering at the beginning of summer and a good second flowering in the fall. An ideal garden rose, best with companions of the same size, it should be used in a bed surrounded by a hedge so that the flowers will stand out above the green wall in all their glory. The shrub needs severe pruning to maintain a balanced shape.

**Origin:** a sport of 'Souvenir de la Reine d'Angleterre.'

## POSSIBLE COMPANIONS

'Mrs. John Laing', another hybrid perpetual and another celebrity among the antique roses, would make a perfect companion for the 'Baroness.' Tall and vigorous, it has a long flowering season and numerous, very large double flowers (45 petals) that are highly scented. The flowers are cup-shaped, silvery pink with purple shadings and borne on long stems, qualities that make it lovely as a cut flower.

Nor should one overlook 'Duchesse de Brabant', one of the most cold-resistant tea roses. Just as famous as the preceding pair, this was the favorite rose of Theodore Roosevelt. It has 5-inch (12 cm) double flowers in shadings that run from pale to dark pink and is highly scented. The flowering is very full and the reflowering excellent, continuing right up to the beginning of winter. The upright shrub grows to 4 to 5 feet (1.2–1.5 m).

# *Chrysler Imperial*
## *Hybrid Tea*

41

they are nearly black, and the flowers can almost be called perfect: velvety purple with intense crimson reflections and 5.5 inches (14 cm) in diameter. It has a scent that no other rose can equal. It has a few faults: a susceptibility to powdery mildew; a lack of vigor; and the flowering, while satisfactory, is not as copious as in other roses of this category.

Another dark red rose is 'Royal William,' winner of two gold medals, with splendidly shaped flowers, large but not overly large, good health, and a pleasant scent. The shrub is strong, branchy, and has solid canes. A recent arrival, it has the qualities to achieve success.

'Magia Nera' by Barni rounds out this series. It is another rose well described by its name, "black magic," which suggests its mysterious dark fascination.

**Height:** 4–4.5 feet (1.2–1.4 m)
**Flower size:** 4–5 inches (10–12 cm)
**Number of petals:** 40–50 (Lammerts 1952)

By now, this rose has found a place among the classics, and competition from more recent arrivals no longer presents much of a threat. Made in America, it has received the highest awards, including a gold medal at Portland and a medal in 1967 for its fragrance; it has also collected honors in Europe. It owes its success to its pretty, tapering buds; the flowers of deep red with a velvety sheen, high-centered, with regular, orderly petals; its copious and recurrent flowering; and its excellent damask fragrance. The shrub is upright and compact, with dark, semiglossy leaves; it is resistant to cold. In warmer climates, it is susceptible to powdery mildew. There is also a climbing form.

**Origin:** 'Charlotte Armstrong' x 'Mirandy.'

### ALTERNATIVE SELECTIONS

'Perle Noir' (1) was created by the Frenchman Delbard, and its name says it all: Its dark red blossoms blend into black, and its buds, almost black themselves, open into large, full (38 petals), noble flowers that do not fade in sunlight. The fragrance is weak. The branchy shrub grows to 3.25 feet (1 m).

A smaller bush is 'Papa Meilland' (2), another very popular hybrid tea, which grows to 32 inches (80 cm). It won a gold medal at Baden-Baden. This rose also has buds so dark that

1

2

102

The Great Stars

# Comte de Chambord
*Portland Rose*

**Height:** 3.25 feet (1 m)
**Flower size:** 3 inches (8 cm)
**Number of petals:** more than 100
(Moreau-Robert 1860)

The Portland roses, dearly loved in the 19th century, never numbered much more than a hundred. This is one of the dozen or so to survive. An upright plant that reaches at most 3.25 feet (1 m) in height, it has very double flowers with an intoxicating fragrance in a warm pink tending toward magenta that is paler at the outer edges. The exterior petals eventually reflex, while those nearer the center are shorter and have a pleasing carefree air. Sometimes they are quartered. The bush is compact and

has pale, elongated, segmented leaves that surround the circular flowers like collars, a characteristic of several Portlands. The flowering is from the end of June on and repeats well. Grace, elegance and a damask scent are among the qualities that have helped this rose survive the passage of time. It is easy to place in the garden and particularly well suited to smaller gardens.

**Origin:** 'Baronne Prévost' x 'Portlandica.'

## ALTERNATIVE SELECTIONS
'Jacques Cartier', made by the same breeder eight years later, is very similar to 'Comte de Chambord' in terms of overall appearance, with the same leaves and the same elegance; the flowers are luminous pink, slightly less cupped and flatter once they

open, at which time they seem a little larger. The fragrance is enchanting. Some experts hold that the reflowering is less abundant.

'Wife of Bath' (1), an English rose, is very compact, very floriferous and very dependable, with flowers of an antique flavor, neither too perfect nor too formal. It is a splendid choice that never disappoints. It may not enjoy the fame of 'Comte de Chambord', but it flowers far more.

**Height:** 3–3.25 feet (0.90–1 m)
**Flower size:** 3.5 inches (9 cm)
**Number of petals:** more than 60
(Meilland 1995)

After less than a decade, this Meilland introduction is already famous. It has been awarded three medals, at Baden-Baden, Monza and Le Roeulx, for its intensely fruity scent that spreads through the air and lingers. A magnificent rose, it cannot fail to please: Its pale pink flowers have darker tones in the folds and are perfectly arranged; the foliage is dark, thick and semiglossy; the flowering is nonstop; and it even boasts excellent resistance to disease.

ALTERNATIVE SELECTIONS
Even more famous and cited in most books, although less often found in gardens, is 'Duet' (Swim 1960), winner of a gold medal from the All-America Rose Selections and another gold at Baden-Baden. It is upright, vigorous and strong. The symmetrical shape of its flowers is particularly pleasing. The magnificent blooms are light pink with a darker reverse, and its reflowering is excellent.

Then there is 'Congratulations', very vigorous, growing to more than 4 feet (1.2 m) and a uniform pink with a touch of coral. Also called 'Rose Sylvia' or 'Sylvia', it is well known and cultivated throughout the world, from New Zealand to Canada, the United States, Europe and South Africa.

'Grand Siècle', a magnificent creation of Delbard, winner of an award at Bagatelle, is highly scented and a luminous pink.

Pink roses tending more to mauve and lilac are 'Manou Meilland' (1), by Meilland, and 'Sterling Silver', a highly scented pink American rose from 1957.

# Glamis Castle
*English Rose*

44

**Height:** 3 feet (90 cm)
**Flower size:** 3.5 inches (9 cm)
**Number of petals:** 80
(Austin 1992)

'Glamis Castle' offers a wealth of leafy branches packed with canes and stems. It is of medium height and has pale flowers sometimes touched with cream at the center; they are deeply cupped and have the gentility and grace of an antique rose; the petals are arranged with a pleasing touch of informality. Flowering is profuse and continuous. All in all, it is perhaps the best of the few white roses from this creator. The fragrance is that very particular scent called myrrh, although to some it seems more like anise. Formal beds, small

gardens and the front row of a border are all excellent sites for this rose, where it will set off red roses such as 'The Dark Lady,' 'The Prince' and 'Sophie's Rose' or will nicely accompany a pink rose such as 'Wife of Bath.' This rose is also well suited to growing in a large container.
**Origin:** 'Graham Thomas' x 'Mary Rose.'

### ALTERNATIVE SELECTIONS
'Winchester Cathedral' (1), a sport of 'Mary Rose', is another white rose with a center touched with yellow. Vigorous but compact, with abundant dark leaves and very reflowering, it grows to 4 feet (1.2 m).

Austin offers another pure white selection: 'Fair Bianca' is small and compact with small, perfect flowers, like those of the famous 'Madame

Hardy' and 'The Nun'—pure and innocent and so shy that no one seems to recognize it, but it is delightful with its semidouble flowers with golden hearts whose shape Austin compares with that of tulips.

1

The Great Stars

**Height:** 4 feet (1.2 m)
**Flower size:** 3–3.5 inches
(8–9 cm)
**Number of petals:** 75–80
(Austin 1984)

Well known and much loved, this rose has withstood the assaults of many newer English roses, none of which has its special beauty, which arises from the fragile evanescence of its flowers. These are perfect round cups with petals that lean toward the center. So pale is the pink that at the edges, it seems composed of nothing more solid than pink light. The flowers are scented of honey. The shrub, with few thorns and smooth canes, has a lovely habit and produces continuous new canes that bear flowers throughout the season at the ends of stems that are as elegant as they are robust.

**Origin:** a sport x ('Iceberg' x 'Wife of Bath').

## ALTERNATIVE SELECTIONS
Many other English roses bear the same beautiful pale pink. 'Chaucer' (1), another veteran, dates back to 1970; it has deeply cupped flowers with the scent of myrrh and excellent reflowering.

'Emily' stands out for its flowers, pretty at every stage—at first cup-shaped, then wide external petals that fold outward; it ends as a splendid rosette. Very scented, only 30 inches (75 cm) tall, it is best used in small gardens and small beds; it is also fine as a container plant.

'Redouté', named for the great illustrator who worked for Empress Josephine, has the qualities and char-

acteristics of 'Mary Rose', of which it is a sport. A highly delicate rose, it has the fineness and purity of an alba.

Also English, also pink that fades to white and also small is 'St. Cecilia', a daughter of 'Wife of Bath'. About 3 feet (90 cm) high, it bears cup-shaped medium-size flowers that are first apricot-pink and then turn very pale. Its foliage is rather skimpy and it shows a tendency to rust. It is strongly scented of myrrh.

1

# *Ingrid Bergman*
## *Hybrid Tea*

## ALTERNATIVE SELECTIONS

More or less of the same tone and intensity of red is 'Asso di Cuori' ("ace of hearts"), which without winning prizes or much recognition has acquired some fame. Many Europeans consider it the best rose for cutting, thanks to the superb shape of the buds just before opening and to the blossoms, which form a large cup when open. It also survives as a cut flower in water for quite a long time. The shrub is leafy and fragrant.

In much of North America, the most famous of long-stemmed roses is 'Mister Lincoln' (1), which is very vigorous and tall, its long branches reaching 5 feet (1.5 m). Besides its use among florists, it is well suited to large spaces in beds. Over a period of almost 40 years (it was released in 1964), it has conquered the public, which appreciates its color, its compact, solid red that does not alter with age and its intense scent. The buds are urn-shaped, the 35-petaled flowers have high centers that give way to large cups 5–5.5 inches (12–14 cm) across. The leaves, opaque and dark green, are not often attacked by disease.

1

**Height:** 4 feet (1.2 m)
**Flower size:** 3.5–4 inches (9–10 cm)
**Number of petals:** 35
(Poulsen 1985, introduced by Mattock)

Among the many, many red roses, this one has enjoyed its share of success, particularly in the 1980s, when it won four important awards, including gold medals at Madrid, Belfast and The Hague. It has all the best qualities of a hybrid tea: strong, rigid canes with few thorns; high, deep red flowers of a typical high-centered form with well-aligned petals; large leaves, abundant, dark and shiny; and good reflowering. The scent, however, is weak.

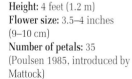

# *Jardins de Bagatelle*
## Hybrid Tea

47

108

**Height:** 3.25 feet (1 m)
**Flower size:** 5 inches (12 cm)
**Number of petals:** 65
(Meilland 1984)

Roses the color of dawn always delight; as Vincenzo Monti once sang, such roses "fill the lap of Aurora." 'Jardins de Bagatelle' has won many medals, including a gold at Geneva, a prize at Madrid and another at Bagatelle for its sweet scent. This is a rose that need fear no rivals. Its flowers are a pinkish cream that is more of a transparent film than a solid color; the stems make it stupendous as a cut flower. A perfect rose for beds, it can be planted with other roses of the same hue to create a dramatic monochrome effect, or it

can be placed beside a pink rose such as 'Silver Lining,' 'Duet' or 'Manou Meilland' for harmonious, delicate shadings.

## ALTERNATIVE SELECTIONS

'Elina', also known as 'Peaudouce' ("sweet skin")—a name that defines it perfectly (although originally it had a more commercial application, having been used for a brand of products for

children)—has won three prizes. It has large, regular flowers with 35 petals that are, in fact, as soft to the touch as skin. The color is also very sweet, an ivory suffused with primrose-yellow. It is a tall, vigorous shrub with copious dense, shiny, dark foliage, robust canes with few thorns and abundant flowering.

'Elina' has given us a worthy offspring, 'Pure Bliss' (Dickson 1994), which is a creamy pink.

Two wonderful American roses that have received very high votes in classifications are 'Garden Party' (Swim 1959), a gold medal winner at Bagatelle, with perfect flowers in a cream that later turns reddish. The other is 'Pristine' (Warriner 1978), winner of two gold medals, with ivory buds and very pale flowers shaded in pink.

'Perdita' (1) is an English rose with the elegant buds of a hybrid tea that open to form delicate rosettes that look as if they're made of wax; the color is a light apricot that immediately shades to cream. Equally great perfection and elegance show up in the scent, which is of tea with a touch of spice. Also suitable for planting in pots.

'Poetry in Motion,' presented by Harkness in 1997, has awakened much interest. Its flowers are cream and primrose yellow.

1

# *Jayne Austin*
*English Rose*

**Height:** 3.25 feet (1 m)
**Flower size:** 3.5–4 inches
(9–10 cm)
**Number of petals:** 100
(Austin 1990)

The pretty shape of these tea-scented flowers is fascinating; at first cups, they then form rosettes, their inner petals arranged around a central button eye and surrounded by broad, extended outer petals. The color is pastel yellow tinged with apricot. The shrub is attractive, compact, healthy and well branched. This is one of the best yellow English roses, although its long branches can make it look unbalanced.

**Origin:** 'Graham Thomas' x 'Tamora.'

## ALTERNATIVE SELECTIONS

'Charity' (1), released by Austin in 1997, has flowers slightly larger than those of 'Jayne Austin', with apricot-yellow centers that grow paler toward the outside and petals that form a shallow cup. Resistant to disease, it reflowers well.

'Pegasus', also by Austin, is from 1995. It is 3 feet (90 cm) tall and has flexible canes, a graceful habit and pretty flowers of an apricot-yellow.

Presented by Meilland in 1998, 'Alphonse Daudet' resembles an English rose. About 3.25 feet (1 m) high, it has superb flowers packed with 80 petals, 4.5–5.2 inches (11–13 cm) in diameter, mimosa-yellow with a touch of peach at the center. The scent is fruity.

'Souvenir de Marcel Proust', by Delbard, and worthy of the name, also resembles an English rose. It won an award for its scent at Nantes in 1995. With the pretty shape of an antique rose, its flowers are double closed cups. Its creator claims this rose "evokes a festive morning full of sun." And just as the sun is luminous and strong, this rose is floriferous and reflowering.

All three of these roses would make perfect companions for 'Jayne Austin' in a bed of solid yellows or yellows with a hint of pale pink chosen from among the English roses.

1

# Just Joey
## Hybrid Tea

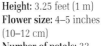

woody bush has opaque, dark leaves with bronzy overtones.

**Origin:** 'Fragrant Cloud' x 'Dr. A. J. Verhage.'

### ALTERNATIVE SELECTIONS

Three other warm-toned roses have ruffled petals that make them worthy of 'Just Joey': A truly audacious idea would be putting them together in the same bed so as to study their subtle color differences and to compare their shapes. Put 'Touch of Class' in the back row, 'Just Joey' and 'July Delbard' (1) in the middle and 'Lilian Austin' in the front row so that its tendency to prostrate growth will create a soft introduction to the bed.

'Touch of Class', a hybrid tea that won a gold medal at Portland in 1988, is among the most highly esteemed roses because of its impeccable flower shape. It has large flowers, coral-orange on a pink base. Its tea scent is weak, but flowering and reflowering are excellent.

'July Delbard' offers a garden the bright lights of its satiny pink flowers suffused with orange. It has very generous flowering, strong canes and dark leaves. Height is 3.25 feet (1 m).

'Lilian Austin', an English rose with flowers in a shade between orange and apricot, flowers constantly. It is less than 3.25 feet (1 m) tall and creates a large, wide bush.

**Height:** 3.25 feet (1 m)
**Flower size:** 4–5 inches (10–12 cm)
**Number of petals:** 32
(Cants of Colchester 1972)

With its almost unique color and its beautifully ruffled, waving petals, this rose is known throughout most of the world. Considered the most popular orange rose, it is not truly orange but a deep apricot with coppery shadows that grow paler toward the edges. The fragrance is dense and fruity. This rose flowers and reflowers and does not fear the onset of autumn. The buds are perfect; the flowers are somewhat less so, but they have a pretty light and last for a long time. Of moderate vigor, the

1

The Great Stars

110

# *Lucetta*
English Rose

50

ROSES IN BEDS

## ALTERNATIVE SELECTIONS

'Belle Story' (1) is another semidouble English rose, in this case a pretty pink color with a darker heart that is revealed only when it opens. Slightly more erect than 'Lucetta' and with a consistently rounded habit, it reaches a height of 4 feet (1.2 m). It is generous in flowering and reflowering.

'Peach Blossom' (Austin 1990) has petals that are indeed as transparent and fragile as peach blossoms. The semidouble flowers, neither large nor small, are scented. It reflowers and offers hips in the autumn.

111

**Height:** 3.25 feet (1 m)
**Flower size:** 5 inches (12 cm)
**Number of petals:** 15–18
(Austin 1983)

Not many English roses have semidouble flowers, but 'Lucetta' is one of them. There is nothing artificial about this rose, which has its own special enchantment. The flowers begin as cups then open to form plates of a very delicate pink with the transparency of Chinese porcelain. The shrub has a wide habit and slightly arching branches, so to avoid clashes, do not plant it near very upright roses. The first flowering is splendid, and after a pause, it repeats regularly but less profusely.

1

The Great Stars

**Height:** 4 feet (1.2 m)
**Flower size:** 5 inches (12 cm)
**Number of petals:** 42–45
(Meilland 1997)

Winner of a gold medal at Monza in 1997, this rose is an interesting addition to the already rich list of fine yellow roses. Its spherical buds open to flowers that have a pretty shape without assuming the typical hybrid tea form. The yellow is solid and strong and not unlike mimosa-yellow, the leaves are opaque, the shrub is vigorous and resistant to disease, and the flowering is long and generous.

## ALTERNATIVE SELECTIONS

'Solidor', another 1984 winner at Monza, makes a good companion to the Meilland roses. An intense uniform yellow, scented and easygoing, this rose does not disappoint.

The same strong yellow can be found in 'Freedom', a rose from 1984 created in Ireland by Dickson that has won three prizes as well as much public favor. Strongly reflowering, its blooms are not very large but are perfectly shaped and a good contrast to the dark leaves.

Another shade of yellow can be found in 'McGredy Yellow' (1), a classic hybrid tea from 1933 that enjoyed great success in its time because of the pretty shape of its yellow-and-cream flowers.

'Peer Gynt', another famous rose much cultivated in northern European gardens, has flowers in an open cup shape in a sulfur-yellow that takes on a pink tinge with age. It has won awards at Belfast and London from the Royal National Rose Society.

'Grandpa Dickson', or 'Irish Gold', is a former celebrity. The winner of five medals, it has enormous 7-inch (18 cm) flowers of the perfect shape so highly esteemed at competitions. The color is a lemon-yellow that takes on pink tones in heat. Its flowering is copious and long, but the appearance of the bush leaves much to be desired, and the scent is weak.

In 1998, Peter Beales released 'Yardley Baroque', a golden yellow rose full of promise.

1

# *Pink Fringe*
*Floribunda*

52  ♀  ◉  ↻

**Height:** 3.25–4 feet (1–1.20 m)
**Flower size:** 4–4.5 inches
(10–11 cm)
**Number of petals:** 18–20
(Interland 1990)

Few of the roses created by the Dutch company Interland ever reach a wide audience, but this one deserves to be in every garden. The first flowering can take one's breath away, and after a brief rest, the flowering continues to the end of the season. The flowers are a delight—they are just barely semidouble and shaped like deep cups with ripply, fringed petals, and the gold tufts of the stamens add a pretty touch of color to the center, where the vibrant pink becomes paler. The shrub is energetic, full of branches in continuous growth and has an ample supply of leaves. It is healthy, easy to cultivate and very decorative. It can be planted alone or in a small group. The drawbacks are that it has no scent and it must be ordered from Holland.

1

## ALTERNATIVE SELECTIONS

'Yves Piaget' (1) is a well-known creation of Meilland (1984). Its spectacular flowers are 5 inches (13 cm) in diameter and packed with 80 serrated petals of an intense pink inherited from 'Paul Neyron.' It has won many prizes, including gold meals at Monza and Tokyo; it has also been selected as the golden rose and the most fragrant rose in the competition at Bagatelle. Its flowering is generous and the foliage semiglossy. The shrub, however, is somewhat untidy and would be best placed in a second-row position, where it will look better and do well because of its outstanding vigor.

Perhaps a little harder to find is a rose from 1983 that won the All America Rose Selection: 'Sweet Surrender.' Its ruffled flowers of 40-odd petals are splendid; also splendid are their pink shade and their scent. This rose is suited to temperate climates.

pretty rosettes packed with petals is 'The Countryman,' a plant that never disappoints, very useful in the front row of a border or a small bed. Upright and packed with lateral branches that increase its width, the shrub has elegant elongated, segmented leaves. It has the strong fragrance of an antique rose.

'Gertrude Jekyll' (1) is very vigorous and upright, capable of great growth in height. Its flowers open from elegantly spiral-wrapped buds into pretty rosettes. They grow in bunches that are not large but so dense that the flowers sometimes look almost crushed. The scent is of such high quality that this rose has been chosen for the production of essential oil.

Upright but shorter, at 3 feet (90 cm), is 'Cottage Rose.' Anything but pretentious and always versatile, it

1

**Height:** 3 feet (90 cm)
**Flower size:** 3.5–4 inches (9–10 cm)
**Number of petals:** 60
(Austin 1994)

This rose has much to recommend it: orderly, geometric rosettes of a lively pure pink with petals that later reflex; flowers borne in groups on the tips of long canes; the intense fragrance of an antique rose; and a pretty shrub with an open habit, short, with rich foliage. It is also easy to cultivate in a container and is ideal for gardens with limited space.

### ALTERNATIVE SELECTIONS
Another English rose that stands out for the luminous pink of its flat,

has medium-size cupped flowers. As its name suggests, it is well suited to small, rustic gardens, as its name suggests.

# Sharifa Asma
*English Rose*

of this rose in a vase with 'Redouté,' 'Eglantyne,' 'Radio Times' and 'The Countryman.'

**Origin:** 'Mary Rose' x 'Admired Miranda.'

### ALTERNATIVE SELECTIONS

Two other English roses bear comparison to 'Sharifa Asma.' 'Eglantyne' (1), a 1994 creation, is a striking pink. Its virtues include perfect flowers in a luminous pink with gilt shadows at the center and a delicious fragrance. A little more than 3.25 feet (1 m) tall, it has pretty branching and is highly resistant to disease.

While only a little older, 'Kathryn Morley' is already a well-loved friend. Always pretty, the soft pink flowers grow on long canes; they have a peculiar lack of symmetry that is once again a sign of grace, not a defect. The outer petals are large and pale, and those toward the center are smaller and a little disorderly. The margins of the petals are delicately serrated. The scent is of myrrh.

**Height:** 3 feet (90 cm)
**Flower size:** 5 inches (12 cm)
**Number of petals:** 85
(Austin 1989)

Although the quintessence of delicacy, this rose does not lack vigor, strength or solidity. The flowers are large and round, full of big petals that grow smaller and tighter at the center, where they fold in on the stamens in an informal way. The color is pink with a touch of gold at the base of each petal. Flowering is excellent and is repeated with great zeal. The bush is vigorous and has long canes bearing flowers on their ends, which bend slightly under the voluptuous weight. For an unforgettable symphony of pink, put cut stems

1

# Sir Frederick Ashton
*Hybrid Tea*

## ALTERNATIVE SELECTIONS

Rose hybridizers offer many white roses; the following are among the most highly recommended. 'Grand Nord' (1) by Delbard, is very elegant and has undergone experiments in many gardens with much success.

By now, 'Youki-San' (from Meilland) has become a classic. Time has done nothing to diminish its fame. It is highly scented.

'Pascali' has three medals to its credit and is considered by many gardeners to be the finest white rose. Its 40-petaled cream-and-white flowers are not very large, but they are well proportioned and last for a long time, either on the shrub or as cut flowers. Some find fault with the small size of the blossoms; they may appear that way simply because the shrub is not densely branched.

'White Masterpiece' was developed in the United States, where it is much loved. Its name refers to the beauty of its enormous double flowers (60 petals). The scent is weak, however.

'Cosmos', a more recent creation of Meilland, has scented, 32-petaled flowers 4 inches (10 cm) in diameter. At 32 inches (80 cm) in height, it is useful where space is limited.

For ivory-white, the choice falls on 'Ice Cream' from Kordes (1993). It is vigorous, of medium height, scented and very floriferous.

**Height:** 4 feet (1.2 m)
**Flower size:** large, very double (Beales 1985)

This is an appealing sport of 'Anna Pavlova.' Beales came upon it by accident while strolling through his own garden. It has all the fine attributes of its parent: an intense scent and full, very double flowers that form deep cups and have slightly ruffled petals. The color is white with a hint of lemon at the center. The shrub, with its rigid canes, is pretty and flowers continuously, but it needs a warm, sunny spot, so is more suitable for warmer, temperate climates.

**Origin:** a sport of 'Anna Pavlova.'

# Sweet Juliet
*English Rose*

## ALTERNATIVE SELECTIONS

'Evelyn' (1) is another well-known and highly valued English rose. It has large, sumptuous flowers, 5 inches (12 cm) in diameter, with a wealth of petals—all of 140. It bears more flowers than does 'Juliet,' and its habit is more open and lower, its branches bending beneath the burden of the flowers. The color is apricot, sometimes with a yellow shading and a hint of pink, which often becomes more intense toward the end of the season. The fragrance is strong—there are good reasons why this rose was named for the famous cosmetic firm Crabtree & Evelyn.

1

**Height:** 4 feet (1.2 m)
**Flower size:** 3 inches (8 cm)
**Number of petals:** 90
(Austin 1989)

The flowers of this rose are not large, but their shape is delicious. So are the color and fragrance, both of which are redolent of ripe apricot. The buds are elegant; the leaves are fine with elongated leaflets; and the shrub is upright and branchy and has many small shoots. This is a refined rose that will take some time to grow into a beautiful, harmonious, compact bush. In some areas, it may need to be protected from powdery mildew.

**Origin:** 'Graham Thomas' x 'Admired Miranda.'

'Admired Miranda,' although disowned by its creator, has many merits and also belongs in this category.

118

**Height:** 3 feet (90 cm)
**Flower size:** 5.5 inches (14 cm)
**Number of petals:** 150
(Austin 1991)

It is among the English roses that one finds the prettiest red roses. 'The Dark Lady,' a shrub with a pleasing shape, low and wide, produces an incredible number of flowers with incredible continuity. The very large flowers are a crimson that later takes on purple tones. From soft, voluptuous flat rosettes, the blossoms become more spherical at maturity. They are always mellow and inviting, almost edible, and they maintain their freshness right up until they shed their petals. The fragrance is strong, of antique roses. A highly recommended rose. In a bed, it should not be accompanied by very upright roses; in a border, it merits the front row.

**Origin:** 'Mary Rose' x 'Prospero.'

1

ALTERNATIVE SELECTIONS

'L.D. Braithwaite' (1), released by Austin in 1988, is a round, open shrub, not too tall, renowned for its dependable flowering. The flowers are large and fully double, soft, in a brilliant crimson that lasts for a long time but may eventually fade to dark pink. The scent is light but good. This is a rose that never disappoints, although its foliage is rather scanty.

'Sophie's Rose,' from 1997, is another English rose with intense crimson flowers in a very pleasing shape. The numerous small petals come together at the center to form a symmetrical rosette. The shrub is decidedly resistant to disease, strong and reflowering.

The Great Stars

# The Prince
*English Rose*

58

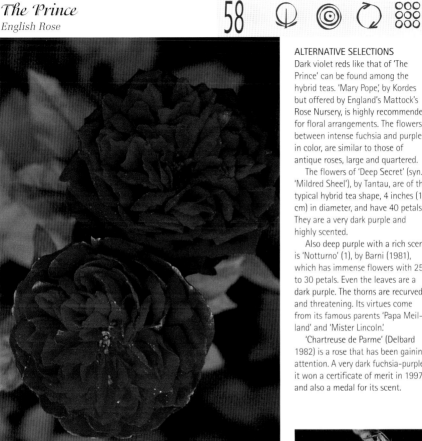

## ALTERNATIVE SELECTIONS

Dark violet reds like that of 'The Prince' can be found among the hybrid teas. 'Mary Pope', by Kordes but offered by England's Mattock's Rose Nursery, is highly recommended for floral arrangements. The flowers, between intense fuchsia and purple in color, are similar to those of antique roses, large and quartered.

The flowers of 'Deep Secret' (syn. 'Mildred Sheel'), by Tantau, are of the typical hybrid tea shape, 4 inches (10 cm) in diameter, and have 40 petals. They are a very dark purple and highly scented.

Also deep purple with a rich scent is 'Notturno' (1), by Barni (1981), which has immense flowers with 25 to 30 petals. Even the leaves are a dark purple. The thorns are recurved and threatening. Its virtues come from its famous parents 'Papa Meilland' and 'Mister Lincoln'.

'Chartreuse de Parme' (Delbard 1982) is a rose that has been gaining attention. A very dark fuchsia-purple, it won a certificate of merit in 1997 and also a medal for its scent.

**Height:** 30 inches (75 cm)
**Flower size:** 4 inches (10 cm)
**Number of petals:** 60–80
(Austin 1990)

Both 'The Prince' and 'The Squire' (one of the parents of 'The Prince') are roses for lovers of the shade of red associated with *Rosa gallica* and the roses derived from the gallicas such as the Portlands and the hybrid perpetuals. It is a deep color—winy, silky, tinged with purple. The flowers are rosette-shaped, and the shrub has a spreading habit, making it ideal for a small bed or the front of a mixed border. An interesting rose that needs time, for it is slow to establish.

**Origin:** 'Lilian Austin' x 'The Squire.'

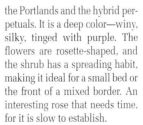
1

yellow and orange. It is a "solar" color that pleases the eye and combines well with green, which it illuminates. 'Whisky Mac' is well known and popular despite the unkind comments sometimes made about it, in particular that it shows a propensity for powdery mildew and has a capricious habit. Such charges are unproven, and it is a pretty rose with flowers of a splendid shade between apricot and gold. Also highly scented.

The flowers of 'Rosemary Harkness' are a pretty mixture of yellow-orange and salmon, and the shrub is attractive—leafy and round. The rose has been awarded two certificates of merit.

'Mojave' (1), winner of four awards, is ranked among the leading selections in its color, which is a decided orange with darker veins. It is somewhat neglected today, perhaps because of its lack of scent.

'Adolf Horstmann', difficult to track down, is a superb golden yellow that looks as though it was just dipped in a vat of molten copper. It has full flowers, large and heavily scented; its leaves are shiny and dark.

The Great Stars

**Height:** 3.25 feet (1 m)
**Flower size:** large, double
**Number of petals:** 40–50
(Kordes 1989)

This rose attracts well-merited attention with its color, a warm yellow with shades of apricot, amber and gold. Also attractive are the well-shaped flowers of classic form and the shiny leaves with metallic glints. The blooms have been exhibited at several contests and are perfect as cut flowers. A good rose, steady and dependable, with an award-winning scent.

**Origin:** 'Golden Sun' x 'Chantré.'

## ALTERNATIVE SELECTIONS
Many roses are of a color between

1

# Amber Queen
*Floribunda*

**Height:** 30 inches (75 cm)
**Flower size:** 2.75–3 inches (7–8 cm)
**Number of petals:** 40 (Harkness 1984)

'Amber Queen' and 'Apricot Nectar' are two highly sophisticated floribundas, quite equal in merit, one with a trace of gilt, the other a deeper shade with more pink. Planted together in a bed, they would create subtle variations in color. It should surprise no one to learn that 'Amber Queen' won the title Rose of the Year in 1984 after receiving many other honors. This is a superb rose for a number of reasons: its color, yellow highlighted with amber; its pretty flowers that form cups when they open in bunches of three to seven blooms; its copious repeat flowering; and its elegant bronze-tinged dark foliage. It also has a neat, compact habit. All in all, a perfect subject for a bed.

**Origin:** 'Southampton' x 'Typhoon.'

## ALTERNATIVE SELECTIONS

'Apricot Nectar' (1) (Boerner 1975) has oval buds and sumptuous 4.5-inch (11 cm) flowers in the perfect hybrid tea form. It flowers without pause and is most at ease in temperate climates. The color is pink-apricot-gold, and its scent is enchanting. It was a first-prize winner at the All America Rose Selection in 1984. It has met some success in England, but it doesn't seem to have made it to continental Europe.

Another floribunda by Harkness that is every bit its equal but a more orange-yellow is 'Anne Harkness.' It has large bunches of flowers in a pretty form and 25 to 28 fringed petals. The flowers are also pretty in a vase. Its scent is slight. Its height is about 3.25 feet (1 m). Flowering is late, and the plant reaches the fullness of its beauty only in August, a trait for which it is highly valued.

'Summer Dream' (Fryer 1989) is the big sister of another splendid rose by Fryer, 'Sweet Dreams.' The cup-shaped flowers growing in dense bunches are enchanting, as is the apricot color. The height is 30 inches (75 cm).

'Glenfiddich', which has a more amber color, has enjoyed great success, so much so that in Great Britain, it seems to be growing in every garden. Its creator, Cocker, a Scotsman, dedicated it to the

famous brand of whisky, with which it shares the same golden shades. Easy to grow and guaranteed to succeed, it is particularly well suited to cold climates.

# Class Act
*Floribunda*

61  ♀  ◉  ○  ⁝

is a robust plant, very healthy, compact, round and dense with leaves. Because of its vigor, it is good as a hedge or as part of a group in a meadow.

### ALTERNATIVE SELECTIONS
'Lady Romsey' (Beales 1985) has elegant buds and semidouble flowers of an ivory-cream with a touch of pink. The scent is slight. The very compact shrub grows to less than 2 feet (60 cm) in height.

'Fiocco Bianco' (1) is a Barni rose (1988) that its creator considers perfect because of its large double flowers, pure white when fully open. It is highly scented, a quality not common in floribundas, and shows exceptional reflowering. The shrub is compact, strong and vigorous. It grows to 24 to 32 inches (60–80 cm) high.

**Synonyms:** 'First Class,' 'White Magic'
**Height:** 32 inches (80 cm)
**Flower size:** 3 inches (8 cm)
**Number of petals:** 20
(Warriner 1981, introduced by Jackson & Perkins)

This rose, awarded a gold medal at Portland, is distinguished by the antique appeal of its delight-ful flowers and for its incredible flowering: The blooms come on and on with such great rapidity that the plant is never bare of flowers until the onset of winter. The large flowers are cup-shaped and have slightly ruffled petals in a creamy white that grows warmer toward the stamens at the golden center. The blossoms are carried atop the canes. This

122

For Light and Color

# *Dusky Maiden*
*Floribunda*

**Height:** 28–36 inches
(70–90 cm)
**Flower size:** 2.75–3 inches
(7–8 cm)
**Number of petals:** 5–7
(Le Grice 1947)

This 'Dusky Maiden' stands out among Le Grice's other 'Maidens' because of her interesting color, an intense crimson that is not easy to find in floribundas. The flowers, which grow in small bunches, open as flat plates and have petals that flutter in the breeze. The flowering is very abundant, the reflowering excellent. The leaves are dark and shiny, the shrub vigorous and well branched. This rose was once famous and deserves to be rediscovered.

**Origin:** ('Daily Mail Scented Rose' x 'Étoile de Hollande') x 'Else Poulsen.'

## ALTERNATIVE SELECTION
A garden in need of a brilliant vermilion rose instead of crimson would do well with 'Sarabande' (1), a rose by Meilland that provides a memorable demonstration of the transience of glory. In 1957, it won five important awards, including gold medals in Geneva, Bagatelle, Portland and Rome, and for years, its name was on the lips of enthusiasts. It was enormously useful wherever a brilliant color was desired. It asserted itself with its large bunches of semi-double flowers that open to reveal a golden center—a wonderful contrast with the vermilion, a quality shared by 'Dusky Maiden.' Today, however, its sun seems to have set. Yet its profuse flowering continues throughout the season. Its height is 30 inches (75 cm).

1

For Light and Color

# Escapade
*Floribunda*

'Greetings.' Of 'Escapade,' suffice it to say that it has charm, and charm is a great quality. It finds time to produce three beautiful flowerings each season. It has few thorns and shiny medium-green leaves. In the company of a white rose such as 'Iceberg,' it would contribute substantially to the composition of a truly delightful flowerbed.

**Origin:** 'Pink Parfait' x 'Baby Faurax.'

## ALTERNATIVE SELECTIONS

For a bluer tone and an even more unusual color, there is 'Lilac Charm,' a pastel mauve with warm shadows from red filaments and golden anthers. The scented five-to-six-petaled flowers, 4 inches (10 cm) in diameter, stand out against the dark foliage, which is upright and compact.

As lilac as its name promises is the English rose 'Lilac Rose' (Austin 1990), which has pretty, flat rosettes with exceptional scent. The shrub is of modest size, no taller than 30 inches (75 cm), but far wider.

'Baby Faurax,' one of the plants that provided the genetic background for 'Escapade,' is a dark lavender polyantha that has been going strong since 1924. This dwarf shrub, only a foot (30 cm) high, is especially useful in gardens where color is needed but space is limited.

**Height:** 32 inches (80 cm)
**Flower size:** 3–3.5 inches (8–9 cm)
**Number of petals:** 12
(Harkness 1967)

Despite the passage of time, this rose, winner of gold medals at Belfast and Baden-Baden, has managed to retain much of its popularity. The outer edges of the small, platelike blossoms are a tender magenta that pales to white toward the center. Not everyone loves this rose, but the color is not aggressive, and perhaps the more one looks, the more it appeals. And the color is one that is gaining favor: The winner of the President's International Trophy in 1997, for example, was the magenta rose

# *Feeling*
*Floribunda*

**Height:** 24 inches (60 cm)
**Flower size:** 2.75–3 inches
(7–8 cm)
**Number of petals:** 20–25
(Barni 1993)

Awarded a gold medal at Baden-Baden in 1994, this rose is one that anyone would love in a vase. It is pretty in any floral composition and worthy of a bride's bouquet. The shape of the blossoms is exquisite, the color is the purest pink with mother-of-pearl reflections; at the center is a touch of peach. It is fragrant. Given its low height and compact habit, this is a rose for any garden, large or small, as well as for a balcony or terrace.

## ALTERNATIVE SELECTIONS

A favorite in Great Britain, although not often seen elsewhere, is 'English Miss' (1), which has the same sterling qualities as 'Feeling.' Upright, with dark, purplish leaves, it has soft pink porcelainlike double flowers that are highly scented. The flowering repeats without pause. Height: 30 inches (75 cm).

Another rose that deserves more widespread use in gardens is 'Kalin-

ka,' or 'Pink Wonder' (Meilland 1970), cast aside by the pitiless laws of the marketplace. Winner of two medals, this rose enjoyed much popularity in its time and displays many virtues: strong scent; vigorous, pleasing growth; pretty leaves as shiny as metal; and blossoms with 28 petals arranged in good order. A fine, delicate rose.

'Many Happy Returns' (2), from Harkness (1991), is fully the equal of the preceding two in terms of delicacy. As its name suggests, this is the ideal rose for a celebration, whether a birthday or anniversary or other occasion. Everything about it is pretty—the leaves, the compact shrub, the buds and the pale pink flowers that grow in bunches.

1

2

**Synonyms:** 'Korresia,' 'Sunsprite'
**Height:** 28–32 inches (70–80 cm)
**Flower size:** 3 inches (8 cm)
**Number of petals:** 28
(Kordes 1973)

'Friesia' has bright yellow flowers, at first cup-shaped and later flat, with petals that curl slightly as though frilled and a strong licorice scent. This rose has three names, a gold medal from Bagatelle, a prize from Hampton Court for its scent and international fame. It is healthy, robust and resistant to cold and disease. Upright but compact and well branched, it has good flowering and reflowering. This is a rose for gardens but is also suit-able for planting in containers and is ideal for those who love the bright color of the sun and prefer plants that need little care. A match with knockout power: Put it in a bed or border with blue pansies.

**Origin:** 'Friedrich Wörlein' x 'Spanish Sun.'

### ALTERNATIVE SELECTIONS

Among the various yellow roses, 'Arthur Bell' is (besides 'Friesia'), the most famous. It has leathery, metallic leaves, 3-inch (8 cm) flowers with 20 petals that stand up to poor weather, very intense scent and early flowering. Its blossoms are a strong, solid golden yellow that fades with age to a creamier shade. But who could call that a defect?

'Allgold' maintains its brilliant yellow right up to the end of flowering. Its blooms are a pretty shape, high-centered, and have 20 somewhat short petals. The compact shrub grows rapidly to medium height and has a bushy shape but is not overly branchy. The scent is light. It's compactness and rapid growth make 'Allgold' a fine choice.

There is also an Italian rose, 'Stelvio Coggiatti', released by Barni in 1998 and named for a great expert and passionate lover of roses. Its virtues include nicely shaped flowers—full, golden yellow rosettes—excellent reflowering, resistance to disease and a pleasing, compact habit.

For Light and Color

# Grüss an Aachen
*Floribunda*

**Height:** 32 inches (80 cm)
**Flower size:** 2.75–3 inches (7–8 cm)
**Number of petals:** more than 60 (Geduldig 1909)

This rose is difficult to classify. Although listed among the floribundas, it came into existence long before those roses were created. David Austin puts it among the English roses, which makes perfect sense because it acts every much like one. The flowers are similar to those of an antique rose, as crisp and fresh as a young girl's ruffle in the 19th century. The color is a light pink that quickly fades to cream; its many petals are arranged with elegant regularity and form a ball as they reflex. Very vigorous and full of branches, it produces flowers tirelessly. The smooth canes have few thorns; the leaves are small and shiny.

**Origin:** 'Grau Karl Druschki' x 'Franz Deegen.'

## ALTERNATIVE SELECTIONS

'Sans Souci' (1), by Barni, is a floribunda worth close attention. Declared the best Italian rose at Monza in 1995 and a gold winner at Baden-Baden, it is 32 inches (80 cm) tall with large flowers of a pinkish cream with apricot shadows. The bush has a balanced, compact habit.

'Chanelle' (2), although hard to find, offers a pastel color and the flowers of a miniature hybrid tea. The cream flowers, medium in size, are suffused with coral; at first cups, they later flatten. Flowering repeats regularly until late autumn.

1

2

For Light and Color

subtle lemon scent and its light green foliage. The best advice for this plant is to hold off pruning it and let it grow into a pretty bush that will then diligently cover itself all over with a mass of white flowers. Even so, care must be taken to deadhead. 'Iceberg' can be planted in the company of any rose to great advantage, but it has the power to support any bed, border or hedge all on its own.

**Origin:** 'Robin Hood' x 'Virgo.'

**ALTERNATIVE SELECTIONS**

Another pretty floribunda with pure white flowers is 'White Diamond', a product of Interland in Holland; it grows to 30 inches (75 cm).

The very interesting floribunda 'White Bouquet' (Boerner 1956) has flowers shaped like a gardenia's, very large and very double. The scent is spicy.

**Height:** 3.25–4 feet (1–1.2 m)
**Flower size:** 3 inches (7.5 cm)
**Number of petals:** 25–30
(Kordes 1958)

'Iceberg,' also known as 'Schneewitchen' and 'Fée des Neiges,' is the world's most famous floribunda and has little need of description. Far from diminishing with the passage of years, its

fame seems only to grow more solid. For one thing, it has no real rivals, since floribundas with pure white flowers are rare ('Iceberg' is as immaculate as its namesake, taking on a pinkish tinge only at the end of the season). Most rose lovers are familiar with the beauty of its long, tapering buds, flowers that open into a cup shape and exhale a

For Light and Color

# Lilli Marlene (or Marleen)
*Floribunda*

**Height:** 28 inches (70 cm)
**Flower size:** 2.75–3 inches (7–8 cm)
**Number of petals:** 25
(Kordes 1959)

Riding the crest of a wave for more than 40 years, this rose's main draw is not the shape or beauty of its flowers but their color, a very intense red between scarlet and crimson that fears neither sun nor rain. It attracts admiring attention from a distance and at close range. Almost everyone is struck by its almost black buds and its velvety cup-shaped flowers that open like explosions of dark light against the leathery green foliage. An easy-to-grow rose, it is generous with its flowers, which last a long time and appear with great regularity. Special care must be taken to protect it against the fungal diseases to which it is sometimes susceptible.

**Origin:** ('Our Princess' x 'Rudolph Timm') x 'Ama.'

### ALTERNATIVE SELECTIONS

'Europeana' (De Ruiter 1963), another very successful floribunda, is less often cultivated today than it was in the past, although no good reason exists for its drop in popularity. It has won four medals for its 40-petaled double flowers, 3 inches (7.5 cm) in diameter—dark crimson rosettes sometimes with a touch of red currant. They grow in very large bunches whose weight bends the branches. It is perhaps the richest-flowering floribunda. Its leaves are also attractive—purple when young and, later, dark green and leathery. This is a rose that should be planted in groups, the plants set close together so that their growing branches will support one another.

Another intensely dark red rose is 'Marlena' by Kordes, winner of two medals. Its sole drawback is its lack of scent. It produces 18-petaled crimson-scarlet flowers. Because it is small, growing to just 18 inches (45 cm) tall, it is very useful where space is limited.

**Height:** 4 feet (1.2 m)
**Flower size:** 4 inches (10 cm)
**Number of petals:** 28
(Harkness 1977)

This has been called a perfect floribunda. In fact, the exquisitely elegant buds, the perfection of the flowers, the porcelain-white of the almost transparent petals slightly tinged with pink in sunlight and the delicious lemony fragrance with a touch of spice have placed this rose among the most beloved and popular in gardens. It has earned acclaim and awards at Geneva, Monza, Rome and in New Zealand, including a medal for its fragrance. Vigorous and upright in habit, it forms a well-balanced bush with dense branches bearing few thorns and semiglossy leaves. It flowers well and reflowers reasonably quickly on new buds. It is the ideal subject for beds but will not disappoint if grown as a specimen plant.

1

**Origin:** ('Rudolph Timm' x 'Dedication') x 'Pascali.'

**ALTERNATIVE SELECTION**
'Ivory Fashion' (1), another well-known floribunda, is noteworthy for the delicacy of its pretty ivory semi-double flowers in the typical hybrid tea shape. It is very dependable, very reflowering and robust. Its flowers are carried on long stems in big bunches high above the canes, making them good for cutting. The shrub is slightly angular and rigid, its only defect.

# Rita Levi Montalcini
*Floribunda*

it shows exceptional resistance to disease.

**ALTERNATIVE SELECTIONS**
'Tournament of Roses' (Warriner 1989) seems to have all it needs to win fame. It is sometimes classified as a hybrid tea, which the shape of its flowers would seem to justify. Little more than 3.25 feet (1 m) high, it has pale salmon flowers. The two awards it has won to date confirm its quality.

Not everyone wants a warm peach or warm apricot rose; some want a rose that is only pink; for those people, Barni offers 'Venere' (1). It is an interesting size, only 20 to 28 inches (50–70 cm) high, and has elegant flowers in rich, perfectly shaped corymbs.

'Sexy Rexy', a pure pink rose with mother-of-pearl highlights, has been judged the best pink floribunda. On the Greek island of Schinos, 200 of these roses have been planted in a single marvelous border. The flowers are pretty and full, rosettes that grow in large bunches, some with as many as a hundred blooms. The bush has dense foliage and small, dark, shiny leaves.

**Height:** 24–32 inches (60–80 cm)
**Flower size:** 2.5–3 inches (6–8 cm)
**Number of petals:** 10–15
(Barni 1991)

This Italian-born rose has won public favor as well as awards, including the much-merited title Golden Rose of Geneva and a certificate of merit at Glasgow. The flowers, their petals arranged in a pretty pattern, are an enchanting shade between apricot and warm pink; the scent is sweet. It also makes a lovely cut flower. The buds are elegant and the foliage dense. The flowering is copious, the bush is compact and vigorous, and last but not least,

1

# Southampton
*Floribunda*

**For Light and Color**

**Height:** 3.25 feet (1 m)
**Flower size:** 3 inches (7.5 cm)
**Number of petals:** 25
(Harkness 1971)

As has been said, floribundas are the roses most often called on to bring light and color into the garden. This rose provides solid proof of their ability. Its blooms, orange bathed in scarlet, are bright without being garish and resemble firelight against the green foliage. The more irreverent call the color orange marmalade. This rose fully merits its fame. Robust and healthy, it prefers cold climates. Well and fully branched, big and tall, it has almost double flowers that open fully, the outer petals pulling back while

the inner ones bend slightly toward the center. Because it tolerates partial shade well, it is suitable for planting in a small wood. In a bed, it could easily accompany a rose of a similar but more delicate color, such as 'Grüss an Aachen' or 'Sans Souci.'

**Origin:** ('Anne Elizabeth' x 'Allgold') x 'Yellow Cushion.'

### ALTERNATIVE SELECTIONS
A good number of roses compete with 'Southampton' for splendor. 'Elizabeth of Glamis', although less famous than the other Elizabeth ('Queen Elizabeth'), is nonetheless greatly appreciated by both competition judges and the public. It is among the most widely planted roses in the gardens of Great Britain. Also called 'Irish Beauty', it wins for

its 4-inch (10 cm) flowers, which are high-centered but flatten as they open; their luminous coral color has lively tints. The scent is intense. It is not a rose for colder climates, nor for very alkaline soils.

'Fragrant Delight' is another rose that must be put in a protected site because it does not do well in cold. Its 22-petaled flowers are salmon-orange with a copper reverse and pleasantly ruffled. The scent is extra-ordinary.

'Marie Curie', a floribunda by Meilland, has a far sweeter color, an almost pastel orange edged with pink. It has large flowers, 3.5 inches (9 cm) in diameter, with 30 to 35 petals, which are slightly ruffled, exposing the stamens. Height is 24–28 inches (60–70 cm).

There is also the world-famous 'Sunset Boulevard' by Harkness, declared rose of the year in 1997. Its name refers not to the famous Los Angeles boulevard but to its color, which is that of a beautiful sunset; its flowers have the typical shape of a hybrid tea but with slightly shorter petals. It has little fragrance but an incredible bloom, absolutely continuous.

# The Times Rose
*Floribunda*

**Synonym:** 'Mariandel'
**Height:** 28 inches (70 cm)
**Flower size:** 3 inches (8 cm)
**Number of petals:** 30
(Kordes 1985)

A color that glows bright scarlet in sunlight, a color like blood; soft rosette-shaped flowers in well-spaced bunches; attractive leaves, dark with bronze tints when young; and exceptional, continuous flowering and excellent resistance to disease make this one of the best selections for creating that famous mass of color so desired by the gardening public. This is by no means a negative judgment but should be taken as an indication of this rose's best use in the garden: Plant it where color is needed—color throughout the season. The shrub is very compact but expansive of habit, well ordered and disciplined.

**Origin:** 'Tornado' x 'Red Gold.'

## ALTERNATIVE SELECTIONS
'Lavaglut' (Kordes 1979) is also called 'Intrigue' but should not be confused with Warriner's 'Intrigue' (a very interesting rose because of its dark plum color); this is another bright red floribunda, with semi-double flowers in the shape of rosettes. The height is 24 inches (60 cm).

Also included among the leading roses is 'City of Belfast,' winner of five medals. With its velvety scarlet-orange, it perfectly meets any need for light and color in a garden. The flowers are on the small side but have ruffled petals. Resistant to dis

ease, always in flower, this rose is faithful to its promises.

There is also 'Paprika,' almost orange-red and a winner of many awards. A celebrity in the 1950s, it is rarely planted today, largely because it is rarely offered. Even so, its very fine qualities remain unchanged.

Also worthy of note is 'Evelyn Fison,' scarlet-orange, winner of two medals, resistant to rain and disease and generous with its flowering, which produces high-centered flowers, similar in shape to those of hybrid teas, in well-spaced bunches.

# SHRUB ROSES

## COLORS OF THE MOST POPULAR REFLOWERING SHRUB ROSES

**White:** 'Nevada,' white 'Fleurette,' 'Jacqueline du Pré,' 'Francine Austin,' 'Sally Holmes'

**Yellow:** 'Graham Thomas,' 'Königin Lucia,' 'Lucinde,' yellow 'Fleurette,' 'Golden Wings'

**Salmon and orange:** 'William Morris,' 'A Shropshire Lad,' 'Colette,' 'Westerland,' 'Fred Loads'

**Pink:** 'Mary Rose,' 'Dapple Dawn,' 'Marguerite Hilling,' pink 'Fleurette,' 'Centenaire de Lourdes,' 'Rosarium Uetersen,' 'Old Blush,' 'Heavenly Rosalind,' 'Rosy Cushion,' 'Bonica 82,' 'Pink Robusta'

**Red:** 'Robusta,' 'Red Coat,' 'Mozart,' 'Marjorie Fair,' 'Scarlet Fire,' 'Cocktail,' 'Eyepaint.'

S
hrub roses, antique and modern, form a vast, eclectic category that combines somewhat randomly roses that are otherwise quite different in terms of type, origin, size and flower shape. Thus the category has something for everyone and for every garden destination except beds. These shrubs can be large or small, and they can have single, double or very double flowers.

If you think of these roses the way you would think of any other shrub, you will more easily understand where and how to place them, which is wherever you would put any kind of shrub—a place where you tend to look often, an important corner, an area in need of embellishment, the middle of a lawn or at its edge, a far corner that needs rounding off with decorative branches and flowers. In small groups, perhaps as few as three, shrub roses can mark off a pathway or form a kind of screen; as individual specimens, they can perform the role of a fine *objet d'art*—attract attention, be a source of admiration much as a statue is. Those with wandering branches can be trained to cover an archway or other support.

What is wanted for such decorative roles is a bush with character, charm and polite behavior; it should be soft and open and have flexible canes. Strikingly beautiful flowers are not of primary importance. The flowers can be large, well designed and packed with petals, but flowers that are small, graceful and pretty may serve the purpose every bit as well. What matters is that the rose can attract attention with that quality sometimes called presence. Is it important that the rose be reflowering? Yes, if its destination is an area of the garden that is highly trafficked. Many of the modern shrub roses are reflowering. Of course, the category of shrub roses includes many antique roses that do not reflower, but in many cases, such as 'Maiden's Blush,' their beauty is so absolute that they cannot be excluded simply because they flower only once. Shrub roses include all the hybrid rugosas as well as the hybrid musks.

The types of roses that should definitely not be treated as shrubs are the hybrid teas, which grow on rigid canes and lack the necessary grace, and the groundcover and patio roses, which lack height.

There is also the matter of finding a place for the species roses and their hybrids. The back of the garden, one of those distant corners that are usually neglected because there is so much work to do to keep the rest in order, often turns out to be the best place to use one of these natural roses, which will have no problems if left alone. Growing wild, their beautiful branches will prove themselves useful for filling in open spaces, those holes too far off to be within the range of usual care. And there are usually wooden structures, sheds, huts or even tree trunks that these plants will hide. The flowering of such roses will be brief but of stark simplicity and dramatic beauty. The most abandoned area of the garden will no longer seem abandoned but will look as if it had been dressed by nature itself.

# *Angela*
*Modern Shrub Rose*

73

cated, but it can create a pretty area of light and add much color to a corner of the garden, especially if planted in groups of three.

## ALTERNATIVE SELECTIONS
Another rose that is not very well known is 'Sorbet Framboise', from the French grower Delbard. This is one of his Great Wild Flower series, which tells us something of its ideal use in the garden. The shiny semidouble flowers, in various shades of raspberry with white centers illuminated by yellow stamens, are graceful and fresh. The scent is light and fruity. Height: 3.25 feet (1 m); very long-flowering.

A slightly different English rose that is attractive when planted in small groups is 'Mistress Quickly' (Austin 1995). It reflowers well, and while its double blooms are not showy, they grow in pretty pink bunches to very pleasing effect. The height is only 30 inches (75 cm).

Another Austin rose that grows into a graceful, winding shrub of 5 feet (1.5 m) in height or more is 'Scintillation'. It has light, semidouble flowers, pale pink, with a very intense scent. It flowers only once, but that one flowering lasts a long time. It has tremendous natural grace, and it is well suited for a position atop a small embankment from which its branches can tumble. Or it can be planted against and wound around a fence. It is equally attractive as a single specimen plant, in which case, it will grow into a small, rangy thicket.

**Height:** 3.25 feet (1 m)
**Flower size:** 2.5–2.75 inches (6–7 cm)
**Number of petals:** 20–25
(Kordes 1984)

This modern rose has the enchantment of an old rose, thanks to the gentility of its flowers, which grow in thick bunches; each cup-shaped flower is composed of petals in various shades of pink that grow paler toward the center. 'Angela' is robust, resistant and healthy. Its flowers are not very large and not of high quality, but it makes up for these defects by the sheer profusion of their growth. The shrub, with a wide habit, covers itself so completely with flowers that one can see only pink. It is not sophisti-

# Blush Noisette
*Noisette*

74

**ALTERNATIVE SELECTIONS**

Two roses that have been forgotten have the same grace and freshness as 'Blush Noisette.' 'Dentelle de Malines,' which is hard to find, forms a pretty bush with elegant arching branches and small flowers in dense bunches, semidouble and double, pale pink. There is only one flowering, but it is magnificent. Created by Lens, it was presented by David Austin in 1983.

Almost unfindable in either gardens or catalogs is 'Lauré Davoust.' It is no doubt growing in the occasional garden, but it will probably go unrecognized. No catalog could describe the enchantment of this rose, with its small, lilac-pink flowers so densely packed with petals that they look like pompoms. And it is known to produce an occasional second flowering. It is believed to be the offspring of *Rosa multiflora* or *R. sempervirens* and resembles 'Félicité et Perpétue,' a hybrid of the latter species. It may well be a rambler, but it is best grown as a shrub. Some claim that it suffers from frost but, if so, only intense frost, because it grows well in Great Britain, at times reaching 13 feet (4 m); it can be protected in winter.

'Spectabilis' and 'Flora,' two other elegant hybrids of *Rosa sempervirens*, resemble 'Blush Noisette' in their fairly low growth and their small, cup-shaped, sweetly scented flowers, lilac that fades to cream. 'Spectabilis' flowers late and sometimes takes everyone by surprise by flowering a second time.

**Height:** 5–6.5 feet (1.5–2 m)
**Flower size:** 2 inches (5 cm)
**Number of petals:** 24
(Noisette 1817)

Some people are surprised to find an important, highly visible spot in a garden reserved for a rose that is so truly modest. But not everyone is drawn to the overwrought displays of certain roses. 'Blush Noisette' has the subtle attractions of gentleness, lightness and simple beauty that many people learn to appreciate in a rose as well as in a friend.

Its bunches of three to six flowers smile out from between the leaves. They form perfect blossoms between pink, lilac and white in color and have a fresh, spicy scent; and they follow one another continuously at the tips of the canes. The shrub is large and has smooth, almost thornless branches that tend to bend and pretty, dark foliage. Set against a wall, it will act like a small climber; it is hard to say how high it will grow.

**Origin:** a sport of 'Champneys' Pink Cluster.'

Alone or in Small Groups

138

ond flowering is good. It needs a half-day of sun.

**Origin:** 'William Allen Richardson' x an unknown rose.

### ALTERNATIVE SELECTIONS

'Francesca' (1) is another yellow variety from the Pemberton group. A shrub with fine foliage with elongated leaflets, its flexible branches are covered in elegant buds and large apricot flowers that slowly pale. They are semi-double and scented. With a height of up to 6.5 feet (2 m), it can be cultivated as a large shrub or trained onto a fence or other structure.

'Agnes' (2), a pretty rugosa created in Canada, is unusual because of its yellow flowers. The flowers are very double, very scented and 3 inches (7.5 cm) in diameter. The color is an amber that pales over time. The fresh foliage is composed of very small leaves. The first flowering is copious, and flowers open intermittently after that. Height: 6 feet (1.8 m).

139

**Height:** 5 feet (1.5 m)
**Flower size:** 4 inches (10 cm)
**Number of petals:** 50
(Ann Bentall 1939)

'Buff Beauty,' one of the interesting group of roses known as hybrid musks, was created by the gardener who served as assistant to the Reverend Pemberton. It fully merits the fame and favor it enjoys. It is the variety with the prettiest color, a warm, intense apricot that seems touched by the sun. The blossoms have a good shape at every stage of their flowering and end as balls of petals. The scent is a rich mixture of apples, bananas and tea. The flexible canes tend to become prostrate, so it is best to wrap

them around stakes, as described on page 142 for 'Cornelia.' This will create a flowering column that will display the blooms, which tend to recline on the stems, to best advantage along the full length of the canes. The foliage is ample, with numerous, medium-green leaves. Flowering is generous; the sec-

Alone or in Small Groups

it has won three medals. The flowers, which grow in big bunches, are small and bright scarlet with white eyes and ruffled petals. The flowering is from June to September; the height is 4 to 5 feet (1.2–1.5 m). Susceptible to blackspot, this rose needs protection. And it is no fan of drought.

Both 'Wilhelm' ('Skyrocket') and 'Robin Hood' (1) are hybrid musk roses that can compete with 'Cocktail' in terms of the intense red of their flowers, a lively cherry-scarlet—although without the white eyes—that stands out against the lush foliage. These roses grow to solid masses of festive color. The first flowering is rich and is repeated in the autumn, just when the graying garden needs a touch of color.

**Height:** 5.25 feet (1.6 m)
**Flower size:** 3 inches (8 cm)
**Number of petals:** 5
(Meilland 1957)

The red of 'Cocktail' is like embers, composed of pure light, with a bright yellow at the center that pales over time. The scarlet of the flowers does not fade, however, but seems to grow only more intense. The blooms blend harmoniously with the small metallic leaves. The scent is light and spicy. This rose does not need pruning—the branches and the bright purple young shoots are best when allowed to grow to their full length. Every few years, cut away the deadwood from the base of the plant to encourage new growth. The blooms grow in small bunches. The flowering is not massive, but it is continuous, so the plant is always embellished. This is a rose for a place, large or small, that faces a house, the spot where the eye falls first. A specimen plant or several grouped together cannot fail to bring joy. It resists cold but does not do well in very cold climates.

**Origin:** ('Independence' x 'Orange Triumph') x 'Phyllis Bide.'

ALTERNATIVE SELECTIONS
Every bit as happy as 'Cocktail' is 'Eyepaint' (syn. 'Tapis Persan'), a floribunda of exceptional vigor that is one of the roses called "hand-painted" because of their quality. Created in New Zealand by Sam McGredy IV,

1

Alone or in Small Groups

English roses. The leaves are dark green and abundant. Very reflowering, it has an intense fragrance; it resists disease and hardly notices rain.

## ALTERNATIVE SELECTIONS

Another recent English rose is 'William Morris' (1), presented by Austin in 1998 and full of promise: A large, vigorous shrub with arching branches that reaches 5 feet (1.5 m), it has apricot-pink flowers in dense, perfectly formed rosettes with small petals at the center and larger outer ones. The scent, while unusual, is very pleasant. The reflowering is excellent. Yet another English rose, 'A Shropshire Lad', with its poetic name, is similar to the above in terms of vigor and health but is a pretty peach color. These are both superb roses, and they attract immediate attention. Visiting them often is a pleasure because they seem to become more beautiful every day.

141

**Height:** 4–5 feet (1.2–1.5 m)
**Flower size:** 3 inches (8 cm)
**Number of petals:** 135–140
(Meilland 1995)

This relatively recent arrival has not yet been fully appreciated. It forms a luxuriant, densely branched bush splendidly covered with coral-pink blossoms with a shape reminiscent of

Alone or in Small Groups

**Height:** 5 feet (1.5 m)
**Flower size:** 2.75 inches (7 cm)
**Number of petals:** 20
(Pemberton 1925)

The Reverend Pemberton named many of the roses he created after women. This is one of those, but it merits special treatment. Its long, flexible canes covered with pale leaves need to be given direction, and one of the best ways of doing so is to build a structure of 3.25-foot (1 m) stakes and train the plant to wrap around it. The result will be a wonderful tower composed of branches and flowers. The buds are strawberry colored, sometimes more orange; they open to form symmetrical rosettes in pastel shades ranging

from pink to pale coral. They grow in numerous flat corymbs at the end of each branch. Their fragrance is deliciously sharp and carries over a long distance. The flowers repeat regularly throughout the season. The main branches should not be pruned, but the side ones can be cut back after flowering. 'Cor-

nelia' is a good rose for marking the end of a pathway, where it can be planted as a central point of interest. If planted with other roses, it looks best with those from the same family—their affinity will create harmony.

### ALTERNATIVE SELECTION

'Francine Austin' (1) has nothing to do with 'Cornelia' but has some of its grace. Like 'Cornelia,' it can be entrusted with important roles in the garden. The small flowers, unruly white balls that follow one another without interruption are composed of minute petals and appear in bunches on thin canes beginning in May. The branches arch to form a pretty shrub with a wide habit. Height: 3.25 feet (1 m); width: 4 feet (1.2 m).

# Dainty Bess
*Hybrid Tea*

and it is covered with dense, leathery leaves, healthy and shiny. The color of the fringed petals is pale pink with a touch of magenta; the light brown stamens give the flowers a special attraction. This rose merits a place in more gardens.

**Origin:** 'Ophelia' x 'K. of K.'

### ALTERNATIVE SELECTIONS

'White Wings' (Krebs 1947) and 'Mrs. Oakley Fisher' (B. R. Cant 1921) are two other roses neglected because of a perceived sin: the possession of no more than five petals. These hybrid teas are essentially the white and yellow-orange versions of 'Dainty Bess'. They are splendid in their simplicity and valuable because their beauty never grows tiresome. They can be planted singly or in groups of up to three, but when used to form a border, they create great light and color. Even though their flowers are simple, they are very effective because they grow in bunches.

The leaves of 'Mrs. Oakley Fisher' are tinged bronze, and it has a pleasant fragrance. The shrub is of medium size.

'White Wings', healthy and robust but a little slow to flower, has peculiar chocolate-colored anthers that stand out against the pale color of the petals. At the center is a cream shadow.

**Height:** 3.25 feet (1 m)
**Flower size:** 4 inches (10 cm)
**Number of petals:** 5
(Archer 1925)

Roses with single flowers do not enjoy the same level of popularity as those considered "true roses." This is a prejudice that should be banished. 'Dainty Bess,' an unusual hybrid tea awarded a medal of honor from the Royal National Rose Society, has single flowers of five petals and is a clear example of how beauty can be found in simplicity and modesty—although, in truth, the large, heavily scented, elegant blossoms of this rose cannot really be called modest. The shrub is upright, its shape pretty, although slightly rigid,

habit, this shrub, a mutation of 'Kordes Robusta', which has red flowers, cuts an excellent figure in any position it is given. It does require space, and if it is not pruned, it will become a very large bush. Height and width: 6 feet (1.8 m).

'Marguerite Hilling' (2), quite famous, has flowers much like those of 'Dapple Dawn', only slightly paler; the shrub is more open, perhaps adapted to even larger spaces, and is generous in flowering. Its leaves are very pale and light. It is often, and to advantage, alternated with 'Nevada', of which it is a sport.

**Height:** 5 feet (1.5 m)
**Flower size:** 5.5 inches (14 cm)
**Number of petals:** 5
(Austin 1983)

Although it is in the shadow created by the bright glow of David Austin's other roses, 'Dapple Dawn' really has no reason to envy the most sumptuous English roses, even if it has only five petals. The exceptional continuity and generosity of its flowering are only the first of its many virtues. There is also the splendid pink of its enormous, attractively shaped flowers with soft petals that flutter in the breeze like wings, light and luminous; all in all, a dramatic spectacle. The shrub is very dense and wide; well branched and covered in leaves, it is strong enough to use as a specimen plant. Resistant to disease, it requires only normal attention and somewhat light pruning, usually just the reduction of its branches by a third. It will support more severe pruning, if needed, and must always be deadheaded.

**Origin:** a sport of 'Red Coat.'

### ALTERNATIVE SELECTIONS
To find equally splendid flowers, one must turn to 'Pink Robusta' (1), a modern variety of *Rosa rugosa* that has few of the species' characteristics. Its leaves are beautiful but not at all typical, although they do bear the accentuated wrinkles. The flowers are large (but not like those of 'Dapple Dawn'), semidouble and a transparent pink, and they follow one another in bunches over a long, long season. With a pretty

Alone or in Small Groups

good. This is a punctual rose and easy to cultivate. It needs little pruning, although dead-wood should be removed to help encourage new growth. If the bush is not deadheaded, its flowering will suffer, although flowers left on will become large orange hips.

**Origin:** 'Eva' x 'Réveil Dijonnais.'

### ALTERNATIVE SELECTIONS

'Eva', highly valued for its single large flowers that grow in bunches, is a bright carmine-pink, pale in the center. Scented. It reflowers and grows to 6 feet (1.8 m).

'Nur Mahal' (Pemberton 1923) is little known. It has 3-inch (8 cm) semidouble flowers with a clean outline and of an intense cherry color that fades to mauve; the petals are pleasantly ruffled. It is 4 feet (1.2 m) high.

Despite its defects—rigid, angular branches and a somewhat loose habit—'Vanity' (1), from Pemberton, 1920, is attractive because of its large, luminous flowers, little more than single, of a shade between pink and cherry. The flowering is copious, and the reflowering is good. A pleasant scent. All of the above roses produce hips if they are not deadheaded.

**Height:** 5 feet (1.5 m)
**Flower size:** 4 inches (10 cm)
**Number of petals:** 10
(Kordes 1939)

Near the end of the 1930s, Kordes added 'Erfurt' and 'Eva' to the group of hybrid musks by Pemberton, invaluable additions because of the intense colors, which blend a range of pas-

tel tints. 'Erfurt' is hardly a sophisticated rose, but it has great force. It has long branches that arch elegantly and stretch to cover a good deal of space. Hanging off the branches amid the shiny bronze-tinted leaves, the flowers are magenta-pink with big cream eyes. The fragrance is of musk, the flowering is long, and the reflowering is

145

**Height:** up to 10 feet (3 m)
**Flower size:** 2.5–2.75 inches (6–7 cm)
**Number of petals:** about 20 (Kordes 1940)

'Fritz Nobis' has thin, pointed buds tinted red; from them open pale pink flowers with a darker reverse, all washed in coral. The flower shape is delightful, the petals forming a crown that curls back slightly around the stamens. The number of flowers cannot even be guessed. The large, open shrub with branches that shoot off in all directions forms a majestic fountain of gray-green leaves suffocated by flowers. Flowering is relatively long and so splendid that one accepts seeing it only once a year. Given its astonishing beauty, 'Fritz Nobis' can occupy an important site, although perhaps not one in the front row, since it is without flowers much of the time. But even without flowers, it is a pretty bush.

**Origin:** 'Joanna Hill' x 'Magnifica.'

1

### ALTERNATIVE SELECTIONS

Roses grow in an international world in which unpronounceable names abound; whether they detract from a rose's chance of fame is unclear, but perhaps such has been the case with 'Rosendorf Sparrieshoop' (1), which is named for the village where the Kordes company has its greenhouses. Its pink flowers, large and almost double with ruffled petals, grow in bunches. It has a slight scent and the grace of a wild rose. In autumn and humid weather, it tends to become spotted.

'Märchenland' is similar to the preceding two. A floribunda by Tantau (1951), it is very vigorous and has an open habit, so it is well adapted to informal gardens. It deserves to be planted more often, not only because its pink semidouble flowers have a modest but authentic beauty but also because the shrub is reflowering and scented. The number of flowers in a bunch can be as many as 40.

# Golden Wings
*Modern Shrub Rose*

83

Canary-yellow in color, it has dark amber stamens. The upright but not rigid shrub has an arching habit with the elegance of the *Rosa pimpinellifolia* (or *spinosissima*) from which it is derived. The leaves are sparse, pale and opaque. If it is not deadheaded, it will produce large hips. This is a rose much loved and visited by bees.

**Origin:** 'Soeur Thérèse' x (*Rosa pimpinellifolia* x 'Ormiston Roy').

### ALTERNATIVE SELECTION

Very similar to 'Golden Wings,' but with semidouble flowers, is 'Windrush' (1) by David Austin. The shrub is about 4 feet (1.2 m) high and vigorous. The generous flowering is followed by large decorative hips if the plant is not deadheaded, an operation always necessary to ensure reflowering.

147

**Height:** 5.25 feet (1.6 m)
**Flower size:** 4 inches (10 cm)
**Number of petals:** 5–7
(Shepherd 1956)

Among the very first roses to flower, 'Golden Wings' stops only when winter arrives; throughout the entire season, it always offers a few flowers. This is not a showy rose, not one that calls attention to itself with spectacular effects, but it is an excellent rose for an informal garden, for it can be wed harmoniously with any other shrub and can thus be included in any garden plan. The flowers are beautiful, much like the wings of gold the name promises, wings that hover lightly, taking flight on flexible branches.

1

Alone or in Small Groups

148

Alone or in Small Groups

**Height:** 4–5 feet (1.2–1.5 m)
**Flower size:** 4 inches (10 cm)
**Number of petals:** 45
(Austin 1983)

'Graham Thomas' is probably the best loved, most famous and most planted of the English roses. The splendor of its flowers, which are the color of sunlight, and the harmony of the shrub itself—upright and round—make this rose a perfect garden plant. Alone it will occupy 21.5 square feet (2 m²); in groups, it forms an island of light. It flowers in May or June, depending on the climate, and continues to produce new shoots that continue the flowering. In a temperate climate, where it will enjoy half-shade, it bears flowers up to Christmas.

**Origin:** 'Charles Austin' x ('Iceberg' x a sport).

## ALTERNATIVE SELECTIONS
There is no lack of shrub roses with pretty yellow flowers suitable for showy positions. Another English rose, 'Golden Celebration' (1), is much the same as 'Graham Thomas', but the gold of its flowers lacks the bronze shadings.

For planting en masse rather than as a single specimen, Austin offers a pretty novelty, 'Mary Magdalene' (1998), which produces bunches of golden semidouble scented flowers. The shrub is practically immune to disease.

'Chinatown' (Poulsen 1963) is a large, attractive floribunda whose vigor suggests it would be best treated as a shrub. It has large, pure gold flowers, 4 inches (10 cm) in diameter, double and flat, which it produces throughout the season without pause.

1

# Lady of the Dawn
## *Modern Shrub Rose*

85

ings, which continue right up to the onset of cold weather, are just as impressive. This rose is pretty at every phase of its flowering and at every moment of the season. A grouping of three plants will prove most attractive in any area of the garden, especially if they are surrounded by green.

**Origin:** 'Interdress' x 'Stadt den Helder.'

### ALTERNATIVE SELECTION

'Marinette' (1) is an English rose created by Austin in 1995. Because of its height and vigor—it will grow up to 5 feet (1.5 m)—it is poorly suited for beds. Well branched and leafy, it has thin, refined buds, very large semidouble flowers that open flat, a cream color suffused with pink and a pleasant scent.

149

**Height:** 4 feet (1.2 m)
**Flower size:** 4–5 inches (10–12 cm)
**Number of petals:** 16
(Interplant 1980)

This rose is almost unknown in some places, as are many of the roses created in Holland, which have difficulty reaching distant markets. Yet this rose has many virtues and not a single defect. It forms an upright shrub with a soft, expansive habit and is dressed to its toes in large, healthy opaque leaves. Its overall appearance is harmonious and balanced. It covers itself with airy, semidouble flowers, just barely pink, with bright centers. The first flowering is spectacular, and later flower-

great deal of joy to any well-trafficked spot. It even tolerates shady sites.

**ALTERNATIVE SELECTIONS**

'Champion of the World' is a good rose known and cultivated by only a few. A hybrid perpetual, it is sometimes classified among the Bourbons. Always in flower, 3.25 feet (1 m) tall, it has arching branches. The buds are crimson, and the double flowers are a mild pink with lilac shadings. Very pretty in the autumn.

Often neglected, 'Madame Lauriol de Barny' (1) deserves more attention. In the United States, at least, its beauty is fully appreciated. Indeed, it is considered one of the best Bourbons because of its silvery pink 4-inch (10 cm) flowers, which are sometimes quartered and have silky, attractively arranged petals. It also has a delicious fruity scent. This rose's single defect? Poor reflowering.

**Height:** 5 feet (1.5 m)
**Flower size:** 2.5–3 inches (6–8 cm)
**Number of petals:** 35–45
(Margottin 1851)

One of the most reliable of the Bourbons, this has highly scented flowers that are deep pink with magenta shadings. The blossoms have a sweet cup shape. Robust and undemanding, it is the most pleasant of the famous trio it forms with 'Reine Victoria,' lilac pink and very fragrant, and 'Madame Pierre Oger,' a delicate porcelain cream. The three roses always go well together. 'Louise Odier' by itself or, even better, planted in a group of three surrounded by a green garden, will add a

1

**Height:** 3.25–13 feet (1–4 m)
**Flower size:** 2–2.5 inches (5–6 cm)
**Number of petals:** 5 (brought to Europe in the 18th century)

This rose is special because of its unusual appearance, its astonishingly long flowering time, the elegance of its narrow, tapering leaves with a purplish tint and its unusual flowers, which are unlike those of any other rose. The flowers go through a sequence of colors, beginning with flame-orange buds. A leathery yellow appears after they open, then they become a coppery pink followed by dark crimson. Each color usually lasts for a day.

The bunches of single flowers with widely spaced ruffled petals call to mind butterflies' wings. This rose may stop growing at 3.25 feet (1 m), or it may keep going, even to 13 feet (4 m). It does not mind cold, but it is sensitive to frost. It prefers protected sites, where it will form a large bush needing only routine cleaning.

### ALTERNATIVE SELECTION
Equally famous, equally adept at flowering and equally old is the first China rose to arrive in Europe, 'Old Blush' (1), which has never left gardens. The quality of its flowers is not particularly high, but its constancy and adaptability make it of value anywhere. It is highly suitable for planting as a hedge.

### A GOOD COMPANION
'Mutabilis' is pretty alone; because of its trick with colors, even a single bush is a colorful vision. But its foliage tends to leave the plant's base exposed, so a good companion would be a groundcover rose such as 'Irène Watts', another Chinese rose, which grows to only 2 feet (60 cm) and offers shades of peachy yellow or coppery red.

1

# *Nevada*
## Hybrid Moyesii

merged in its first early flowering by large white flowers with petals like plates, although these can also be a surprising pink, according to the season, the soil and the humidity. It will then give the occasional new flower. Alone or in a group of three, perhaps combined with 'Marguerite Hilling,' it will always be a pretty ornament for an informal garden. It is best to eliminate the deadwood every two or three years to encourage new growth and keep the shrub from becoming overly woody and losing its shape. If a shrub has already become old and haggard, prune it drastically, cutting it back to 24–32 inches (60–80 cm).

**Origin:** 'La Giralda' x *Rosa moyesii*.

### ALTERNATIVE SELECTIONS
'Jacqueline du Pré' (Harkness 1989), a more recently arrived rose, could easily substitute for 'Nevada'. It has dark, shiny leaves and highly scented ivory semidouble flowers, sometimes with rosy shadings. The pretty, rounded flowers open to reveal the burnished gold of the stamens.

Even more recent is 'The Compass Rose,' offered and highly recommended by Mattock's Rose Nursery in Oxford. It has white, cup-shaped 15-petaled flowers. In 1995, it was acclaimed as the year's most highly scented rose.

**Height:** 6 feet (1.8 m)
**Flower size:** 5 inches (13 cm)
**Number of petals:** 5
(Dot 1927)

No garden should be without this shrub, and in fact, it can be found almost everywhere. All this splendid rose lacks is fragrance. Resistant to disease and mistreatment, it has few thorns and large, arching branches and is covered with small, semiglossy gray-green leaves. It prefers cool climates, in which it can grow into a truly impressive shrub. It should be given plenty of space so that it can grow as it pleases. It should not be pruned, since that could destroy the grace of its branches. The shrub will be literally sub-

# Paul Neyron
*Hybrid Perpetual*

**Height:** 3.25–5 feet (1–1.5 m)
**Flower size:** 5 inches (12 cm)
**Number of petals:** 65
(Levet 1913)

This rose was embraced during the second half of the 19th century, primarily because of its flowers, which at the time, were extraordinarily large. Their plump buds open to form cups with an intense fragrance, the flowers are crimson-pink with a touch of magenta and edged in silver, and they maintain their color to the end; the short petals are quartered but in a casual way. This rose wins out not by its quality or refinement but by force of character. The flowering is very showy, beginning toward the middle of June, and repeats well in autumn. The large shrub has wide leaves and few thorns. It grows naturally to more than 5 feet (1.5 m), but pruning it back will maintain it at the desired size. It was named for a medical student who died during the Franco-Prussian War.

**Origin:** 'Victor Verdier' x 'Anna de Diesbach.'

## ALTERNATIVE SELECTIONS

Another rose distinguished by the power and richness of its color is 'Yolande d'Aragon', with sumptuous pink flowers. Once enormously popular, it fully deserves to be rediscovered. A Portland, it is capable of reflowering, and its round, heavy flowers, of a pretty design, are a lively, luminous pink well suited for cutting. The only defect is that it tends to grow thin at the base, but this can easily be remedied by planting a groundcover rose in front of it. The best would be one with small flowers in a color that reinforces 'Yolande' such as 'Flower Carpet'. White groundcovers that would set it off are 'White Flower Carpet', 'Kent' and 'Yorkshire'.

'Ulrich Brünner Fils' is another possible choice, whether planted alone or in groups, in the middle of a garden or along the side. A large, very floriferous shrub, it has two flowerings of pink-crimson blooms, a rich scent and pretty leaves. It is a rose suited to the Victorian technique of "pegging": fastening the tips of the canes to short stakes, or pegs, stuck in the ground around the bush so that the branches will grow out along them for their entire length, creating pretty garlands.

Alone or in Small Groups

# Red Coat
## Modern Shrub Rose

**Alone or in Small Groups**

**Height:** 5 feet (1.5 m)
**Flower size:** 5.5 inches (14 cm)
**Number of petals:** 5–7
(Austin 1973)

This rose offers much satisfaction, is easy to place and is of great use wherever there is enough room for it—an area of at least 6.5 by 6.5 feet (2 by 2 m). The bright crimson of its airy flowers contributes greatly to the beauty of a natural garden. The first flowering is generous, as are those that come later, for this rose is zealous in reflowering, which it does without pause, keeping the bush dressed in a splendid red livery. The effect of the whole could not be more brilliant. It can be pruned back by half to obtain a more

compact shrub or by a third to maintain it.

### ALTERNATIVE SELECTIONS
'Robusta' (1), a rose by Kordes from 1979, is a descendant of *Rosa rugosa*, but its pretty, shiny leaves are not typical of the species. The luminous blood-red flowers grow in small groups, have five petals and are about 2.75 inches (7 cm) in diameter; they are scented. The flowering is copious and the reflowering excellent. A vigorous rose, this needs neither pruning nor any special cures or treatments. Its growth is luxuriant, and it has forbidding thorns. It grows up to 6.5 feet (2 m) tall. It is best suited to a part of the garden that is left to itself. Plant this rose in groups rather than as a single specimen, and the shrubs will form a dense, intricate green thicket, hedge or screen.

Also by Kordes, who specializes in

dark roses, is 'Morgenrot' (1985). It has large, single flowers of bright vermilion with a highly visible white eye and grows in bunches. It is highly useful where space is limited, since it grows only 32 inches (80 cm) high.

1

# *Rokoko*
## *Modern Shrub Rose*

91

only because of a lack of initiative on the part of sellers. About 4 feet (1.2 m) high, it produces numerous bunches of semidouble flowers in various shades of cream, the center and stamens of which are highlighted in a more intense shade. The flowering is generous. The name promises a sweet color and a sweet scent, and the promises are kept. The graceful, natural habit, exuberant foliage and complete lack of pretense make this an ideal addition to the "wildest" garden.

To create an even brighter spot of color, try planting 'Bordure Nacrée' at the feet of 'Bouquet Vanille'. Its flowers, of a color between rosy cream and amber, grow in large, dense bunches. Another rose you could try for the same purpose is 'Irène Watts', whose flowers are a blend of apricot, peach and coral.

1

**Height:** 4.6 feet (1.4 m)
**Flower size:** 3 inches (8 cm)
**Number of petals:** 25–30
(Tantau 1987)

This elegant rose, decked out with dark, opaque leaves, has a harmonious habit and large, full flowers in a pleasant pastel tone between cream and pink. What's more, it defies colder cli-

mates. Little known, it is offered in the Kordes catalog. It merits greater use for a number of reasons, not the least of which is that modern shrub roses with delicate colors are not common.

### ALTERNATIVE SELECTIONS
'Bouquet Vanille' (1), by Delbard, is another shrub rose with a delicate tint that, like 'Rokoko', is little known,

# Stanwell Perpetual
## Hybrid Pimpinellifolia

**Origin:** *Rosa damascena* x *bifera* x *Rosa pimpinellifolia*.

## ALTERNATIVE SELECTIONS

Shrubs with a round, delicate shape, an elegant appearance, a height of about 3 feet (90 cm) and black hips include 'William III', with semidouble crimson flowers that turn plum; 'Single Cherry', carried by Kordes, which has single cherry-colored flowers and is also pretty in the fall, when its black hips show against the copper foliage; and 'Mrs. Colville', which has crimson-purple flowers with white eyes. Forms with very pretty double flowers include 'Double White' and 'Double Pink', each the color of its name.

If a 'Stanwell Perpetual' is located anywhere near a wall, nothing could be better than draping 'Robbie Burns' (1) onto that wall. 'Robbie Burns' also pleases with the simplicity of its flowers, similar to those of a wild rose. Single and pale pink, almost white at the center, they open to form pretty plates. The plant has pale, thin branches covered with tiny thorns and minute leaves. After its long flowering, it may produce a few more blooms in the autumn.

**156**

**Height:** 5 feet (1.5 m)
**Flower size:** 2.75 inches (7 cm)
**Number of petals:** 60
(introduced by Lee 1838)

This rose should be in every garden, large or small. It is not pompous and does not draw attention to itself, but it possesses a beauty composed of grace, elegance and simplicity that can awaken a deep response in those who see it. To those unfamiliar with it, *Rosa pimpinellifolia*, formerly *spinosissima*, comes as a surprise. 'Stanwell Perpetual' is a spontaneous hybrid that was found in the village of Stanwell and raised in the Lee nursery in Middlesex, England. True to its name, it is perpetually in bloom in mild climates, often from March to December. The shell-pink flowers, enormously abundant, open flat and are composed of soft petals that curve toward the center, where there is often a green button eye. In fertile soil, it can grow to a 6.5-by-6.5-foot (2 by 2 m) shrub, but it needs no other attention, not even dead-heading, for the spent blooms fall by themselves. Light pruning will be needed after the first large rush of flowers, and overall cleaning is necessary at the end of winter. Try planting three as close together as possible at a focal point of the garden, or plant them with other hybrid pimpinellifolias to create a small harmonious group. The selection is tempting.

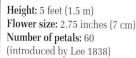

Alone or in Small Groups

1

**Height:** 10 feet (3 m)
**Flower size:** 1.5–2 inches (4–5 cm)
**Number of petals:** 15
(Penzance 1894)

Around the end of the 19th century, the English lawyer Lord Penzance created a small family of roses based on *Rosa eglanteria*, a common hedge rose similar to the dog rose. The Penzance roses with the brightest colors are 'Amy Robsart,' 'Meg Merrilies,' 'Greenmantle' and 'Autumn Fire.' 'Amy Robsart' produces splendid pink flowers with a pale center in June. The plant has the typical apple-scented leaves, especially after a rain, and highly decorative branches, dense with thick thorns. Attractive, round scarlet hips in the autumn add color to the winter landscape. The flowers inevitably remind some people of Shakespeare, whose sonnets and plays are full of references to roses; the best remembered of these is probably Juliet's "That which we call a rose by any other name would smell as sweet." And keeping Shakespeare's works in mind, we might choose to plant our wilder roses on a cliff or hillside where "the wild thyme blows," in the company of primroses, violets and honeysuckle. In the back of a garden, this rose can be used to create large, intricate tangles.

**Origin:** *Rosa eglanteria* x a Bourbon or a hybrid perpetual.

### ALTERNATIVE SELECTIONS

'Autumn Fire' ('Herbstfeuer') produces large bunches of semidouble, dark red scented flowers. Sometimes a few blooms appear in the fall, when the shrub matches its summer splendor with abundant pear-shaped orange hips set off by golden foliage.

'Meg Merrilies' is a prickly shrub with bright crimson semidouble flowers and abundant bright red hips. Both flowers and leaves are scented.

'Greenmantle' has aromatic leaves and white-centered single flowers of a pink so strong it is almost red.

For the Back of the Garden

# Canary Bird
## Hybrid Xanthina

94  ♎  ☉  ✕  ⣿

**Height:** 6.5 feet (2 m)
**Flower size:** 2 inches (5 cm)
**Number of petals:** 5
(1907)

One of the first roses to flower, early in April, 'Canary Bird' has an open shrub as tall as it is wide. The fascination of this rose, as with 'Helen Knight,' which it closely resembles, is its long, dark, pendulous branches covered in splendid leaves of 9 to 13 leaflets which display the abundant flowers to best advantage. The blooms are a luminous canary-yellow. Flowering lasts for a month and is spectacular despite the simplicity of the flowers. An occasional late bloom appears and then black hips. This is a satis-fying rose that can be used wherever the delightful elegance of its branches would be of use. It does not require any special attention, only that dead branches be cleared away. 'Canary Bird' is also available as a tree rose; it is one of the best.

Here is a short list of yellow-flowered roses and their hybrids: *Rosa ecae* and its varieties 'Golden Chersonese' and 'Helen Knight,' which have bright yellow flowers; *R. foetida*, which has intensely bright yellow flowers reminiscent of wet lacquer; *R.* x *harisonii* ('Harison's Yellow'), the American rose known as "the yellow rose of Texas," which has bright yellow double flowers; *R. xanthina hugonis*, with pale yellow flowers; *R. pimpinellifolia* 'Ormiston Roy,' with light yellow flowers; *R. primula*, with primrose-yellow flowers and leaves that smell of incense.

**Origin:** probably *Rosa hugonis* x *Rosa xanthina*.

# *Frühlingsmorgen*
Modern Shrub Rose

95 ☿ ☉ ✕ ⣿

**Height:** 6 feet (1.8 m)
**Flower size:** 4 inches (10 cm)
**Number of petals:** 5
(Kordes 1942)

Of the small group of roses derived from *Rosa pimpinellifolia*, all of them dedicated to spring, 'Frühlingsmorgen' is the one that most honors the joys of that season. Its flowers are delicate—large, single and cherry-pink with primrose-yellow at the center, where the stamens project a dark shadow. When it flowers in May, it spreads its scent through the air as if to announce good weather. Flowering lasts the entire month, and sometimes a few blooms appear later. In autumn, if offers purple hips. This is one of the prettiest

roses for marking the border of a garden or planting along the sides of a sloping path or a stairway.

**Origin:** ('E.G. Hill' x 'Cathrine Kordes') x *Rosa pimpinellifolia altaica*.

## THE COMPANIONS OF 'FRÜHLINGSMORGEN'

'Frühlingsgold' (1), "spring gold," the best known of this series, has won much recognition for the gold color of its flowers, which are slightly smaller than those of 'Frühlingsmorgen', 2–4 inches (5–10 cm) in diameter, and its good scent; 'Frühlingsanfang' ("beginning of spring") is as ivory as the first light of dawn and very scented. 'Frühlingsduft' ("scent of spring") has double flowers

between yellow and apricot in color and is as fragrant as its name suggests; 'Frühlingszauber' ("spring magic") has crimson flowers that tend toward silvery red; 'Frühlingsschnee' ("spring snow") is early-flowering and has pale flowers; and 'Frühlingstag' ("spring day") has semidouble yellow-gold flowers.

1

# Lady Penzance
## Hybrid Eglanteria

96 ♀ ☉ ✕ 🎱

**Height:** 6.5–10 feet (2–3 m)
**Flower size:** 2–2.5 inches (5–6 cm)
**Number of petals:** 5
(Penzance 1894)

'Lady Penzance' and 'Lord Penzance' (left and lower left) make an attractive couple. The surprise is their offering of flowers with the color and transparency of fresh ice cream. Descendants of *Rosa eglanteria*, they have the delicious leaves of the family, scented of apple. 'Lady' is the more colorful, an intense red bathed in yellow and salmon, even copper, and the gleam that illuminates its petals from the center reveals that its other parent was *R. foetida bicolor*, celebrated for its enamel-orange coloring. The flowers of 'Lord Penzance' are of the same tone but more delicate and have lemon-yellow stamens. They flower in May; later are round hips, which are useful in the kitchen. It is best to place roses like these in a natural garden—or at least in the more informal section of a garden. If such a space does not exist, they can be planted at the gateway to a path leading out to the countryside, for example, or just outside the garden—in fact, in any spot that would mark the outer border of the garden. No one will protest.

   **Origin:** *Rosa eglanteria* x *Rosa foetida bicolor.*

# Maiden's Blush
*Alba*

**Height:** 3.25 feet, 6.5 feet (1 m, 2 m)
**Flower size:** 3 inches (8 cm)
**Number of petals:** up to 100 (prior to 1500)

Two forms of this rose exist, identical in all ways except size: 'Great Maiden's Blush' grows to 6.5 feet (2 m) tall, and 'Small Maiden's Blush' reaches only 3.25 feet (1 m), so the choice depends entirely on the space available. This is a very old rose, its origins lost in time. What is certain is that it was being cultivated at Kew Gardens in 1797. Its great age gives it a certain weight, but even without the aura of antiquity, it would be one of the most fascinating roses in any garden. It can be used alone or in a border, but it would not be good for a front-row position because of its short flowering season, June to July. Even so, its beauty demands a site within view, and its scent will attract attention. Those who know this rose wait with anticipation as the short buds, blunt at the top and crowned by sepals, open to form soft pink flowers, more creamy toward the edges, which are "of shocking beauty as soon as they open," in the words of Gertrude Jekyll. Neither particularly large nor perfect, they hold an enchantment that is hard to explain—but perhaps not impossible. Suggestions for the rose's appeal can be found among the names by which it was known in the past: 'Cuisse de Nymphe' ("thigh of the nymph"), 'Cuisse de Nymphe Emue' ("thigh of the passionate nymph"), 'La Séduisante' ("the temptress") and 'La Virginale.' The name 'Maiden's Blush' is only a recent effort to slightly redirect the enthusiasm. The bush itself is attractive, growing increasingly open year by year because of the suckers that rise from the roots. The leaves are glaucous and elegant and have seven leaflets. The scent is alluring, delicate, sweet and agelessly seductive.

**Origin:** probably *Rosa alba* x *Rosa centifolia*.

# Rosa x alba maxima
## Alba

**Synonym:** *Rosa alba plena*
**Height:** 8 feet (2.5 m)
**Flower size:** 3 inches (7.5 cm)
**Number of petals:** 200

This rose is truly ancient. Roman legions took it to England, where it was later adopted as the emblem of the Stuarts. Because of their boundless exuberance, this rose and *Rosa alba semi-plena* have been referred to as tree roses. They grow into enormous, hardy bushes that live practically forever. They are also exquisite, with bunches of soft, cream-colored flowers that offer a wonderful freshness and form a splendid white cloud that can illuminate the darkest corner of any garden. Such corners are dark because they are in shade, and of all the roses, albas are the most tolerant of shade. When the flowering is over, nothing remains but the shrub's large, glaucous leaves, so this is not a rose for a front-row position. As the season advances and the various fungal diseases arrive, the bush can be pruned down to an acceptable size; if left alone to grow wild without pruning, no harm will come, since the next year will bring healthy new leaves. This is an easy rose to grow and has no special needs in terms of soil, position or nourishment.

Besides the form *Rosa alba semi-plena*, which has semidouble flowers, is *R.* x *alba suaveolens* (1), also semidouble and highly scented.

**Height:** up to 10 feet (3 m)
**Flower size:** 4–5 inches
(10–12 cm)
**Number of petals:** 5–7

Despite its name, no rose is simpler than the *Rosa complicata*. The only difficulty with it is tracing its origin. It is probably a spontaneous cross between *Rosa gallica* and *R. canina* or *R. x macrantha*. Its broad petals form a circular cup of bright pink with a touch of white at the center, which is brightened by yellow stamens. The cups spread out along the branches, covering them in a color that glows vividly in sunlight, and then fold back on themselves in the evening. The flowering is capricious and single but long.

It is very effective once the shrub reaches maturity. This rose will grow well in even the poorest soil. It can be left intact, as it will grow only wider by way of side shoots, or it can be cut back to a desired size. It is susceptible to blackspot, but there is no need to fuss—the rose will survive.

### ALTERNATIVE SELECTIONS
Few *Rosa gallica* roses are not double, but in 1982, Peter Beales created the splendid 'James Mason' (1), the flowers of which are little more than single but make up for it by being enormous, highly scented and a dazzling velvety red. There is one abundant flowering in mid-June.

A change in direction brings us to *Rosa roxburghii*, which stands out because of its angular, contorted branches, bark that sheds, elegant leaflets, very large pale pink flowers and pretty hips bristling with setules. *R. roxburghii plena*, with double flowers, is stupendous.

## Rosa farreri persetosa
Species Rose

100

**Height:** 5 feet (1.5 m)
**Flower size:** 0.6 inch (1.5 cm)
**Number of petals:** 5
(introduced 1915)

Also known as *Rosa elegantula* 'Persetosa,' this rose was brought by Farrer from China. It holds the prize for the smallest leaf size, but its small leaves give the bush, which would otherwise look ponderous, a sense of lightness. Also very small are the thorns, and the lilac flowers are small and almost insignificant. But the hips, elongated and with sepals that flutter from the crown, are very decorative in the fall. This rose can be planted in half-shade.

## Rosa x macrantha
Shrub Rose

101

**Height:** 5 feet (1.5 m)
**Flower size:** 3–3.5 inches (8–9 cm)
**Number of petals:** 5 or more
(found in 1823 in France)

Another pretty selection for the "wild" garden, this has a dense, open habit and long, prostrate branches and is ideal for covering a slope. The flowers are large and delicate, pale pink and single or semidouble, and they bloom from mid-June on. The scent is enchanting. There is also a variety with only semidouble flowers, 'Daisy Hill.'

   **Origin:** *Rosa gallica* x *Rosa canina.*

# *Rosa moyesii*
Species Rose

102

**Height:** 10 feet (3 m)
**Flower size:** 2.5 inches (6 cm)
**Number of petals:** 5
(introduced by Wilson in 1894)

The ephemeral flowers, a lively crimson red, are borne on the big bush in small groups that open in succession, so the flowering seems longer than it is. And when it is over, the tiny leaflets remain, graceful and elegant. Fall brings the splendor of bulbous orange hips. A hybrid is the famous 'Geranium.'

165

# *Rosa woodsii fendleri*
Species Rose

103

**Height:** 6.5 feet (2 m)
**Flower size:** 1.5 inches (4 cm)
**Number of petals:** 5
(1888)

This superb bush, originally from the United States, is upright and has gray canes armed with sharp thorns and densely covered by leaves composed of five to seven leaflets. The highly scented flowers are a bright lilac-pink and appear from June to August. The round hips are a waxy red and appear in hanging bunches that stay on the plant for a good part of the winter. Very decorative, this makes a great, colorful show in the autumn.

For the Back of the Garden

# BORDERS, HEDGES, ESPALIERS

"*B*order" and "mixed border" are general and rather vague terms used to describe similar situations. For the purposes of this book, however, a border is a single row of plants that acts as a border, meaning that it follows the edge of a path or is placed alongside a stairway or the length of a wall. A mixed border is a much wider area of soil— it's really a long, narrow bed wide enough to accommodate several rows of roses. A border, which can also be a mixed border—the sort for which English gardens are famous—can be planted with roses and any other plants. These are usually arranged according to height, the lowest in front and the tallest at the back. Such a bed is one of the centerpieces of garden, made even more inviting by the bright colors of the flowering plants. Even more important and spectacular is a double border along the sides of a grassy path leading to a pavilion, a gazebo, a belvedere or other point of interest—a place to pause.

A border is the ideal place to plant antique roses, for their often straggly habits and the brevity of their flowering make them poor choices for beds. To achieve a border of roses that are always in flower, however, means turning to modern roses.

One of the greatest pleasures for any gardener is combining different plants in a border, whether they are all roses or roses and other plants. If nothing else, such operations are opportunities to display personal taste. They also require a certain amount of thought, since the gardener must bear in mind the characteristics of the plants, their heights and colors, the shapes of the flowers and even the type and quality of their leaves. The goal is always harmony. Gallicas combine well with one another, as do damasks and musks, but planting roses of

168

## VARIEGATED ROSES

*Some roses have truly capricious coloring, streaked and striped. In some cases, delicate tints are combined; in other cases, the colors contrast sharply. Before the arrival of humans, such combinations were created by nature, the oldest known being*

*'Rosa Mundi,' or Rosa gallica versicolor (left), much cited in Roman days and in the Middle Ages. Fanatical collectors, people who are passionate about all curiosities, or those who simply have the space to spare in a garden could create a border planted only with variegated roses; their combined blooms would be truly spectacular. There are certain very famous examples, but nearly every class of rose offers a few examples:*

*'Camaieux' and 'George Vibert'* *(gallica), a pale pink striped with purple*

*'Honorine de Brabant' (Bourbon), lilac and purple stripes*
*'Variegata di Bologna' (Bourbon), purple stripes on a creamy white background*
*'Ferdinand Pichard' (hybrid perpetual), carmine with broad white stripes*
*'Vick's Caprice' (hybrid perpetual), an unusual combination of lilac, white and pink, with stripes, veining and spots of a darker pink*
*'Stars 'n' Stripes' (miniature), a famous example with striking stripes of white and strawberry-red.*

different types together requires more skill. Shrub roses must be selected on the basis of their characteristics, including the shape of the flowers. A rose with simple flowers will probably look out of place amid a group with more pompous and complicated arrangements of petals. A rose with dull leaves will clash with one that has shiny, metallic leaves.

Much care must go into matching colors. Pastel tints go well with one another; strong colors should be dealt out parsimoniously. A pale pink will work with a dark pink; pink goes with yellow; any color goes with white. Orange-reds clash with purples and violet-reds. One secret: To make a bed or border seem larger, keep paler colors toward the outside of the group and darker ones in the middle.

A hedge is a kind of border but much thicker and higher. More important to the definition of "hedge" is the role it plays, which is that of a more-or-less impenetrable barrier which makes a sharp separation between two different parts of a garden or marks the boundary of the garden area so as to create intimacy.

Although they are not evergreen, roses can make perfect hedges. Such comparatively colorless evergreen plants as laurel, berberis and holly should be reserved for places where their perennial green is truly indispensable, where there is something that must be hidden for the entire year or where the eyes of strangers might otherwise intrude.

'Mozart.'

Furthermore, although they lose their leaves, some types of roses have such densely interwoven branches that they form screens every bit as effective as those made by evergreens. In addition to creating the desired barrier—rendered truly impenetrable by the presence of fearsome thorns—the architectural interweaving of a rosebush serves a decorative function as well. The rugosa roses are the queens of hedges, especially in cold climates. Anyone doubting this need only witness the beauty of these roses in Scandinavian countries, where they are used abundantly in public and private gardens.

Finally, there are always places in a garden where one senses the need for a low dividing line—nothing as rigid or final as a wall, just a separation that draws a line but leaves what is on the far side visible. What is wanted is a sense of height in an area where the horizontal dimension has become monotonous. The answer is an espalier, be it on a wooden trellis or just a length of wire stretched between stakes. The perfect roses to train onto such a support are climbing shrubs or climbing roses that are not overly high such as the so called pillar roses.

# Belle Isis
## Gallica

♀ ◎ ✕ ⁝⁝

could easily be mixed in among these gallicas. Very pale, as are most of the albas, just touched with pink and moderate in size, it is perfect for a mixed border. Even though its flowers are small, only 2.5 inches (6 cm) in diameter, this is probably the jewel of the family. The petals reflex completely at maturity; the flowers, a splendid shape, are densely packed with petals arranged

**Height:** 4 feet (1.2 m)
**Flower size:** 2.5–2.75 inches (6–7 cm)
**Number of petals:** 45–55
(Parmentier 1845)

If the flowers of 'Belle Isis' disappoint in terms of size, it is likely because we have become accustomed to the exaggerated size of modern roses. Pale pink with petals arranged in delicate curves toward the center, the flower is a flat cup with a button eye at the center. Flowering is very abundant in summer. The scent is of myrrh. The canes have few thorns but do have hispid setules. The shrub is upright, compact and round and has small, gray-green leaves. This rose merits its fame.

## GOOD COMPANIONS

Another gallica with pale colors is 'Duchesse de Montebello'. In cultivation since 1834, it continues to please with its extremely delicate flowers in a pink that evaporates to white. They are 2.75 inches (7 cm) in diameter, double and fragrant. Given full sun and rich, well-fertilized soil, it will become a dense shrub and flower generously at the end of May. Its height is 4 feet (1.2 m).

There is also 'Duchesse d'Angoulême' (1), also called 'Wax Rose' because of the translucent appearance of its flowers, which are soft, pale, ephemeral, deeply moving. Since the shrub does not grow to more than 5 feet (1.5 m), it could be used toward the front of a border just behind a groundcover rose of a slightly more vivid tint such as 'Surrey' or 'The Fairy'.

'Félicité Parmentier' (2), an alba,

one against the other. It needs good fertilization and plenty of rich, moist soil. Height: little more than 3.25 feet (1 m).

All these roses are pretty combined with other flowering plants.

Antique Roses for Borders

# Blanche Moreau
*Moss Rose*

**Height:** 4–5 feet (1.2–1.5 m)
**Flower size:** 3 inches (7.5 cm),
very double
(Moreau-Robert 1880)

This was one of the most popular white roses of the 19th century, along with 'Madame Hardy,' which has much larger flowers. What makes this rose singular is the sharp contrast of the fabric-like enamel-white flowers with the dense moss of the buds and the darker-colored thorns. The pretty flowers, which grow in bunches, are cup-shaped, very double and sweetly scented and have a green button eye. Flowering is in June, although a few late blooms sometimes appear. The shrub has an open, loose habit and thin canes.

**Origin:** 'Comtesse de Murinais' x 'Quatre Saisons Blanc' ('White Moss').

## ALTERNATIVE SELECTIONS
'Alfred de Dalmas' and 'Mousseline' are both very pale, almost white, moss roses that are so similar they are often mistaken for each other. Both have elegant soft, fragile, mother-of-pearl petals, and both are pleasing because of the sharp scent given off by their mossy calyxes. They are reflowering.

Two other very pretty white roses, white but not snow-white, can compete with 'Blanche Moreau.' The first is 'Unique Blanche,' also called 'White Provence,' a centifolia rarely planted today but well worth rediscovering. Its long buds, surrounded by leafy sepals, are pretty, and the large flowers are enchanting, a silky white touched with pink with a

group of small, thin petals tucked into the center. The shrub is elegant and particularly pretty near water. It may flower a second time.

The second is 'Boule de Neige,' which as a Bourbon, has a long flowering, from the end of June to September; its flowers are a light ivory, like balls of snow that the dawn edges in pink and the rising sun will later turn white. The upright shrub has thin canes with few thorns and dark, shiny, leathery leaves.

## GOOD COMPANIONS
These white roses can be used to create a pretty border with 'Souvenir de la Malmaison.' Toward the far end of the garden, the border could end with the soft cushion of a ground-cover rose such as 'Avon' or, if a brighter color is wanted, 'Essex' for pink or 'Oxfordshire' or 'Regensberg' for an even more daring contrast.

appear in June, are very full, globular, silvery pink and quartered and flat when completely open. They have an intense scent that wafts through the air, especially on warm days. The shrub's canes are well provided with thorns, its leaves are rough and opaque, and its habit is open. This is a rose for collectors or for the last row in a border.

### ALTERNATIVE SELECTIONS

For a true moss rose, the best choice is still the original, 'Common Moss' (1), also known as 'Old Moss.' In cultivation since the 18th century, it has held up well. Its flowers are pale pink, and the flower stems and calyxes are covered with a reddish green mosslike growth. Very scented. Height: 4 feet (1.2 m).

Another excellent *Rosa muscosa* (moss rose) is 'Général Kleber,' highly valued for its large flowers, which are pale to dark pink with lilac shading and have soft, ruffled petals at the center around the button eye. Highly scented, the shrub is compact and covered densely with leaves.

**Synonyms:** 'Crested Moss,' *Rosa centifolia cristata*
**Height:** 4.25 feet (1.3 m)
**Flower size:** 3 inches (8 cm)
**Number of petals:** more than 100 (Vibert 1827)

Vibert claimed to have discovered this rose growing on the broken-down wall of a convent in Fribourg, Switzerland, in 1820.

All its given names refer to a singular characteristic that makes it unique among roses: the impressive fringe, originally mistaken for moss, that surrounds and overwhelms the fantastic buds. Thanks to the fringe, the buds often look like tiny three-pointed hats similar to the famous *chapeau* associated with the French emperor. The flowers, which

Antique Roses for Borders

**Height:** 4–5 feet (1.2–1.5 m)
**Flower size:** 3–3.5 inches (8–9 cm)
**Number of petals:** more than 100
(raised at the Roseraie de l'Hay in the 19th century)

One of the most popular gallicas, this has short, pudgy bright red buds that open into pretty flowers. The densely packed petals form orderly flowers, but they are so short that the cup they form looks flat, much as if it had been sliced in half. The color is a dark crimson with purple and mauve accents that becomes decidedly purple; but the plants vary—some are crimson, some tend toward a wine color, and still others are closer to violet. The blossoms are joined in groups of four or five, and the shrub is upright, dense with canes that bear few thorns and covered with somewhat rough leaves. The flowering lasts about four weeks, beginning with the onset of summer; it lasts a little longer than does that of other antique roses, but it is still a good idea to flank this rose with a few that remain in flower longer, perhaps some with pink flowers instead of red—'Chambord,' for example, or an English rose with an antique flavor such as 'Wife of Bath.' 'Charles de Mills' needs rich soil and protection from powdery mildew, which attacks late in the season. This rose will happily tolerate half-shade.

## ALTERNATIVE SELECTIONS

Two other gallicas can be used with 'Charles de Mills' to create a lively border of red and pale pink. The first is 'Assemblage des Beautés,' with 2.75-inch (7 cm) flowers, double rosettes in a bright cherry-red. They are very well shaped and scented. 'Duc de Guiche' is the second, a magnificent gallica, scented, with large crimson-purple flowers whose petals are arranged symmetrically and reflex as they mature. It needs rich, dense soil.

A bright cherry-red can also be found in two hybrid perpetuals that offer the obvious advantage of reflowering: 'Dupuy Jamain,' with large 30-petaled flowers, and 'Ardoisée de Lyon,' with nicely shaped blossoms, quartered and shaded purple and violet. There is also 'Arthur de Sansal,' a Portland that stands out for the pleasing shape of its blossoms and their intense dark purple-crimson with deeper shades.

Antique Roses for Borders

**Height:** 5–5.5 feet (1.5–1.7 m)
**Flower size:** 3–3.5 inches
(8–9 cm)
**Number of petals:** more than
100

Nothing is known of this rose's origin, but it appeared in European gardens early in the 20th century. It is named for the French painter Fantin-Latour (1836–1904), famous for his pictures of lush roses, of which this could easily be one. The flowers are enchanting; growing in small sprays, they are flesh-pink with darker centers. Flowering occurs once, in June, but it is very copious. This rose does not completely resemble a centifolia, and its smooth, semi-glossy leaves indicate some Chi-

nese ancestry. It can be used in a border, perhaps with other antique roses, to ensure color for the entire season; plant lower-growing roses in the front row. Pink companions could be 'Surrey,' 'Nathalie Nypels' and 'The Faun.' Nancy Steen, a grower in New Zealand, planted 'Fantin-Latour' beside a smoke bush (*Cotinus*), creating interesting color and texture contrasts. 'Fantin-Latour' can be planted without support, but it is a good idea to prune the branches after flowering, cutting back the central branches by a quarter and the laterals by two-thirds. Also advisable are treatments to protect it from powdery mildew, which arrives in the middle of summer.

### ALTERNATIVE SELECTIONS
Two pretty centifolia roses that can substitute for or be combined with 'Fantin-Latour' are 'Juno' and 'Reine des Centefeuilles.' 'Juno' is 4.6 feet (1.4 m) high, with blossoms typical of its class, 3 inches (8 cm) in diameter, full and round with a button eye at the center when fully open. The color is a luminous pale pink. Scented. The shrub is relaxed with an arching habit; because of the weight of the flowers, it is a good idea to give the branches some kind of support.

'Reine des Centefeuilles' is a true queen, with flowers even larger and more original that those of 'Juno.' When fully open, they are flat and appear to have been neatly trimmed with scissors. The very double flowers are deep pink.

# La Ville de Bruxelles
*Damask*

other damasks with clematis, letting the clematis climb over the roses, combining their colors in a soft mixture. Pretty with the pink roses would be the lavender of clematises 'Vyvyan Pennell,' 'William Kennet' and 'Mrs. Cholmondeley.'

### ALTERNATIVE SELECTIONS

'Marie Louise', a damask that was part of the collection at Malmaison, also has very large flowers that open flat and then form balls. The color is a luminous mauve-pink, and the blooms are dense with highly scented petals. The dark-leaved shrub grows to just over 4 feet (1.2 m), and when in flower, its branches sometimes bend all the way to the ground.

'Ispahan' is the most famous of the damasks, as popular today as it was in the 19th century, perhaps in part because of the generosity of its flowering. It is the first and last rose to come into flower. The pink of the blooms is rich, and the flowers are double and opulent, at first quite orderly but later relaxed and untidy. The fragrance is extraordinary.

**Height:** 4–5 feet (1.2–1.5 m)
**Flower size:** 4 inches (10 cm)
**Number of petals:** 45–55
(Vibert 1849)

This rose is loved for its broad flowers, which are decidedly large for an antique rose. They are pure pink and have an intense scent. The shape of the blossoms is delightful the

petals are aligned in quarters and expose the usual button eye; the outer petals reflex lazily over the smaller ones. The shrub is packed with pale branches; it has a compact habit, but the branches arch gently when carrying the full weight of the flowers.

For an original border, combine 'La Ville de Bruxelles' and

Antique Roses for Borders

three to form a small hedge, in a border or in a container on a balcony. Lovers of potpourri will find themselves delighted by it. It loves full sun, where it will flower profusely, but it accepts half-shade.

### ALTERNATIVE SELECTIONS

'Rose du Roi', another Portland, is so named because it grew in the garden of Louis XVIII at St. Cloud. It has even greater historical importance, since it is the rose from which all the hybrid perpetuals are descended. It is also very useful today because of its low habit and soft flowers, which are crimson-purple and have a strong fragrance. The reflowering is very good.

Three moss roses offer shades of very dark red: 'Deuil de Paul Fontaine' (1), as dark as the "mourning" its name indicates; 'Capitaine John Ingram', with crimson-purple-brown flowers and dark foliage; and 'Nuits de Young', as black-violet as the night, its only light the golden stamens; it exhales a strong aroma of resin.

**Height:** 3.25 feet (1 m)
**Flower size:** 2.5 inches (6 cm)
**Number of petals:** more than 40

This rose was brought from Iran by Nancy Lindsay, a great lover of roses, who found it growing in a garden of ancient Rescht (Rasht). It is strongly characteristic of a gallica. It is enchanting because of its sharply defined rosettes, which are erect on the branches and carried on short stems; the flowers are packets of short, silky petals of an intense shade between fuchsia and purple—a color that shines. The flowering is copious, and the reflowering good. With its compact, bushy habit, it occupies little space and can be planted anywhere—alone, in a group of

1

# Tuscany Superb
*Gallica*

**Height:** 4–5 feet (1.2–1.5 m)
**Flower size:** 3.5–4 inches
(9–10 cm)
**Number of petals:** 30
(Rivers, introduced by Paul
in 1848)

This rose is superb, an exceptional shrub that tends to expand. The flowers, which appear in mid-June, are a sweet, velvety, dark crimson-brown; the petals, large and round, form a cup that partly hides the yellow disks of stamens. Probably a sport of 'Tuscany,' another famous rose, 'Tuscany Superb' is superior in all ways—for the wealth and size of its flowers, which have larger and more numerous petals; for its vigor; and for its larger leaves.

## ALTERNATIVE SELECTIONS
'Belle de Crécy' (1) is another gallica with a singular dark red color. Dedicated to Madame Pompadour, the favorite of Louis XV, it has very double but rather small 3-inch (7.5 cm) flowers that are flat and quartered; the central petals bend toward the green button eye. Its color is almost indescribable—cherry and purple that take on violet shadings and end up lavender and gray. The fragrance is very intense, and the flowering is reasonably long. The roots should not be allowed to dry out.

Any list of dark, intensely colored gallicas must include 'Sissinghurst Castle,' previously known as 'Rose des Maures' and renamed after being rediscovered in her garden by Vita Sackville-West. It has 3.5-inch (9 cm) flowers of a brown-crimson-purple shade rather like that of 'Tuscany' but for a few streaks of white at the base of the petals.

## GOOD COMPANIONS
Roses with intensely purple-red flowers work well in a border with silver-leaved companion plants such as lavender, sea ragwort (*Senecio cinerea*), *Artemisia* 'Silver Queen' and lamb's-ears (*Stachys byzantina*; *S. lanata*). A fairly low shrub such as a white-flowered *Potentilla* would make another good companion, as would highly floriferous roses such as 'Iceberg' and 'Fleurette.'

1

# White Meillandécor
## Groundcover Rose

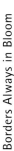
Borders Always in Bloom

**Height:** 32 inches (80 cm)
**Flower size:** 2.5 inches (6 cm), double
(Meilland 1988)

This is one of a group of roses used widely in Mediterranean gardens and once known as Meidiland roses. The name Meillandécor is intended to indicate their function: Much as pieces of furniture decorate a room, these roses are designed to decorate a garden, "to create the landscape," as the Meilland company explains. The Meillandécor roses form an impressive team: 'Alba' and 'White,' 'Magic,' 'Perle,' 'Ice,' 'Fuchsia,' 'Rouge,' 'Scarlet,' 'Bingo,' and many more. Immense bunches of flowers, dense foliage com-

posed of small, shiny leaves that descend all the way to the base of the plant, a wide habit that includes them in the class of groundcover roses, and astonishing flowering and reflowering all make these shrubs highly useful for planting in the first row of any kind of border and, in fact, in any area of a garden.

Their heights vary greatly. The largest, which can reach nearly 5 feet (1.5 m), are 'Alba Meillandécor,' medal winner at Frankfurt in 1989, and 'Scarlet,' which is best used in hedges. The heights of the others range from 20 to 32 inches (50–80 cm). The lowest is 'Magic Meillandécor,' which has pale pink-magenta flowers, scented and semidouble, and grows to just

20 inches (50 cm). 'White' has pure white flowers; 'Perle' is pearly and almost double with a clump of smaller petals at the center; 'Ice' is semidouble and icy white; 'Fuchsia' is that color and semidouble; 'Scarlet' has double flowers of a bright scarlet; 'Rouge' has simple flowers of a very brilliant red. 'Bingo Meillandécor,' the winner of three awards, is very interesting. Its single flowers are a pale pink verging on white, and it blooms continuously. 'Perle,' 'Magic,' 'Scarlet' and 'Rouge' are all available as tree roses.

### ALTERNATIVE SELECTION
The qualities of 'Pearl Drift' (1) are guaranteed by its splendid parents, 'Mermaid' and 'New Dawn,' an unusual coupling. 'Pearl Drift' produces masses of pink buds that become big, graceful cup-shaped semidouble flowers with large white petals touched with pink. The shrub is well balanced; very dense, it has a wide habit and shiny green-and-bronze leaves and dark thorns. It will tolerate shaded sites.

1

# Bonica 82
## Modern Shrub Rose

113 ⚓ ◉ ↻

**Height:** 3.25–5 feet (1–1.5 m)
**Flower size:** 2 inches (5 cm)
**Number of petals:** more than 40
(Meilland 1982)

Two prestigious awards in America and Germany, a gold medal at Belfast and a lesser prize at Bagatelle greeted the launching of this French rose, which in 1998, was included in the classification of best shrub roses. This is such a pleasing, healthy rose that we can begin by listing its defects: lack of fragrance, small flowers that will not satisfy those eager for a "mass" effect and the shrub's rather loose habit. Its virtues include delicate rosette-shaped flowers in luminous pink with large, round, ruffled petals. The

blooms appear along the full length of the branches from early in the summer onward. The small, semiglossy leaves are graceful. This rose is well suited to elegant borders, perhaps with 'Surrey' in front of it and, if the bed is wide enough, 'Fritz Nobis' behind it.

**Origin:** (*Rosa sempervirens* x 'Madame Marthe Carron') x 'Picasso.'

### ALTERNATIVE SELECTIONS
'Charles Aznavour' (1), also by Meilland, is a floribunda, and the winner of five medals; it has the same type of flowers—as though chiseled by the hand of an artist—in a creamy white with touches of pink. The flowers are double, numerous and 4 inches (10 cm) in diameter. More orderly and compact than 'Bonica 82',

it grows to about 32 inches (80 cm).

For a more sugary pink, there is 'Clos Fleuri' (Delbard 1992), another French rose. It is the offspring of 'Centenaire de Lourdes', whose qualities it has inherited. It has very double flowers, tremendous flowering and a scent of hay and strawberries. Its resistance to disease is strong. The height is 32 to 36 inches (0.8–1 m). 'Clos Fleuri' is also available in yellow, white and bicolor versions.

1

**Height:** 3–4 feet (0.9–1.2 m)
**Flower size:** 3.5 inches (9 cm)
**Number of petals:** 15
(Delbard-Chabert 1958)

Known but not well enough, this rose never fails to meet expectations, never promises more than it can give. The flowers, which grow in bunches of five to ten, have ruffled petals of a soft pink slightly tinged with coral and paler at the base. The flowers are numerous and succeed one another with few pauses. The shrub has such a very broad habit that in favorable conditions, it will grow up to 6.5 feet (2 m) wide; it is resistant to everything and requires no particular treatment—it can be left alone and not even pruned.

It is pretty by itself, in a border or combined with other plants in a mixed border; it can easily be accompanied by antique roses. There is also a 'Centenaire de Lourdes Rouge' with red flowers, but it does not have the same delicacy.

**Origin:** ('Frau Karl Druschki' x a sport) x a sport.

### ALTERNATIVE SELECTIONS

'Pink Parfait' is another floribunda that enjoyed much favor in the 1970s, as indicated by the four medals it received. Created in the United States by Swim, it has established a firm foothold in Europe, where everything that is said about it is good. It has the elegant buds of a hybrid tea, nicely shaped flowers in a pleasing blend of pink on a cream base and prolific flowering. The flowers stand up well to rain and make perfect cut stems. Other characteristics: thin canes, almost without thorns, semiglossy leaves, no fragrance, height of 32 inches (80 cm).

In 1998, Mattock's launched 'Centenary', a rose created for that English nursery by Kordes. It has already won three medals. A vigorous floribunda, it has drawn attention for its splendid semidouble flowers in various shades of pink, their ruffled petals and their intense scent. The shrub is upright and disease resistant and has an abundance of shiny, dark leaves.

# Heavenly Rosalind
*Modern Shrub Rose*

seems more like a wild rose of the hillside. And it has a very great virtue: Rather than producing all its flowers in two or three weeks, it continues to offer its small bunches a few at a time from May all the way into October. The blooms are fragile cups, light and transparent, as immaterial as puffs of air. They are the palest pink with white centers and have only the slightest fragrance. At sunset, they fold their petals to protect themselves during the night.

### ALTERNATIVE SELECTION
'Rosy Cushion' (1) is a well-established rose. Its flowering, unlike that of 'Heavenly Rosalind,' is quite striking and very long. the flowers are 2.75 to 3 inches (7–8 cm) in diameter and pink with white centers; they grow in large corymbs at the ends of the branches, which bend almost to the ground, and cover the plant like a blanket. After a rest period, the flowering repeats, less strikingly. It is considered a groundcover rose, but given its height and the length of its branches, its placement calls for good judgment: It should be given the space it needs. It can be left on its own without pruning in a border, along a row of trees or by a wall.

**Height:** 4.6 feet (1.4 m)
**Flower size:** 3 inches (8 cm)
**Number of petals:** 5
(Austin 1995)

Noble and distinct, this rose has something of the appearance of a wild rose. It is a joy to have such a pretty, simple plant in one's garden; without even a hint of the artificial about it, it

Borders Always in Bloom

**Height:** 4–5 feet (1.2–1.5 m)
**Flower size:** 3 inches (7.5 cm)
**Number of petals:** 20–30
(Kordes 1960)

'Lavender Lassie' looks like a vigorous floribunda, and unlike other hybrid musks, it does not produce long, wandering canes but instead forms a compact shrub. It is not an impressive rose at first glance but a gentle one, a rose one is happy to have in the garden. Its flowers are flat rosettes of a tender lilac-pink with magenta shadings and the enchanting look of antique roses. The flowering is heavy and repeats regularly. It is known to be resistant to disease and easy to care for. Sometimes its growth is so vigorous that it reaches 10 feet (3 m).

### GOOD COMPANIONS

'Lavender Dream' (1), Interplant, 1984, is a shrub rose whose parentage goes back to the polyantha 'Yesterday'. Its color, intense lilac, is one that takes some getting used to, but it becomes increasingly pleasing over time. When planted with the softer

color of 'Lavender Lassie', it creates a surprising effect, the contrast being further emphasized by the shapes and types of flowers.

'Lavender Dream' produces a mass of small 16-petaled flowers similar to those of phlox, making it a great carpet to roll out in front of the larger roses in the group. This is a fine rose for sites with half-shade, particularly in climates with a burning sun that might damage the color—another advantage of this rose, since every garden has places where shade is a problem.

Roses of this color usually combine well with white roses. The first to come to mind is 'Francine Austin', whose small rosettes like a multitude of snowflakes will do well against the flowers of 'Lavender Lassie'. 'Jacqueline du Pré' would make another good companion.

# *Lichtkönigin Lucia*
### Modern Shrub Rose

♀ ☉ ✕ ⣿

in the middle of a large border, with perhaps a Chinese 'Mutabilis' behind it for a striking contrast in flower shape. 'Norfolk' or 'Ghent' would be good in the front row.

## ALTERNATIVE SELECTIONS

'Mountbatten' (1) is a famous floribunda developed by Harkness, who drew on all the prettiest and most famous yellow roses for creating it. Backed by its potent family tree, it won four medals and was declared rose of the year in 1982. For more than a decade, it has reigned as one of the best yellow roses. Its vigor, height and very upright habit make it better for a border than for a bed. The dark semievergreen leaves are an ideal backdrop for the bunches of flowers in a solid yellow that is reminiscent of the color of mimosas and never garish. The flowers are pretty in bud and pretty when open. It reflowers and is disease resistant.

## GOOD COMPANIONS

The yellow of these roses goes very well with the white of 'Margaret Merril', 'Class Act' and 'Jacqueline du Pré' as well as that of hybrid teas such as 'Cosmos', 'Pascali' and 'Sir Frederick Ashton'.

**Height:** 5 feet (1.5 m)
**Flower size:** 3 inches (8 cm)
**Number of petals:** 30–40
(Kordes 1966)

The flowers of this rose are an intense lemon-yellow. They are full and grow singly and in small groups and have nicely ruffled petals. The rose has been in gardens for several decades now and has many virtues: It is dependable and richly scented; it has a splendid autumn flowering; it is luxuriant and packed with leaves; and it resists frost and disease well. The decorative stamens are a bright amber color that adds a touch of gold to the lemon of the petals, which could otherwise seem rather cold. This plant would go well

**Height:** 28 inches x 3.25 feet (0.7 x 1 m)
**Flower size:** 2.5 inches (6 cm)
**Number of petals:** 18
(Poulsen 1991)

This is one of a group of roses named for counties of Britain. It capably fills its role as a groundcover and is also highly valuable for its color, which is somewhat rare in this category. Since it forms a dense shrub, very expansive and fully covered with pretty bronze-shaded leaves, it merits being admired on its own, not merely as a secondary player to other roses. It could easily be used in a pretty border along a pathway or to divide two areas of a meadow. Its gift is continuous bunches of small, pretty flowers in a splendid combination of lighter and darker shades of apricot. An irreplaceable rose, this pleases wherever it grows, even alone in

a container. And it has a delicate, pleasing scent.

### ALTERNATIVE SELECTION

'Blühwunder' (1), launched by Kordes in 1995, offers a similar color, a blend of salmon and coral tones. While it is far less endearing, it can deliver a greater impact. Its impressiveness lies in the exceptional size of its clusters of up to 50 flowers, sometimes packed too densely. The flowers are semidouble and borne high on glossy foliage. It has the subtle scent of apples.

Borders Always in Bloom

## The Herbalist
*English Rose*

119

185

**Height:** 3 feet (90 cm)
**Flower size:** 4.5–5 inches
(11–12 cm)
**Number of petals:** 26
(Austin 1991)

*Rosa gallica officinalis*, known since earliest antiquity and valued for its presumed medicinal qualities, is no longer grown in gardens, having been replaced by hundreds of far less humble varieties with much longer flowering times. 'The Herbalist,' however, offers the same flower with more copious flowering. Austin named it for its resemblance to the antique rose of apothecaries. It has pretty magenta flowers, large and semidouble and illuminated by the stamens. The shrub has a pretty habit, erect but grace-ful; it is branchy, has thin canes and is easy to care for. It will fit easily into in a mixed border because the pale green of its leaves and the bright color of its flowers combine well with blue and white.

For a classic matching, plant 'The Herbalist' with catmint (*Nepeta mussinii*) or dwarf lavender. For a symphony of magenta and lilac, plant it with 'Escapade' or 'Charles Rennie Mackintosh' roses.

**Origin:** a sport x 'Louise Odier.'

### ALTERNATIVE SELECTIONS
'Portland Rose' (1), or 'Duchess of Portland', is another rose with a luminous color, in this case, a bright cherry that does not fade. This is the rose that gave birth to the group of Port-land roses, which are few in number but always interesting. An excellent garden shrub, 3 feet (90 cm) high, it has large, luminous semidouble flowers and offers two pretty flowerings, in the summer and in the autumn. Deadheading must not be overlooked.

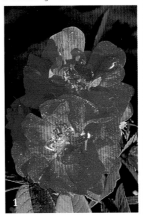

BORDERS, HEDGES, ESPALIERS

Borders Always in Bloom

can be fronted by 'Emily,' which is only 30 inches (75 cm) high and an almost white pink, or by 'English Garden' or 'Wife of Bath.'

**Origin:** 'Graham Thomas' x 'Yellow Button.'

### ALTERNATIVE SELECTION
Meilland has its own luminous yellow offering: 'Toulouse Lautrec' (1), 1993, which won an award at Monza for its scent. Its large, very double flowers are gracefully relaxed in the antique style.

**Height:** 4 feet (1.2 m)
**Flower size:** 4.5 inches (11 cm)
**Number of petals:** 140
(Austin 1991)

A delightful fresh, pure yellow, an equally fresh scent and flowers in the enchanting shape of flat rosettes packed with short petals as delicate as tissue paper all make this rose a pleasing addition to a mixed border. Its habit is elegant and upright, and it has thin, flexible canes that after the first copious flowering, tend to lengthen while still bearing flowers. With its soft yellow, it does well in a border of English roses, combining well with the pink of 'Heritage,' 'Chaucer' and 'Mary Rose' or the white of 'Glamis Castle.' In the border, it

1

# *Ballerina*
*Hybrid Musk*

121

**Height:** 5 feet (1.5 m)
**Flower size:** 2 inches (5 cm)
**Number of petals:** 5
(Bentall 1937)

Sometimes 'Ballerina' is classified among the hybrid musks and at other times among the polyanthas. The latter classification is justified by its phlox-like flowers. Whichever it is, it is adorable and special. Its dainty flowers are magenta with white centers and grow paler over time. The flowers grow in very large corymbs on the tips of the canes as well as on the side branches. Individual flowers look like butterflies that have just alighted, weightless and fluttering, although as the name suggests, when viewed en masse, they are like the airy dress of a dancer. They carry a slight fragrance of musk that is also reminiscent of sweet peas. The plant has few thorns and pale, semiglossy, very healthy leaves. The shrub is reflowering and does not grow much in height because its long, flexible canes bend elegantly down-ward. The branches may grow up to 5 feet (1.5 m) long, but the plant itself never exceeds 3.25 feet (1 m) in height. It should never be pruned, which would destroy its grace, but it should be cleaned and renewed every year to eliminate old canes and stimulate new growth. A large hedge or group of 'Ballerina' in flower can be spectacular and moving.

## ALTERNATIVE SELECTIONS

'Marjorie Fair', also known as 'Red Ballerina', is the red-flowered variant. Its color, of course, is brighter, and the overall effect is less delicate. 'Mozart' is a darker pink version.

'Yesterday' (1) is a polyantha with the same type of flower as 'Ballerina'. Its grace and lightness are also reminiscent of 'Ballerina'. It is lower-growing and produces a profusion of tiny, sweetly scented cups that are renewed on canes produced during the season. The color is lilac-violet, paler at the center. This rose has made itself famous and brings a new color to gardens. Pretty in a container or as a potted plant on a patio or terrace, it also goes well in the front row of a border.

BORDERS, HEDGES, ESPALIERS

187

Hedge Roses

# Baronne Prevost
*Hybrid Perpetual*

**ALTERNATIVE SELECTION**

'Mary Rose' (1) is an English rose that creates an equally pretty hedge. It is full of branches and leaves, and the pauses in its flowering are few. It has been around for many years but has yet to be replaced because of its many virtues. Resistant to disease, it is also very vigorous, with large, full flowers of no particular quality but capable of creating a pretty effect with their bright, luminous pink. It is also adapted to the coldest climates. Height is 4 feet (1.2 m). 'Mary Rose' has given us two important English roses that are mutations of it: 'Winchester Cathedral' and 'Redouté'.

1

**Height:** 4–5 feet (1.2–1.5 m)
**Flower size:** 3.5–4 inches (9–10 cm)
**Number of petals:** about 100
(Desprez 1842)

One of the first hybrid perpetuals, this rose is still among the best, perfect for making a thick hedge and highly valued for its pretty flowering in June followed by a magnificent autumn display. The flowers are a striking pink and very double; they open flat in a pleasing design. The outer petals eventually form a crown around the densely packed shorter central petals, which are arranged around the button eye. The leaves are rough and the canes prickly. This rose is not suitable for humid climates.

Hedge Roses

# Blanc Double de Coubert
*Hybrid Rugosa*

123

of the flowers, their extraordinary springtime fragrance of violets comes as a surprise. The flowers open in succession beginning in June, earlier in more temperate climates, but the reflowering is weak. As always with rugosas, the shrub loves cold climates and sandy soils. If it does not like its site, it will stop growing short of 3.25 feet (1 m). It is not overly full of branches and leaves, but it has the pleasant, healthy leaves of a rugosa, with deep wrinkles and a crumpled fabriclike texture.

**Origin:** *Rosa rugosa* x 'Sombreuil.'

## GOOD COMPANIONS

To create a dense, attractive hedge, you can alternate 'Blanc Double de Coubert' with some branchier rugosas: 'Snowdon,' a creation of Austin, has double medium-size pure white flowers, and after the first flowering, they repeat throughout the summer. There is also 'Schneezwerg' (1), with rather small white semidouble flowers with yellow stamens at the center. The flowering is long, and at the end of the summer, the white flowers contrast with the red hips (2).

**Height:** 5 feet (1.5 m)
**Flower size:** 3 inches (7.5 cm)
**Number of petals:** 18–24
(Cochet-Cochet 1892)

This is a rose of great fascination because of its elegant buds and its immaculate flowers that evoke visions of eternal snow and a sense of cool freshness. Because of the chilly whiteness

1

2

BORDERS, HEDGES, ESPALIERS

189

Hedge Roses

# Claire Rose
*English Rose*

**Height:** 4 feet (1.2 m)
**Flower size:** 4 inches (10 cm)
**Number of petals:** 200
(Austin 1986)

What first attracts attention to this rose is its incredible wealth of petals. The flowers, an evanescent, luminous pink, are a true surprise. When completely open, they lie as flat as though cut with scissors and present packets of small, silky petals pressed against one another so tightly a pin could not be inserted among them. The compactness of these flowers when held in the hand is surprising, and so is their weight, yet the stems bear them high above the dense foliage. This is a different kind of rose,

and it comes with a single defect—spotting in humid weather, a problem shared by many of its companions, so it is not a good choice for rainy areas. Its reflowering is weak, but that would be asking too much.

**Origin:** 'Charles Austin' x (a sport x 'Iceberg').

## ALTERNATIVE SELECTIONS
Two other English roses flaunt lavish flowers with equal pride. The scented flowers of 'Brother Cadfael' (1) are of an astonishing size. Immense pink balls, almost like peonies, they never fully open, as though hiding their heart like a secret. The blossoms of the second flowering are more modest. Height: 3.25 feet (1 m).

Austin created 'Walter Raleigh' in 1985 but no longer includes it in his catalog, perhaps judging it inelegant. It is, however, a rose of enviable robustness that makes up for its possible lack of elegance by giving strikingly enormous, very double flowers of a warm, vibrant pink. These, too, seem like the flowers of an arboreal peony, and their antique-rose fragrance wafts far and wide. Very thorny and covered with big leaves, it can create an impassible barrier.

1

**Height:** 4 feet (1.2 m)
**Flower size:** 3 inches (8 cm)
**Number of petals:** 24–30
(prior to 1583)

An ancient rose of obscure origins, this was known as 'Rosa Francofurtana' until being rebaptized in the 19th century in honor of the empress who did so much for roses. It is magnificent because of the flowers' intense magenta-pink with darker veining and paler reflections and rippling papery petals. Not a typical gallica, it displays affinities with *Rosa cinnamomea*. The shrub is full of branches that bear few thorns and has gray-green rather rough foliage. The shrub is relatively low growing, rounded and compact, and it can form a hedge. It is most suitable for a less sunny area of a garden. It is pretty in flower as well as later, when it produces large, decorative hips shaped like a child's top.

### ALTERNATIVE SELECTION
'Président de Sèze' (1), also called 'Madame Hébert' and 'Jenny Duval', is another gallica for use as a hedge.

Its bunches of very double flowers, 4 inches (10 cm) in diameter, first form superb thick pillows composed of petals facing the center and then take on a spherical form. But what makes this rose singular is its color, or colors: an intense magenta but also violet and lilac and silvery gray with lavender on the edges, tints that the flowers assume in succession as they age. Height: 4 feet (1.2 m). It is also fragrant.

1

Hedge Roses

192

# Fleurette
*Modern Shrub Rose*

126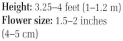

**Height:** 3.25–4 feet (1–1.2 m)
**Flower size:** 1.5–2 inches
(4–5 cm)
**Number of petals:** 5
(Interplant 1978)

If this rose did not exist, we would feel its absence. This is not the kind of rose that creates a sensation but one that forms the backbone of the garden. It has no pretensions and is always orderly. No other shrub is capable of flowering for three seasons and still remain attractive in the winter, as does this one, thanks to its shiny semievergreen leaves. Aside from this, 'Fleurette' is available in three colors. The classic version has bright pink flowers with white centers; in 1989, Interplant presented a variety with white flowers, deliciously fresh; and in 1992, the yellow-flowered version appeared, its flowers an infinity of small suns shining against the green. These are roses to put anywhere, making the selection on the basis of color. They are highly useful as hedges or planted in groups, each group composed of a single color. The shrub has an attractive, roundish shape and is so densely packed with foliage that it blocks out all view of the ground, for which reason, it is also used as a groundcover. There is one inconvenience: 'Fleurette' is carried only by the more alert rose specialists.

**Origin:** 'Yesterday' x a sport.

to 16 inches (40 cm) in diameter in a dazzling vermilion that some authorities claim is more salmon-pink. There is no question that the splendor of these flowers is what attracts attention to this rose. The large flowers have attractive, rippling petals and a light scent; the leaves are shiny and pale, and the shrub is healthy and vigorous. Used as a hedge, it can bring to life the most listless and insignificant corner of a garden. Immensely generous with its flowers, it has excellent reflowering. Because of its merits, it received the gold medal of the National Rose Society in 1967.

**Origin:** 'Dorothy Wheatcroft' x 'Orange Sensation.'

### ALTERNATIVE SELECTION

'Red Blanket' (1) can serve the same purpose. Its flowers are slightly smaller and are of a sweeter red, a color between geranium and vermilion, and they grow in small groups. The shiny leaves are leathery, healthy and almost evergreen. All in all, it's a calmer plant but quite beautiful and imposing as a hedge. An isolated specimen will eventually form a large, very pleasing umbrella.

**Height:** 5 feet (1.5 m)
**Flower size:** 2.75 inches (7 cm)
**Number of petals:** 7–10
(Holmes 1968)

Despite its single flowers, this is a popular rose, and everyone knows how hard it is for the public to appreciate roses of this type. But its flowers grow in immense bunches measuring up

Hedge Roses

and a single specimen plant gives pause, leading the viewer to admire and appreciate it as a vision of beauty.
**Origin:** 'Ophelia' x 'Trier.'

### ALTERNATIVE SELECTIONS

Two similar hybrid musks can be used to create informal but elegant hedges. 'Pax' has creamy white semi-double flowers, the largest in the family, and behaves much like a climber; 'Prosperity' has creamy white, highly fragrant double flowers that grow in large bunches.

A different selection is 'Sally Holmes' (1). It has neither the refinement nor the charm of 'Penelope' but is nevertheless gaining more and more favor; recently, *The American Rose Annual* chose it as the shrub of the year. It has been called a flower machine, and in fact, dense bunches of single, creamy flowers borne high on the canes are always present somewhere on the plant. It needs a lot of space, because given the right climate, meaning temperate, it can grow quite large; against a trellis or wall, it will scramble more than 6.5 feet (2 m) and equal that in width.

### GOOD COMPANIONS

The luminous colors of 'Penelope', 'Pax', 'Prosperity' and 'Sally Holmes' go well with *Geranium grandiflorum*, *G. sanguineum* and *G. robertianum* and, in a temperate climate, with a *Pelargonium* with scented leaves.

**194**

**Height:** 5 feet (1.5 m)
**Flower size:** 3 inches (7.5 cm)
**Number of petals:** 18–24
(Pemberton 1924)

Among the many delightful roses created by the Reverend Pemberton, this is rightly considered the favorite. The flowers are fragile, airy and trembling. In bud, they are a delicate color that recalls seashells or the palest coral; just after opening, this color evaporates into cream and then white. It is scented like an antique rose. The spring flowering is abundant and dramatic, and the autumn reflowering is almost its equal. If the flowers are not deadheaded—and they should be—there will be hips in the fall, at first green and then pink. The arching canes, which are a little rigid and extend outward, have few thorns. The leaves are large, semiglossy and abundant. The plant should not be pruned but left to express itself, forming a fountain of leafy branches. A hedge of several 'Penelope' bushes is radiant,

1

Hedge Roses

# Queen Elizabeth
*Grandiflora*

129

**Height:** up to 6.5 feet (2 m)
**Flower size:** 3.5–4 inches (9–10 cm)
**Number of petals:** 35–40
(Lammerts 1955)

This is a classic grandiflora, a type with characteristics intermediate between the hybrid teas and the floribundas. From the first group, it takes its high-centered flowers and, from the second, its numerous bunches of rich flowers. 'Queen Elizabeth' has enjoyed boundless success; in Pretoria, it was once declared "the most popular rose in the entire world." Offered by every nursery, it is planted in nearly every garden. When you see a pink rose, you can be almost certain it's this

one. And no one can deny that it is a rose of quality—the flowers are beautiful and so is the sweet pink color. It also has pretty, leathery leaves, shiny and dark. The scent is very weak, however, and something else seems to be missing. Allure? Furthermore, because of the shrub's extraordinary vigor and because it bears its flowers very high on long canes on a large bush, it this is not an easy rose to combine with others. Perhaps its best place in a garden is a spot where several can be grown together as a large, showy hedge. Or one can cultivate a single specimen.

**Origin:** 'Charlotte Armstrong' x 'Floradora.'

## ALTERNATIVE SELECTIONS
Another floribunda (or grandiflora) with the large flowers of a hybrid tea, one that is making room for itself among the many of its class, is 'L'Aimant', which Austin offers in its catalog. By now a favorite of many, it has pink flowers with petals that ripple slightly. The repeat bloom is excellent, the flowers coming abundantly and in rapid succession. They are very fragrant. Vigor, beauty and shiny, healthy foliage make this the ideal plant for many places in the garden. It makes a spectacular hedge, although a smaller one than 'Queen Elizabeth' produces.

Another rose for a large pink hedge is 'Felicia', a hybrid musk that is second to none in terms of popularity. The pretty flowers, not large, are flesh-pink with a touch of silver. They begin in the classic shape of a hybrid tea and become less composed as they open. The scent is of musk. Over time, the color pales slightly. The May flowering is immense and provides a full month of glory, then silence until September, when the flowering is again pretty. This makes it ideal for positions of responsibility, to do honor to a meadow and to show off alone. To make a hedge, space plants 4 feet (1.2 m) apart. A mixed hedge could be created by alternating this rose with red-berried barberry (*Berberis*).

scent is intense and spicy with a touch of pepper. There are two flowerings, between which the shrub, which resembles a big umbrella, is always bearing a few blossoms. It needs no special attention; every three or four years, the larger canes should be removed at the base to encourage new growth. To make a dense hedge quickly, space the plants 4 feet (1.2 m) apart. In a naturalistic garden, it can be used alone or planted in a group of three.

196

**Height:** 6 feet (1.8 m)
**Flower size:** 3.5 inches (9 cm)
**Number of petals:** 20–40
(Cochet-Cochet 1901)

This rose is named for the rose garden in Paris's Parc de Bagatelle. And it makes the prettiest possible hedge with its striking color. Densely branched and fully dressed in leaves down to its base, this rose forms a solid wall of green impenetrable to the eye and, given its thickly interwoven branches and the threat of its thorns, impenetrable to passage. The lovely buds begin to open early in June; the flowers come in small groups and are a dark crimson evocative of a particular shade of peony. The

**ALTERNATIVE SELECTION**
The rugosa 'Hansa' (1), with double, strongly scented purple flowers, is another choice for a pretty hedge; it also makes an excellent specimen plant, growing nearly as wide as it does high—4 feet (1.2 m). Very floriferous and reflowering, it produces large, decorative red hips.

Hedge Roses

# Scabrosa
*Hybrid Rugosa*

**Height:** 4–5 feet (1.2–1.5 m)
**Flower size:** 4–5 inches
(10–12 cm)
**Number of petals:** 5
(prior to 1830, introduced by
Harkness 1950)

A foundling, this rose spent a long time wandering unknown from garden to garden until Jack Harkness rediscovered it. A typical rugosa, it has attractive rippled, cedar-colored leaves with visible wrinkles and large, pretty flowers of a bright magenta that is very dark at first and illuminated by a vibrant clump of stamens bursting with pollen. Flowering is in June; reflowering, when it occurs, is far weaker. When the spring show is over, the plant

immediately covers itself with hips, which begin as shiny green balls and become large orange fruit in very decorative bunches. The shrub, dressed to its base in foliage, expands a great deal by way of its numerous canes and can form an enviable hedge—robust, intricate and healthy.

**ALTERNATIVE SELECTION**
Created in 1907 in Germany, 'Carmen' (1) is another rugosa but much less well known. Its dense growth of numerous high, erect canes make it ideal for a hedge. The color of its flowers, single and medium size, is an interesting dark crimson that emanates light and contrasts sharply with the yellow stamens and the dark green leaves.

1

**Origin:** 'Golden Glow' x a hybrid of *Rosa eglanteria.*

### ALTERNATIVE SELECTION

'Maigold' has many of the character-istics of the pimpinellifolias from which it is descended. Highly robust, like all the Kordes roses, it is resistant to all ills, including frost and disease. Its short buds open to large, semidouble flowers, luminous, strongly scented, yellow-bronze: a glorious welcome to spring. The early flowering is long and is followed by occasional blooms. The energetic canes grow to about 10 feet (3 m).

198

**Height:** 8 feet (2.5 m)
**Flower size:** 3.5–4 inches (9–10 cm)
**Number of petals:** 65–75
(Kordes 1956)

This is a both a climber and a large shrub. Its flowers have a pretty antique shape—large, heavy and flat—and are yellow with rich splashes of orange and pink. The leaves are tinted bronze when they are young but later become dark and shiny. The canes, thick with thorns, begin growing upright and later arch. The flowering is early and does not repeat. This is an interesting climber to let scramble up a trellis to form a dividing wall in a garden or to lean against a support.

Espaliers

# *Madame Hardy*
*Damask*

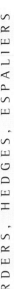

**Height:** 5.25–6 feet (1.6–1.8 m)
**Flower size:** 2.75–3 inches (7–8 cm)
**Number of petals:** about 200
(Hardy 1832)

It is possible that Eugène Hardy, director of the Jardins du Luxembourg in Paris, obtained this rose from a centifolia, but in truth, no one knows its origin for sure. Its flowers show affinities with those of the gallicas. It has been cited many times as the prettiest white rose of the past. The buds are elegant, wrapped in feathery calyxes, and they open to even more elegant flowers, an immaculate white with sharp features, quartered; the external petals are reflexed, while the inner ones pay homage to a feathery button eye. The scent is of fruit, most of all lemons. The flowers last a long time, more than a month if it doesn't rain, and under their weight, the branches bend to the ground. The leaves are pale, glaucous and opaque; the canes are furnished with thorns of various sizes. Sometimes the shrub is compact; sometimes it is more open. It does well when planted beside a support. Every three or four years, it must be renewed by a pruning to remove about 24 inches (60 cm) of its height. Graham Thomas recommends putting stems of 'Madame Hardy' in a vase with those of 'Belle de Crécy,' and the same combination is possible in the garden— the winy red of 'Belle' at the feet of the snowy candor of 'Madame.' A pair of sublime blooms to bring enchantment to the early days of summer.

## ALTERNATIVE SELECTION

Not long ago, David Austin put 'Snow Goose' on the market, a delightful rose that seems to have had Noisettes as parents. Its small, white, scented flowers are borne in bunches along the full length of the canes continuously until well into winter. The long, flexible canes reach 6.5 feet (2 m) and are splendid when trained onto an espalier.

# Queen of Denmark
*Alba*

thorny. It has slightly rough dark gray-green leaves. Flowering is early in June. The fragrance is divine. Great effect can be achieved by planting blue lupines at its feet.

### ALTERNATIVE SELECTION

'Aloha' is a rose of intense, uniform color, a hybrid tea shrub or climber that grows to 6.5 feet (2 m) high and is one of the few American roses to be well received in Europe. A versatile plant, it can be used as a hedge or a pillar rose. It has numerous pleasingly large heavy flowers that appear continually on long canes. Moderately scented, the flowers are pink with a darker reverse and have the pretty shape of the roses of the past. When arranged on an espalier, they are very attractive. This is a very dependable rose, even if it is not overly sophisticated. The leaves are dark and leathery. The buds promise little but open to form round, regular cups. A robust plant adapted to cold climates, it is not prone to disease. To avoid possible attacks of powdery mildew, attach it to a support in such a way that air can circulate among the branches.

**Synonym:** 'Königin von Dänemark'
**Height:** up to 6.5 feet (2 m)
**Flower size:** 3 inches (8 cm)
**Number of petals:** about 20
(Booth 1816)

Impetuosity, a tendency to wander and an arboreal appearance make this rose well suited to growing against a supporting structure. Trained to a trellis, for example, it will create a pretty green screen that will later be covered with splendid double flowers. Sometimes quartered, the flowers are pink with a touch of carmine at the center, the reflexed outer petals fading to white. This is not a typical alba; it is more subtle in appearance, more branching and more

Espaliers

of its flowers, a velvety violet-purple with touches of gray; very decorative. The calyxes are wrapped in the thick aromatic moss characteristic of this type of rose. 'William Lobb' is spectacular planted near 'Madame Hardy' or with a pink rose, which makes an even sweeter contrast—'Queen of Denmark' would be a good choice.

### ALTERNATIVE SELECTIONS

For a rose with a very intense and unusual color, choose 'Reine des Violettes' (1), which is very popular and deservingly so. It grows to 6.5 feet (2 m). Its buds are the color of dark grapes and open to form 75-petaled flowers of carmine, cherry, mauve and, finally, violet. The smooth, glaucous leaves are a perfect backdrop. This rose needs rich soil, and it must be deadheaded to make the flowering last longer. The last flowers have the most intense color.

'Tour de Malakoff' is also known as 'Black Jack' because of its dark color, an unusual shade that some people find extraordinary and others quite ugly. Its large flowers are a dark mauve that turns to gray. The canes reach more than 6.5 feet (2 m) and should be trained against a support.

**Synonym:** 'Old Velvet Moss'
**Height:** more than 6.5 feet (2 m)
**Flower size:** 3 inches (8 cm)
**Number of petals:** 20–40

This rose, born in 1855, is an audacious choice for those looking for a rose to drape over a trellis or create a small separation in a green space. The choice is audacious because of the color

Espaliers

# GROUNDCOVER ROSES

*A* groundcover is a plant with a prostrate or semiprostrate habit and dense enough foliage to cover and hide the ground. Ideally, it should not be much more than a foot (30 cm) in height, but it should grow wide enough to spread across the bare earth like a green skin. In nature, there is no such thing as bare ground, and if we do nothing to cover the soil we shovel and turn over to make a garden, nature will see to it and cover it with weeds. Rather than accept nature's weeds, we may as well select the plants ourselves, the only other solution being mulch. Like mulches, groundcovers prevent weed growth and stop erosion.

Many plants are suitable as groundcovers, and many are quite attractive when planted with roses: *Globularia*, strawberry, *Alchemilla*, *Vinca* and even violets. Not too many years ago, an entire series of roses was created to meet this need, filling in the spaces between the biggest and tallest roses and creating pleasing and sometimes surprising effects. Whether the blooms of these groundcover roses are simple or imposing, the flowering is almost always copious and long. In many cases, the foliage is also attractive and has very small, shiny, healthy leaves. Some of the plants are compact, some form true round cushions—'Avon,' 'Little Bo-Peep' and 'Essex' are of this type—others throw out long canes that slither across the ground like snakes. Such roses can sometimes be too vigorous, invading all of a garden's space, so they should be used only where there is enough room.

Indeed, since this category embraces roses of diverse origins and types, knowing the character of the rose you plant is essential for avoiding mistakes that could prove costly. The series that John Mattock has named after the counties of Britain (such as 'Sussex') consists of roses that are by now quite famous. More than enough of them exist to satisfy all tastes. Most are the work of two breeders, the German Kordes and the Dane Poulsen, the leading specialists in this type of rose. Highly luxuriant groundcovers such as 'Smarty,' 'Grouse' and their companions named for birds, 'The Pheasant' and 'Partridge,' put down roots along the branches and create intricate masses of foliage. Because of their great vigor, they are equally well suited to growing as ramblers; set against a support such as the trunk of a tree or a fence, they will happily scramble upward.

*Note: In the entries for these roses, the size is given as two numbers: the height and width of the plant, respectively.*

*Top: 'Heidesommer'; above: 'Castore.'*

# *Avon*
## Groundcover Rose

136 ♀ ⊚ ↻

**Size:** 16 inches x 3 feet
(0.4 x 0.9 m)
**Flower size:** 1.2 inches (3 cm)
**Number of petals:** 18
(Poulsen 1992)

This rose forms a delightful cushion of tiny green shiny leaves on which an incredible mass of small double flowers rests several times each season.

If you did not know they were roses, you might take them for daisies. They are white with a touch of pink. Deadheading this plant takes several hours, but being in the company of 'Avon' for whatever reason is always a pleasure. It is the most decorative plant imaginable, perfect as a groundcover but also perfect in a terracotta pot or a border.
**Origin:** 'Pink Drift' x a sport.

### ALTERNATIVE SELECTIONS
The same year as he released 'Avon', Poulsen also introduced 'Little Bo-Peep' (1), which is its twin. It produces innumerable tiny flowers, as pretty as those of 'Avon', in a very pale pink.

'Schneeküsschen' is an equal offering from Kordes, 1 foot (30 cm) high with tiny flowers of the hybrid tea type, pure white and double; they grow in bunches.

# *Essex*
Groundcover Rose

137 ♇ ☉ ⌀

206

Compact Bushes with Wide Habits

**Size:** 20 inches x 3.25 feet
(0.5 x 1 m)
**Flower size:** 6 inches (2.5 cm)
**Number of petals:** 5
(Poulsen 1988)

A truly original rose, this has made a name for itself, winning a gold medal at Dublin. The very small, pale, shiny green leaves form a magnificent cushion that blocks out all view of the ground; the tiny flowers, bright pink with a white eye, grow in well-spaced corymbs, both large and small. 'Essex' is a jewel that delights even those who are not fond of roses with single flowers. It has a copious, long flowering and excellent reflowering.

**Origin:** 'The Fairy' x a sport.

ALTERNATIVE SELECTION
The Japanese rose 'Nozomi' (1), by Onodera, 1968, is a different kind of rose but also a small jewel in its own way, which is why it has conquered so many Western gardens. It is almost a miniature rose, with long, thin, flexible canes that grow erect then bend down to the ground forming something like a bubbling brook. The flowers, which look like little butterflies, are tiny 5-petaled roses of a pearly white touched with pink; there is also a slight scent. The only drawback is that it leaves open ground, obliging the gardener to perform the tedious task of weeding. Splendid when left to run down a slope, it is also splendid in the tree form. Size: 1 x 4 feet (0.3 x 1.2 m).

# *Flower Carpet*
Groundcover Rose

138

ers, growing in bunches of 15 to 25, are semidouble and dark pink with paler reverses. Easy to care for, and the outcome is never in doubt. This rose will cover the ground but can also be used to decorate a windowsill or balcony or grow in a container.

**Origin:** 'Immensee' x 'Amanda.'

### ALTERNATIVE SELECTIONS

'Bordure Vive' (1), a polyantha by Delbard, is equally useful in the garden, but its flowers are more of a cyclamen pink. Slightly lower, it measures 12 by 20 inches (30 x 50 cm). Like its sisters 'Bordure Nacrée', 'Bordure Vermillon', 'Bordure d'Or' and 'Bordure Magenta', it is a recommended groundcover, but it is also good as a border, in a small bed or planted in a colorful grouping.

1

**Size:** 2 x 3 feet (0.6 x 0.9 m)
**Flower size:** 2.5 inches (6 cm)
**Number of petals:** 15–20
(Noack 1990)

Called 'Heidetraum' in Germany, this rose has achieved celebrity. Awarded a certificate of merit by the Rose Society, a gold at The Hague and at Dortmund, it is an invaluable rose even though it seems to lack that "touch of class." Its virtues are its incredible flowering, which repeats without pause; its intense flower color, which enlivens the foliage; the semievergreen leaves themselves, which cover the plant almost all year long; and last but not least, a strong resistance to disease. The buds are plump, the flow-

**Synonym:** 'Frau Dagmar Hartopp'
**Size:** 32 inches x 4 feet
(0.8 x 1.2 m)
**Flower size:** 3–4 inches
(8–10 cm)
**Number of petals:** 5
(Hastrup Nursery, Denmark, 1914)

The only difficulty here is lingering confusion about the name. This hybrid rugosa possesses an enchantment different from the other groundcovers, since it puts most of its growth into its width, covering the ground with dense, compact branches. The pointed buds are elegant, the flowers grow in pale, airy bunches of a transparent pink tinged with silver, their pallor emphasized by the creamy stamens. The splendid leaves are the typical rugosa type with visible wrinkles; they look like crepe and are a cedar-green. It flowers in June and produces flowers sporadically until its second flowering in the autumn. If it is not dead-headed, it will form hips like pink radishes. Given favorable conditions, it will grow to more than 3.25 feet (1 m).

### ALTERNATIVE SELECTIONS
There is also a 'Frau Dagmar Hastrup' with yellow flowers (1), which made its appearance in 1997. From Dickson, there is also 'Red Dagmar,' a red sport with a lower habit and a sweet scent.

'Mrs. Doreen Pike' (2), from David Austin, is interesting not only for its low habit, wide and very compact, but for its delightful double flowers of a warm, luminous pink, large and highly scented, that look as if they were made of crumpled fabric. They grow in such dense bunches that they seem already gathered for a vase. The flowering is long and continuous, and the foliage is wonderful.

Compact Bushes with Wide Habits

# Gwent
*Groundcover Rose*

140 ♎ ◉ ◯ ⣿

209

**Size:** 20 inches x 4 feet
(0.5 x 1.2 m)
**Flower size:** 1.2–1.6 inches
(3–4 cm)
**Number of petals:** 14–16
(Poulsen 1992)

The Danish breeder Poulsen, known as an ingenious creator of small roses, was responsible for this jewel in the collection of roses named for British counties. Its habit is low and wide, and the foliage is composed of tiny dark green leaves against which the semidouble flowers, lemon-yellow as buds and then even paler, stand out with a stark beauty; the two colors create a pleasing contrast that lasts all summer and into the fall. The slightly ruffled petals never become fully flat.

Few groundcover roses have yellow flowers, and this is far and away the prettiest.

### ALTERNATIVE SELECTIONS
'Dunwich Rose' (1) has much of the grace and beauty of 'Gwent.' In fact, its elegant, soft habit, its mass of delightful tiny leaves and decorative prickles (those of the *pimpinellifolia* species) would make it seem the preferable plant except for one thing—it has only one, albeit copious, flowering. The flowering is not to be missed, however, and afterward, the plant bears tiny hips (2). Not for use in a border or mixed with taller roses, this is a plant for the informal garden, a site near a pond or a large rock. It could always be used as part of a large group, perhaps a happy island composed of other *pimpinellifolia* roses, both red and pink.

GROUNDCOVER ROSES

Compact Bushes with Wide Habits

# Little White Pet
## *Hybrid Sempervirens*

141

**Size:** 20 inches x 3.25 feet (0.5 x 1 m)
**Flower size:** 2 inches (5 cm)
**Number of petals:** 50 (Henderson 1879)

This rose has been around for quite a while, but it is one that will never willingly be abandoned. It is the prostrate version of the famous 'Félicité et Per-

pétue,' and it has the same pink buds and enchanting white rosettes touched with pink. Flowering repeats from April to the onset of winter. In temperate climates, it does not lose its leaves. It also has a delicate fragrance. It can be placed wherever the gardener desires—tumbling out of a container; covering the ground, which it performs with

diligence; growing among taller roses, since its color goes well with any other; or illuminating a neglected corner of the garden with the gentle touch of its white snowflakes.

**Origin:** hybrid or sport of 'Félicité et Perpétue.'

### ALTERNATIVE SELECTIONS

'Snow Carpet' (McGredy 1980) lives up to its name. Its flowers, made up of densely packed petals, create a miniature blanket of snow 8 inches (20 cm) high and 3.25 feet (1 m) wide from June to October.

'Elegant Pearl' (1), from Interplant, is a daughter of 'Nozomi' and is truly elegant, with creamy flowers of more than 40 petals and its pretty and repeated flowering. About 20 inches (50 cm) high and the same width, it is packed with branches and leaves.

Compact Bushes with Wide Habits

# Nathalie Nypels
*Polyantha*

142

**Origin:** 'Orléans Rose' x ('Comtesse du Cayla' x *Rosa foetida bicolor*).

### ALTERNATIVE SELECTION
One of the least known of the groundcover series named for British counties is 'Northamptonshire' (1), by Mattock, 1990. It is similar to 'Nathalie Nypels' and to 'Cécile Brünner' because of its perfect pink buds that open to small mother-of-pearl pink flowers which last for a long time and grow in large bunches held fairly high above the foliage.

1

**Synonym:** 'Mevrouw Nathalie Nypels'
**Size:** 24 x 32 inches (0.6 x 0.8 m)
**Flower size:** 2.5 inches (6 cm)
**Number of petals:** 30–35
(Leenders 1919)

A longtime lodger in our gardens, this rose has no fear of losing its place. It is kept on because it is so absolutely trustworthy, with its dense foliage, which stays low but expands to hide the ground, and its continuous flowering. The flowers, which come in big, well-spaced bunches, are pretty and pleasing even though they are not always perfect. Pink with a touch of salmon, they have a nice fragrance.

## *Norfolk*
*Groundcover Rose*

143

an uncommon quality in a groundcover rose. Equally delightful are the flowers—double, perfectly shaped, bright yellow rosettes borne on the branches in small groups. The plant is compact, full of medium-green leaves and has a pleasantly wide habit; the reflowering is excellent. This rose must be deadheaded.

### ALTERNATIVE SELECTIONS
'Penelope Keith' (1) cannot be called a particularly pretty rose, but it never fails to perform its duty. Not all roses manage to flower and reflower with such reliable promptness. Upright and compact, about 2 feet (60 cm) high, it is always covered with pretty bright green leaves and bunches of high-centered flowers that eventually form rosettes with pointed petals, golden yellow with a touch of orange and pink; darker stamens. The bunches are borne high above the foliage, and the overall effect is orderly, lively and pleasant.

**Size:** 28 inches x 3.25 feet
(0.7 x 1 m)
**Flower size:** 1.2–1.6 inches
(3–4 cm)
**Number of petals:** 80–90
(Poulsen 1990)

The salient characteristic of this rose is its delicious, intense fragrance, which impregnates the air many yards around it—quite

212

Compact Bushes with Wide Habits

# Oxfordshire
*Groundcover Rose*

144

**Size:** 1 x 4 feet (0.3 x 1.2 m)
**Flower size:** 2.5 inches (6 cm)
**Number of petals:** 15–20
(Kordes 1996)

This recent acquisition might as well be called the creeping twin of 'Surrey,' which it combines with very well—the tall 'Surrey' with 'Oxfordshire' spreading low at its feet. Its pink flowers, somewhat large for its class, form open cups of ruffled petals and are produced continuously. It is compact and dense despite the long canes that take off in all directions. Excellent.

213

# Polluce
*Groundcover Rose*

145

**Size:** 20 inches x 4 feet (0.5 x 1.2 m)
**Flower size:** 1.4 inches (3.5 cm)
**Number of petals:** 10–12
(Barni 1987)

In Italian, the heavenly twins Castor and Pollux are called Castore and Polluce. 'Castore' has light pink flowers; those of his twin are crimson. The flowers grow in bunches; flowering is long and repeated on new canes or side shoots. The plant should be pruned short to maintain its compact shape and to prevent the long canes from becoming disorderly.
  **Origin:** 'Tesorino' x 'Happy.'

Compact Bushes with Wide Habits

## Queen Mother
*Groundcover or Patio Rose*

146

**Size:** 18 x 18 inches
(0.45 x 0.45 m)
**Flower size:** 2.5 inches (6 cm)
**Number of petals:** 20
(Kordes 1990)

Dedicated to Britain's Queen Mother, this rose was designed for use in a container and as a groundcover, duties it performs with nobility, discretion and a good deal of grace. Resting against the shiny foliage, the bright pink flowers look much like freshly laundered handkerchiefs, starched and ironed. There is also a subtle scent.

    **Origin:** *Rosa wichuraiana* x 'Toynbee Hall.'

214

## Snow Ballet
*Groundcover Rose*

147

**Size:** 16 inches x 4 feet
(0.4 x 1.2 m)
**Flower size:** 3 inches (8 cm)
**Number of petals:** 45–50
(Clayworth 1977)

Created in New Zealand, this rose is, of all the roses inspired by snow, the one that most deserves the name. With a glacial beauty, the flowers are composed of small, narrow, tightly packed petals that cover the smooth, leathery leaves like thick new-fallen snow: truly a ballet of snowflakes. The scent is slight. The flowering is long, the reflowering good.

    **Origin:** 'Sea Foam' x 'Iceberg.'

## Suffolk
*Groundcover Rose*

215

**Size:** 10 inches x 3 feet
(0.25 x 0.9 m)
**Flower size:** 1.6 inches (4 cm)
**Number of petals:** 5–9
(Kordes 1988)

This rose is appealing for its unusual very dark color, between crimson and scarlet, which is enlivened by the yellow stamens; for its completely prostrate habit, covering the ground with canes loaded with small dark leaves; and for the abundance of its flowers. It is resistant to disease and produces tiny orange-red hips in the autumn.

**Origin:** ('Sea Foam' x 'Red Max Graf') x a sport.

### ALTERNATIVE SELECTIONS

'Sommerabend' (1), by Kordes, 1995, is highly recommended. It produces bunches of small single flowers, dark red and shaped like plates. The shrub is a foot (30 cm) high and has prostrate canes full of small, shiny leaves.

For a brighter color, a vermilion that attracts attention, there is Warner's 'Pathfinder' (1995). The semidouble flowers have pleasantly rounded petals and yellow eyes. The leaves are small and shiny; the shrub grows to 2 feet (60 cm) high and 3 feet (90 cm) wide.

1

turns slightly paler over time. The only pruning necessary is a light cleaning; however, any long canes that spoil the balance of the shrub should be cut off low.

**Origin:** 'The Fairy' x a sport.

### GOOD COMPANIONS

An attractive border can be made by planting 'Surrey' in the back row, 'Oxfordshire' alternated with *Geranium sanguineum* or *G. robertianum* in the middle row and cushions of 'Avon' in the front row. 'Surrey' can also be used to create a small bed on its own; those so inclined might want to surround it with a blue border of forget-me-nots (*Myosotis*) in the spring and replace them with annual lobelia for the summer flowering.

**Size:** 2 x 4 feet (0.6 x 1.2 m)
**Flower size:** 2–2.5 inches (5–6 cm)
**Number of petals:** 20–22 (Kordes 1985)

This highly esteemed rose, in widespread use in gardens, is known in Germany under the name 'Sommerwind.' It grows a little too high for a groundcover rose, but this occurs primarily when it is in flower, for the big bunches of flowers are borne on long canes. It forms an attractive, heaped-up bush with shiny, very healthy leaves. The flowers are open cups, pure pink, with ruffled petals. It is always flowering, and the bunches last a long time without spoiling, although the color

Compact Bushes with Wide Habits

# The Fairy
*Polyantha*

150 ♀ ◎ ○

**Size:** 28 inches x 3.25 feet
(0.7 x 1 m)
**Flower size:** 1.2 inches (3 cm)
**Number of petals:** 30–34
(Bentall 1932)

This polyantha makes an ideal groundcover even though it was created long before the word "groundcover" had been applied to a rose. It is still among the best—irreplaceable, in fact. It produces enormous, well-spaced corymbs with tiny pale pink flowers; the flowering begins somewhat late, but there are still flowers on the plant when winter arrives. It is very floriferous and very decorative wherever it is planted—dense with shiny pale leaves that cover the entire area, never leav-

ing openings through which the ground can be seen. Given suitable soil, climate and water, it can grow to a voluminous, shaggy bush. Pruning takes time and effort; the shrub must be cleaned out, and the long canes that have borne that year's flowers must be removed.

'The Fairy' has a sister named 'Lovely Fairy,' but this newer version does not seem to have met with much success. The flowers are carmine-red, grow in less copious bunches and are less dense; the bush is also less floriferous. But these are not the reasons for its failure to win fans; this is more closely related to its color, which is dull, and, even more seriously, to its lack of allure.

**Origin:** 'Paul Crampel' x 'Lady Gay.'

## GOOD COMPANIONS
'The Fairy' goes well with 'Snow Ballet'; the two could be used, for example, along the sides of a pathway. Or one could combine two different shades of pink in a border, perhaps alternating 'The Fairy' with 'The Faun' or even making a bed packed with the two of them.

218

# White Flower Carpet
*Groundcover Rose*

151 ♀ ◉ ⟳ ⁝

## ALTERNATIVE SELECTIONS

The series of roses named for British counties includes two interesting groundcovers with white flowers. The first is 'Kent' (1), a round pillow of leaves covered with semi-double pure white flowers that can defy humidity and rain. Size: 2 x 3 feet (60 x 90 cm).

Then there is 'Yorkshire', with bunches of pale flowers that last for the entire summer and fall. Scented. Size: 3 x 2 feet (90 x 60 cm).

**Size:** 1 x 2 feet (0.3 x 0.6 m)
**Flower size:** 2.5 inches (6 cm)
**Number of petals:** 20–22
(Noack 1993)

This is a number-one choice among groundcover roses. The companion to 'Flower Carpet,' with which it can be combined, is also useful because there is never enough white in a gar-den. Almost creeping, eternally covered with its relatively large flowers—open plates of pure white—resistant to all diseases, to cold and to rain and even delicately scented, it is not a rose to forget.

**Origin:** 'Grouse' x 'Margaret Merril.'

## Pink Bells
*Groundcover Rose (Miniature)*

152 ⚓ ◎ ✕ ⦂

**Size:** 2 x 5 feet (0.6 x 1.5 m)
**Flower size:** 1.2 inches (3 cm)
**Number of petals:** 35
(Poulsen 1983)

This rose cannot be discussed without also mentioning 'White Bells' (1) and 'Red Bells' (2), for the three form an inseparable trio. These are unlike all others, truly miniature roses with leaves as delicate as lace, flowers that look like symmetrical bows and thin, elegant branches. Every part of these plants is delicate, almost immaterial, like sprays of water from a fountain. 'Pink Bells' has very pink flowers, those of 'White Bells' are white bathed in yellow, and 'Red Bells' has crimson flowers. Flowering begins in May in tem-

perate climates, a little later where it is colder, and lasts four weeks or even longer. Pruning can be handled in two ways. You can leave the branches to grow as they wish, cleaning the plant only after it has flowered and again early in the spring, or you can prune the plant back very low after flowering to give it a more compact and orderly

habit. In that case, the long canes of the new vegetation will develop the following spring.

**Origin:** 'Mini Poul' x 'Temple Bells.'

# Sea Foam
## Groundcover Rose

shoots as soon as they lose their flowers.

**Origin:** 'White Dawn' x 'Pinocchio.'

### ALTERNATIVE SELECTION

'Swany' (1), by Meilland, 1978, is a well established rose. A descendant of *Rosa sempervirens*, it is considered a creeping miniature. Its leaves are bronze when young, then grow darker and very shiny. Its flowers are initially pompoms then open to form rosettes; at first, they have a pink center, but when fully open, they are pure white. Very dense and very vigorous, the branches are almost completely prostrate. An ideal site is atop a low wall down which the plant can throw its pretty branches; several bushes planted in this way make a spectacle that will repeat throughout the season.

**Size:** 2 x 10 feet (0.6 x 3 m)
**Flower size:** 2–2.5 inches (5–6 cm)
**Number of petals:** 45–55 (Schwartz 1964)

Long shoots, packed with pretty leaves, wrap around themselves to form cylinders, climb up a trellis or run across the ground. These shoots are covered with a first dazzling flowering of hundreds upon hundreds of flowers and then flower again and again well into the winter. The flowers come in both large and small bunches in a creamy white that turns pinker in the fall. This rose won a gold medal at Rome. It is best to let the branches grow and cut back the side

Semiprostrate Bushes with Long Canes

# Smarty
*Groundcover Rose*

154 ♀ ☉ ✗

221

**Size:** 32 inches x 10 feet
(0.8 x 3 m)
**Flower size:** 2 inches (5 cm)
**Number of petals:** 7
(Ilsink 1975, introduced by
Dickson)

Vigorous—almost too vigorous—this rose grows and
spreads to cover a large area
with a mass of foliage. Its
branches sometimes exceed 10
feet (3 m) in length and are covered with small thorns and
large, opaque leaves. The flowers are numerous at the first
flowering and rather large, barely pink and paler at the center;
the reflowering is weaker. A
perfect groundcover for a wild
area, a slope to cover or a ditch
to invade. Best of all is to plant

it with anoth-
er rose of a
brighter color
but equal vigor
such as 'Ferdy,'
one of the Meidiland
series with double flowers in a
bright pink, or 'Rosy Carpet'
(Interplant 1984), with single
flowers, bright pink with white
eyes, and long canes that grow
to 5 feet (1.5 m).

## ALTERNATIVE SELECTIONS
Three other roses of lush, uncontrol-
lable growth are the "game birds":
'Grouse', which in Germany is known
as 'Immensee' or 'Kordes Immensee'
(Kordes 1984), has scented flowers
in a pale pink, single, with heart-
shaped petals; 'Partridge', called
'Wiesse Immensee' in Germany, with
white flowers; and 'The Pheasant' or

'Heidekönigin', with
bright pink double
flowers. 'St. Tiggy-
winkles' (1), Kordes,
1998, is delightful, has
won medals in Great
Britain and Germany and has
luminous pink flowers and splendid
leaves. It is reflowering. Size: 3 x 6.5
feet (0.9 x 2 m).

# THE SMALL PROTAGONISTS

*Preceding pages: 'The Faun.'*

*Planting a large-flowered rose such as 'Canterbury' next to a small-flowered groundcover rose such as 'Essex' creates an effective contrast.*

## CREATORS AND THEIR FAMOUS MINIATURES

**De Vink:** *'Tom Thumb,' crimson with white eyes; 'Cinderella,' white; 'Sweet Fairy,' pink*

**Pedro Dot:** *'Para Ti,' white and yellow; 'Perla de Alcanada,' carmine; 'Perla de Montserrat,' pink edged with silver*

**R.S. Moore:** *'Little Buckaroo,' dark red; 'Baby Darling,' orange; 'Lavender Lace,' lavender; 'Stacey Sue,' dark red with lighter red edges*

**Meilland:** *'Colibri,' orange; 'Lady Meillandina,' pink; 'Lutin,' pink*

**Tantau:** *'Baby Masquerade.'*

*P*atio roses are a new category, and what they have in common is their size, not any particular botanical characteristics. These are small roses—and hardy ones—that fit the space limitations of a patio, terrace or balcony. Because such locations offer so little room for plants, patio roses also tend to be impeccable, roses that flower punctually and are otherwise covered with glossy, healthy leaves.

The dividing line between patio roses and groundcover roses is not clear, and a certain amount of confusion has made its way into the subject. Several groundcovers can indeed serve on a terrace, but true patio roses are less easily adapted to use as groundcovers because most of them are upright plants and do not have spreading habits. Many floribundas (the smaller ones) and many polyanthas can be cultivated in the small spaces of terraces, patios and courtyards. Of course, by nature, patio roses and groundcover roses have much in common, most of all elegant growth, small, glossy leaves and a modest size. Wherever they are placed, they can always be used together easily.

There is also the category of patio climbers, although right now, all the members of this category come from the same creator, E.H. Warner of Bradley Nurseries in Devonshire, England. These are small climbers, no larger than 6.5 to 8 feet (2–2.5 m), but they boast the same characteristics as their full-size brethren: very small, very shiny leaves, flowers ranging from medium to small in size and very long flowering periods. These plants have an extraordinary grace and, not surprisingly, have awakened great interest. Perfect on a balcony, they are stupendous in a garden when growing on a support, which they will wrap around, or trailing along a pathway, marking the four corners of a herb garden or draping over a garden gate.

The smallest of all roses, the miniatures, are really more *objets d'art*, more like Meissen or Delft porcelains than flowers. Certainly, they are purchased as if they were decorative objects to put on a shelf or to line up in a pretty row on a table or terrace. They are not and cannot be part of the structure of a terrace or small garden. And because of their size, they are out of place in a real garden—with their tiny dimensions, they cannot compete with other roses or flowering plants. People buy miniatures as decorations without knowing their names, much as they buy azaleas in flower to brighten a corner for a season.

Some kinds of miniature roses have become well known. There are, for example, those of the Meillandin series, which the Meilland company has been turning out in great numbers for several years. These little plants in their many colors have invaded the market, filling florists' shops. In addition to these is the Symphonie series in 'Gold,' 'Pink' and 'Orange.' In Italy, there is the Rampichella series by Nino Sanremo, small climbers loaded with flowers in white, pink or red. In the United States, 60-odd varieties have been turned out by Ralph S. Moore of Visalia, California, certainly the most prolific creator of miniatures.

**Height:** 30 inches (0.75 m)
**Flower size:** 6.3 inches (16 cm)
**Number of petals:** 12
(Austin 1969)

David Austin declares this to be the prettiest rose with single (or almost single) flowers, and it is hard not to agree. The immense pink flowers, warmly lit by the stamens, are of an almost indescribable beauty. The silky petals vibrate slightly as though shivering, then stretch and fold back with voluptuous softness. The bush is slightly angular, broad and low, with a not very generous supply of large leaves. This rose is not usually included among the patio roses, which in general have smaller leaves and flowers, but it is a rose that can fit very well on a terrace in a container, where the glory of its flowers, in almost continuous bloom, can be fully enjoyed.

**Origin:** ('Monique' x 'Constance Spry') x a sport.

### ALTERNATIVE SELECTION
Finding a rose that resembles 'Canterbury' is not easy. 'Everest Double Fragrance' (1), Beales, 1979, a rose that has not been given its due, is unlike it but does have the same color and the same power of enchantment. It is a floribunda with flowers that begin in the hybrid tea shape then open to 25 vibrant petals. The petals are broad, as are the flowers—4 inches (10 cm)—the color is between pale pink, coral and ivory, and the fragrance is intense. It grows to 28 inches (70 cm) and more, has an upright habit and dark leaves marked by deep veining.

Patio Roses

# Charlotte
*English Rose*

**Patio Roses**

**Height:** 30 inches (0.75 m)
**Flower size:** 3.5 inches (9 cm)
**Number of petals:** 80
(Austin 1993)

'Charlotte' is less known and less planted than the other English roses, although for no obvious reason. Its creator recommends it as a rose of superior quality. Although not a typical patio rose, it is ideal for use in a large container. Its habit is compact and harmonious, and it is nicely branched. The pale yellow flowers are like closed cups. There is even a hybrid tea scent. The flowering is long and copious and occurs intermittently throughout the season.

**Origin:** a sport x 'Graham Thomas.'

### ALTERNATIVE SELECTIONS

'Happy Child' (Austin 1993) is a small English rose with bright yellow flowers and a well-balanced, arching habit. It also has particularly interesting leaves, so glossy they seem waxy and as leathery as a camellia's. It also has the delicate scent of tea.

Another bright yellow rose is 'Molineux' (1), winner of several awards, including a medal for its intense tea scent, although it is not yet popular with the public. The rosette-shaped flowers are a deep yellow. The compact, orderly plant usually stops growing at just over 2 feet (60 cm) and is rarely without flowers.

Another selection in this category is 'Goldmarie 82', a small floribunda created in 1958 and later presented by Kordes in an improved version. The large double flowers, which are fragrant, have copper shadows; the leaves are very dark and shiny. A robust plant, it is resistant to rain, cold and disease; it is very floriferous and can be useful anywhere—in a pot, on the far edge of a meadow or in a group bringing light to a garden.

# Crystal Palace
*Patio Rose*

157

coral that become even paler when the flowers are fully open, at which time, they form perfect cups full of ruffled petals. The bunches are large for such a small shrub and arrive encircled in shiny leaves.

## ALTERNATIVE SELECTIONS

'Bordure Nacrée' (1) is a small rose 16 to 20 inches (40–50 cm) high, which its creator, Delbard, suggests using in a border. But it is just as delightful in a container. Its cushion of leaves supports dense bunches of small double flowers of a festive and luminous color that blends shades of cream, apricot and pink. It is always in flower.

'Irène Watts' is a Chinese rose remembered by only a few, yet it is one of those that deserve respect. The orange buds open to small flowers of pinkish ivory with peach shadows. The flowers are a splendid shape, composed of small petals wound into spirals at the center and surrounded on the outside by larger, flatter petals. It is 2 feet (60 cm) high, scented and blooms continuously.

**Height:** 2 feet (0.6 m)
**Flower size:** 3.5 inches (9 cm)
**Number of petals:** 25
(Poulsen 1995)

This delightful rose, fresh and nicely scented, looks so much like spun sugar that one has to fight off the urge to taste it. The color is enchanting, a cream with warm shades of peach and

**Origin:** ('Lilian Austin' x a sport) x ('Iceberg' x 'Wife of Bath').

## ALTERNATIVE SELECTIONS

Two roses merit attention here, most of all because they bring to the terrace some of the fascination of antique roses, a rare virtue in this category. For those not fond of gaudy yellows is 'Eurostar' (1), a patio rose created by Poulsen and put on the market by Mattock in England in 1995. It seems in every way a rose from the past, with its rather large, splendidly shaped and sweetly scented flowers in a pale sulfur-yellow. The rose also possesses the qualities of new roses—shiny leaves, solid resistance to disease and generous flowering.

There is also 'Comtesse du Barry', by Meilland, 2 feet (60 cm) high. It has double flowers of 50–60 petals, 2 to 2.5 inches (5–6 cm) in diameter, that form sweet cups in a pale yellow tending to sulfur, the petals bending softly toward the center. The flowering is uninterrupted.

**Height:** 32 inches (0.8 m)
**Flower size:** 3–3.5 inches (8–9 cm)
**Number of petals:** 140
(Austin 1986)

One of the less voluminous English roses, this rose's orderly, contained habit and, of course, its beautiful flowers make it the jewel of any patio or terrace. The large, perfectly symmetrical rosettes are of an unusual color—small, bright yellow hearts surrounded by a crown of large petals that grow paler toward the outer edges. It has an absolutely delicious tea scent. Very floriferous and very recurrent.

1

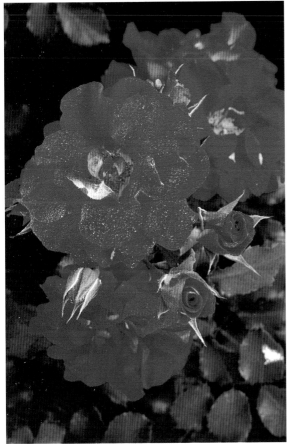

ly packed with healthy, metallic leaves. The flowering is continuous. This rose has received certificates of merit and other distinctions. It is also available in a tree form.

### ALTERNATIVE SELECTIONS

'Heidekind' (1) is another rose of a changeless bright cherry red, with full, double, medium-size flowers that grow in large bunches; the erect shrub reaches 32 inches (80 cm).

For vermilion, a brighter, more brilliant red, 'Trumpeter', only 18 inches (45 cm), offers its immense bunches of flowers that a rain will bend all the way to the ground. The flowers are blood-red, have 35 petals and are 2.75 to 3 inches (7–8 cm) in diameter. This is one of those roses

**Height:** 20 inches (0.5 m)
**Flower size:** 2.75 inches (7 cm)
**Number of petals:** 45
(Kordes 1994)

Sometimes when praising a flower, one is moved to exclaim, "It looks fake!" The judgment is double-edged, of course, and in this case, it is almost too apt. The flowers of this rose last for-

ever and stay forever the same, apparently made of a substance that looks a lot like plastic. They are pretty the first day, pretty a week later and pretty the week after that, and so on. The color is a shrill crimson-scarlet, mottled here and there with spots of white light, and the reverses are silver. The plant is a round shrub, low and compact, dense-

that never give problems, never get sick and never stop flowering.

'Top Marks', declared rose of the year in 1992, is by Fryer; it truly has earned the highest marks in many classifications. It forms a wonderful 18-by-18-inch (45 x 45 cm) pillow of an incredible number of 35-petaled rosette-shaped flowers in blazing vermilion. The flowers last every bit as long as those of 'Festival', forever fresh, forever vivid.

Patio Roses

rose, one might say, and in a certain sense it is, but it draws attention to itself all the same. It even has the subtle scent of a mandarin orange. The shrub is branchy and compact and has small, shiny dark leaves. Flowering is continuous.

## A GOOD COMPANION

It is the daring who get ahead in life. When choosing companions for roses with glowing colors, it is better to emphasize them rather than try to disguise them. If 'Mandarin' is growing in a large container, put at its feet 'Cambridgeshire' (1), one of that famous line named for British counties. It has a prostrate habit and will direct its 28-to-32-inch (70–80 cm) branches beyond the edge of the container, spilling out its festive semidouble rosettes in cherry, scarlet and gold that will bloom in profusion for the entire season.

**Height:** 16 inches (0.4 m)
**Flower size:** 2 inches (5 cm)
**Number of petals:** 45–50
(Kordes 1987)

Sometimes a rose or other plant is pleasing because of the astonishment it causes: 'Mandarin' is one of these. It is not a complete novelty, since it had a famous predecessor, 'Masquer-ade.' These are multicolored roses, as cheerful as the gay decorations strung up for a small-town festival. 'Mandarin' had its moment in the limelight when it won the gold medal at Belfast. The flowers, dark pink in bud and similar to miniature hybrid tea blooms, open to reveal an exultation of yellow and orange that turns to cherry. An ugly

Patio Roses

# Pretty Polly
*Patio Rose*

small hybrid tea blooms. It was the rose of the year in 1976, and its size, habit and long, continuous flowering make it a model for its category. It has medium-green semiglossy leaves and a slight scent. At the end of the season, care must be taken to protect it from powdery mildew.

**1**

**Height:** 18 inches (0.45 m)
**Flower size:** 2 inches (5 cm)
**Number of petals:** 24–28
(Meilland 1989)

This minute plant would be pretty in a terracotta pot or in a small border in a small garden. Its waxlike flowers are a light pink with a darker heart, double and well shaped. The leaves are

healthy, shiny and numerous; the flowering is continuous. The shrub is rounded and somewhat compact.

**Origin:** 'Coppelia' x 'Magic Carrousel.'

### ALTERNATIVE SELECTION
'Gentle Touch' (1), by Dickson, has graceful pink flowers with 10 to 15 pointed petals that look much like

THE SMALL PROTAGONISTS

231

Patio Roses

# *Regensberg*
*Patio Rose*

**Height:** 20 inches (0.5 m)
**Flower size:** 2.75 inches (7 cm)
**Number of petals:** 20
(McGredy 1980)

This popular rose is a festival of colors. It is noteworthy for the harmonious shape of its low shrub, which has attractive glossy leaves, dark and often tinted bronze. The flowers are a bright pink with pale pink and white stripes and spots and silver reverses. The flowering is continuous throughout the season. The blooms appear in small bunches. This is one of the series of Hand Painted roses made in New Zealand by Sam McGredy, and the color does look as though applied by an artist with a brush. This

won a gold medal at Baden-Baden.

The first Hand Painted rose, 'Picasso,' a bright pink on a white background with cherry brushstrokes, created an immediate sensation. Today is it less often planted because it is subject to disease. A daughter of 'Picasso,' 'Matangi,' with ver-

1

milion brushstrokes on white, has won four medals and is considered an excellent rose for both beds and containers. It is a healthy rose with profuse flowering and good reflowering. Among the Hand Painted roses is also a pale pink one with darker veins and white stripes, apparently known to no one: 'Laughter Lines,' with very abundant and continuous flowering. It would be fun to assemble the various Hand Painted roses in a group in a corner of a terrace or in containers on a patio—a small collection of roses signed by the artist.

# Scepter'd Isle
*English Rose*

163

dense with branches and only 30 inches (75 cm) high. The medium-size flowers are a transparent pink that grows paler at the outer edges; they first form a cup, then a rosette, then an elegant cupola of extended petals. The scent is good.

'Nancy Steen' (Sherwood 1976), a good floribunda, has been almost completely forgotten, perhaps because it hails from New Zealand and does not have the temperament of a happy traveler. Named for a great gardener, it deserves to be rescued from oblivion. The flowers are large and double and grow in highly scented bunches; they are a delicate pink shaded with coral and have creamy centers. The plant is upright, 30 inches (75 cm) high and has copious shiny, dark leaves tinted bronze. The flowering is more or less continuous.

**Height:** 3 feet (0.9 m)
**Flower size:** small
**Number of petals:** about 50
(Austin 1996)

This is a graceful shrub with graceful cup-shaped flowers, the inner petals huddled around the warm pad of the stamens, the outer petals slightly reflexed, all in a luminous pink. The flowers are very numerous and borne high on the canes. This is an excellent subject for a big container, from which it will tirelessly endow a terrace or patio with its splendid color and a strong scent of myrrh.

## ALTERNATIVE SELECTIONS
'Dr. Herbert Gray' (1), by Austin, 1998, is another rose eminently suited to container-growing. It is

Patio Roses

# Sweet Dream
*Patio Rose*

164

**Height:** 18 inches (0.45 m)
**Flower size:** 2 inches (5 cm)
**Number of petals:** 35–45
(Fryer 1988)

One of the most successful patio roses, this enchants with sharply defined rosette flowers in a splendid apricot; very double, they grow in large, long-lasting bunches, showing the perfection of silk flowers. The plant is small and compact and always covered with flowers; it is as suitable for a small border as for a terrace or balcony. If one of its branches grows a little too long and threatens to throw the shrub out of balance, simply prune it back.

ALTERNATIVE SELECTIONS
Other patio roses come in similar shades of warm apricot. 'Peek-a-Boo' (Dickson 1981) was among the first. Upright and only 18 by 18 inches (45 x 45 cm), it is almost a miniature. Its apricot flowers become pinker over time. They grow in bunches.

'Cider Cup' (1), by Dickson, 1988, merits greater use. The flowers have 18 petals in a pretty arrangement and are a luminous apricot. More modern, and also by Dickson, is 'Sweet Magic', a rose with a stronger color that is making a name for itself. Its flowers are a gilt orange that glows like a flame in the sun; they are even scented, a rare quality in a rose of this class.

1

briefest intervals, over such a long period that in warmer climates, they continue almost until Christmas. The plant requires no care beyond watering and moderate fertilization, after which it asks only to be deadheaded so as to always look its best.

**Origin:** 'Sea Foam' x 'San Valentino.'

### ALTERNATIVE SELECTION

'Raubritter' (1) has similar small pink flowers in perfectly round closed cups borne high above the foliage in attractive bunches. It is one of the few hybrids created from *Rosa* x *macrantha*. The flowering is enormously abundant, thoroughly overwhelming the small shrub, but it is not repeated. This is a wonderful rose in the standard, or tree, form.

**Size:** 28 x 40 inches (0.7 x 1 m)
**Flower size:** 1.2 inches (3 cm)
**Number of petals:** 25–30
(Barni 1982)

As sweet as its name ("little treasure"), this is a rose to grow in a garden, on a balcony or on a terrace, wherever there is enough room. This small rose will return the favor with faith-ful and continuous flowering. Truly a rose that merits its name. It can be used as a groundcover because of its wealth of small, shiny leaves and its habit, which is upright but also wide. The flowers are like little cups of pink silk, and modestly, they do not reveal their hearts. They grow in terminal corymbs and are produced, with only the

1

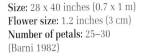
Patio Roses

thickly covered (all the way to its base) that the branches cannot be seen. The flowering is very long and repeated. All that is missing is scent. This rose must be ordered from Holland.

**ALTERNATIVE SELECTIONS**

'Milrose', by Delbard, has few equals in terms of the duration and abundance of its flowering. At first, the flowers are cup-shaped, then they form rosettes, somewhat double, that rise over the shiny foliage in large bunches like a bouquet.

'Pink Hit' (1), by Poulsen, 1994, is another patio rose with fairly large

**Height:** 28 inches (0.7 m)
**Flower size:** 2–2.5 inches (5–6 cm)
**Number of petals:** 50
(Poulsen 1990)

'The Faun' has perfectly symmetrical quartered flowers, of a harmonious, well-balanced size, neither too small nor too large, with the delicacy of silk; they are pretty in bud and every bit as pretty at the last moment of their life. Countless flowers blanket the shrub, which is nicely shaped, wide and covered in shiny, pale, healthy leaves. A rose to plant wherever there is space—in the garden, a container, a border or on a balcony or patio. It can also be used as a groundcover, since it is so

flowers and an orderly form packed with petals. There is also 'Sun Hit', with sunshine-yellow flowers. The height of both is about 2 feet (60 cm). Their habit is compact and upright.

Patio Roses

pure white with small sulfur-yellow hearts, grow in bunches that stand out against the intensely bright green leaves. The canes, also green and almost without thorns, show the plant's wichuraiana heritage. This is a gracious rose, easy to care for and reflowering.

**Origin:** *Rosa wichuraiana* x a polyantha.

### ALTERNATIVE SELECTIONS

'Hakuun' is a pretty floribunda, white with a few touches of cream, created by Poulsen in 1962 and then lost in oblivion only because of the absurd laws of the marketplace and the constant thirst for novelty. It is appealing with its small colored buds, soft bunches of semidouble flowers with ruffled petals, pale leaves and slight scent. The bush is harmonious, low, compact, orderly.

With an evocative name that describes it well, 'Tumbling Waters' (1) is a small shrub about 3 feet (90 cm) high with a wide habit. It was created by that great master of small roses, Poulsen, who presented it in 1997. It has not yet had time to acquire the popularity it deserves. It is enormously pleasing, with its unusually large pyramidal corymbs of white semidouble flowers that really do seem to tumble down the pretty foliage.

**Height:** 2 feet (0.6 m)
**Flower size:** 1.6 inches (4 cm)
**Number of petals:** about 20
(Turbat 1910)

A polyantha, although it has large flowers for the class, this rose has survived the passage of years, proof that it has never stopped bringing pleasure. Its semidouble flowers,

1

# Little Rambler
## Patio Climber

shades of amber. 'Nice Days' arrived in 1994 with a sweet scent and petals that overlap like roof tiles, but its orange-salmon tones are very bright.

'Little Rambler,' however, is thoroughly adorable, the most endearing and fascinating of this group of rambler-climbers. They can be called ramblers because they have the right appearance—many thin, flexible canes and tiny, elegant leaves. And they can be called climbers because of the way they behave—a long flowering that repeats after a pause of half the summer. 'Little Rambler' is a rose of enormous grace, every aspect of which is small if not minuscule. The very pale pink flowers are scented and grow in elegant little bunches. Unless given support, it will behave like a groundcover.

**Height:** 6.5 feet (2 m)
**Flower size:** 0.75 inch (2 cm)
**Number of petals:** 30–35
(Warner 1994)

This is one of a new and very interesting series, the patio climbers. As of now, its creator, Chris Warner, has presented only five. The first two came in 1988. 'Warm Welcome,' which was greeted and helped on its way by two medals, has scented flowers in a pretty shape but in an orange-vermilion that is rather aggressive for a rose presented as "delicate." The same can be said of 'Laura Ford,' which was also greeted with a medal and is descended from a famous patio rose. Its color is a dazzling golden yellow with

Patio Roses

# Open Arms
*Patio Climber*

169

**Height:** 6.5 feet (2 m)
**Flower size:** 1.5–2 inches (4–5 cm)
**Number of petals:** 10
(Warner 1995)

This is another small rambler for a balcony or tiny garden. The shiny, abundant foliage is delightful with its pointed leaflets and soft canes. The flowers, slightly more than single and in a pink that gradually grows paler, are as delicate as those of a fruit tree or a wild rose. This rose never tires and is a perfect choice where space is limited.

239

# Trier
*Hybrid Multiflora*

170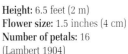

**Height:** 6.5 feet (2 m)
**Flower size:** 1.5 inches (4 cm)
**Number of petals:** 16
(Lambert 1904)

Although this is not one of the patio climbers, it could be. 'Trier' was one of the pillars of the hybrid musks created by the Reverend Pemberton. It is a pretty rose, not bulky, with flexible canes and elegant semi-glossy pale-green leaves. Its flowering is not showy, but it blooms continuously in small clusters, the flowers ivory on a straw yellow base.

THE SMALL PROTAGONISTS

Patio Roses

## Daniela
*Miniature Rose*

171

**Height:** 10 inches (0.25 m)
**Flower size:** 2 inches (5 cm),
very double
(Kordes 1987)

The flowers are fairly large and have narrow, pointed petals that form very orderly but unusual rosettes almost like the flowers of a zinnia. The color is a pale pink that does not fade with time. The leaves are semiglossy and pale and grow densely on the small, compact shrub.

## Longleat
*Miniature Rose*

172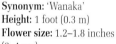

**Synonym:** 'Wanaka'
**Height:** 1 foot (0.3 m)
**Flower size:** 1.2–1.8 inches (3–4 cm)
**Number of petals:** 40
(Sam McGredy IV 1978)

This small, tidy, well-disciplined bush is a particularly graceful example of the always graceful miniatures. Its flowers are perfect, of a vivid orange-red and practically eternal; they have a slight scent to prove that they are real.

Origin: 'Anytime' x 'Trumpeter.'

Miniature Roses

# Petit Four
*Miniature Rose*

173

**Height:** 14 inches (0.35 m)
**Flower size:** 1.8 inches (4 cm)
**Number of petals:** 12
(Ilsink, introduced in 1982)

This very small rose bears a highly appropriate name, since it is as inviting as a tiny pastry. The semidouble flowers with notched petals form flat crowns and are a vivid pink that pales slowly over time. It has a slight scent and reflowers at a good interval after the first flowering.
**Origin:** 'Marlena' x a sport.

# Rosmarin
*Miniature Rose*

174

**Height:** 1 foot (0.3 m)
**Flower size:** 1.2 inches (3 cm)
**Number of petals:** 50–60
(Kordes 1965)

'Rosmarin' offers big bunches of pretty flowers, very full, a silvery pink with carmine eyes that darken over time. The central petals of the rosette-shaped flowers form a star. Very floriferous. The shrub is compact and full of dark leaves. Kordes has put an improved variety on the market called 'Rosmarin 89.'
**Origin:** 'Tom Thumb' x 'Dacapo.'

Miniature Roses

# COLD-CLIMATE ROSES

## CLIMATIC ZONES: HOW COLD IS COLD?

*The agriculture departments of the United States and Canada have devised systems of dividing their countries into climatic zones based primarily on the lowest average winter temperature. The zones are approximately the same for the two countries, and both have produced maps that make it easy to see what zone you live in. The United States Department of Agriculture zone map can be found at www.usna.usda.gov/Hardzone/. The Agriculture Canada map is easiest to get to through the CRS website. A few nurseries provide zone maps as well, as do some gardening books, especially those geared to cold climates. Below are the average minimum temperature ranges for zones 1 through 9.*

| Zone | Fahrenheit degrees | Celsius degrees |
|------|--------------------|-----------------|
| 1 | below –50 | below –45 |
| 2 | –50 to –40 | –45 to –40 |
| 3 | –40 to –30 | –40 to –35 |
| 4 | –30 to –20 | –35 to –29 |
| 5 | –20 to –10 | –29 to –23 |
| 6 | –10 to 0 | –23 to –18 |
| 7 | 0 to 10 | –18 to –12 |
| 8 | 10 to 20 | –12 to –7 |
| 9 | 20 to 30 | –7 to –1 |

"*B*ut will it grow *here?*" is the cry of many a northern gardener. Depending on the particular rose and the amount of work you are willing or able to do, the question has three possible answers: no, maybe and an emphatic yes.

There are also at least three approaches to growing roses in cold climates. One gardener prefers to treat tender roses as annuals: "Buy an inexpensive but floriferous rose in spring, enjoy the flowers through a single season, and expect no more," he says. "If it survives the winter, it's a bonus." Not the words of a true rosarian, perhaps, but it is certainly a valid way to go about rose-growing in a harsh climate. A second approach, for those inclined to do a certain amount of work, offers some tried-and-true techniques for growing tender roses beyond their expected range. Books and articles on the subject are easy to come by, one of which is Douglas Green's *Tender Roses for Tough Climates* (see Bibliography).

A third alternative is to investigate roses bred to survive very cold winters with little or no protection. A number of the roses described earlier in this book would be quite suitable for growing in cold climates. Many of those by Kordes (Germany), Austin (England) and Poulsen (Denmark), for example, thrive happily in the less harsh areas of cold-climate purgatory. However, a multitude of North American cultivars has been developed in the northern United States and Canada specifically for those climates. Dr. Griffith Buck created many lovely roses at Iowa State University, and Agriculture Canada's breeding program for hardy roses has produced a wide range of beautiful, long-flowering roses in two different series—the Parkland series, designed to defy Manitoba's tough prairie winters, and the Explorer series, developed in Ottawa, Ontario, and L'Assomption, Quebec.

The roses described in this chapter were hybridized either by Griffith Buck or through Agriculture Canada's program. All are hardy to zone 3 or 4 (see Climatic Zones: How Cold is Cold?), and some can probably be coaxed through a zone 2 winter. For information about other Buck roses, see the website www.extension.iastate.edu/pages/hancock/hort/educ/GBRoses.html. For more information about Canada's Explorer and Parkland series, see the website of the Canadian Rose Society (CRS) at www.mirror.org/groups/crs, where you can find the complete Agriculture Canada listing.

Many choices besides the roses featured here are available, however. The CRS website includes a wealth of information about what roses will grow where (see Rose Associations for further contact information for the CRS). As well, many nurseries that specialize in roses are happy to share expert advice (see Specialized Nurseries). Whenever possible, contact a nursery that is close to you. Those with Internet access may find the website www.helpmefind.com/rose to be very useful. A database that includes a great many roses, it normally provides hardiness-zone information for the roses and lists nurseries where each can be obtained.

# *Alexander MacKenzie*
Modern Shrub Rose / Climber

**Height:** 5–6.5 feet (1.5–2.0 m)
**Flower size:** 2.5 inches (6–7 cm)
**Number of petals:** 40–50
**Climatic zone:** 3
(Svejda 1985)

The attractive, deep red cup-shaped flowers, which grow in clusters of 6 to 12, resemble those of grandifloras or hybrid teas. The canes of this climber may die back to ground level in colder zones, depending on the harshness of the winter, and elsewhere, it may need deadwood pruned away in spring. Highly resistant to powdery mildew and blackspot. Explorer series.

## Captain Samuel Holland
*Modern Shrub Rose / Climber*

**176**

**Height:** 6 feet (1.8 m)
**Flower size:** 2.75 inches (7 cm)
**Number of petals:** 23
**Climatic zone:** 3
(Ogilvie 1991)

One of Canada's Explorer series, 'Captain Samuel Holland' produces medium-red to magenta semidouble flowers, borne singly or sometimes in clusters of up to 10. It flowers continuously when grown in full sun. The vigorous, bushy plant is lush and well-foliated, and as it has a trailing growth habit, it works well as a climber. This winter-hardy rose is resistant to powdery mildew and blackspot.

246

## Carefree Beauty™
*Modern Shrub Rose*

**177**

**Height:** 4 feet (1.2 m)
**Flower size:** 4.5–5 inches (11–12 cm)
**Number of petals:** 15–20
**Climatic zone:** 4
(Buck 1977)

One of the most popular of Buck's roses, it has large, fragrant rose-pink flowers that grow in clusters throughout the summer. The plant has a bushy, upright spreading habit and is well clad in large, leathery dark green leaves. Orange-red hips appear in fall. Good tolerance to blackspot and powdery mildew. Also known as Audace® and 'Katy Road Pink.'

# Champlain
*Modern Shrub Rose*

178

**Height:** 3.25 feet (1 m)
**Flower size:** 2.5 inches (6–7 cm)
**Number of petals:** 30
**Climatic zone:** 3
(Svejda 1982)

Outstanding for its free and continuous flowering throughout the summer and fall, 'Champlain' produces lovely velvety dark red flowers in clusters. The lush-looking, bushy shrub is well-foliated and has a spreading habit. Usually needs some deadwood pruned away in spring. Good resistance to powdery mildew; moderate resistance to blackspot. Explorer series.

247

# Charles Albanel
*Rugosa / Groundcover*

179

**Height:** 20 inches x 36 inches wide (0.5 m x 1 m)
**Flower size:** 2.75–3.5 inches (7–9 cm)
**Number of petals:** 20
**Climatic zone:** 2
(Svejda 1982)

This hardy, vigorous low shrub produces medium-red flowers freely and repeatedly in early summer and then sporadically through the rest of the season. Large, attractive orange-red hips appear in fall. The plant tolerates partial shade and is highly resistant to powdery mildew and blackspot. Explorer series.

# Country Dancer
*Modern Shrub Rose*

180

**Height:** 2.5–5 feet (0.8–1.5 m)
**Flower size:** up to 4 inches (10 cm)
**Number of petals:** 15–30
**Climatic zone:** 4
(Buck 1973)

'Country Dancer' offers lovely cupped flowers of rose-red, deep pink or medium pink, depending on light exposure and weather conditions. Its clove-scented flowers, which become paler with age and make long-lasting cut flowers, appear from late spring to freeze-up. The vigorous, compact shrub has an upright, bushy habit and an abundance of dark green leaves. Very disease-resistant.

248

# Cuthbert Grant
*Modern Shrub Rose*

181

**Height:** 2.5–3.25 feet (0.8–1 m)
**Flower size:** 4 inches (10 cm)
**Climatic zone:** 3
(Marshall 1967)

Winner of the 1970 Award of Merit from the Western Canadian Society for Horticulture and also chosen as Manitoba's centennial rose, 'Cuthbert Grant' has large, velvety deep crimson flowers. The semidouble cup-shaped flowers bloom in June and September on a vigorous, upright shrub with glossy green foliage. Excellent resistance to powdery mildew and blackspot. Parkland series.

## De Montarville
*Modern Shrub Rose*

 **182**

**Height:** 3.25 feet (1 m)
**Flower size:** 2.75 inches (7 cm)
**Number of petals:** 26
**Climatic zone:** 3
(Agriculture Canada 1997)

From June to September, this upright shrub bears dark red buds that open to pretty medium-pink blooms which become mottled when the flowers are fully open. Blooms appear singly and in clusters of up to four. Little spring pruning is needed. Resistant to powdery mildew and tolerant of blackspot. Explorer series.

## Frontenac
*Modern Shrub Rose*

 **183**

**Height:** 3–3.5 feet (1 m)
**Flower size:** 3.25 inches (8 cm)
**Number of petals:** 20
**Climatic zone:** 3
(Ogilvie 1992)

'Frontenac,' another of the Explorer series, has deep pink semidouble flowers that grow in clusters of up to eight. Very floriferous. Peak bloom is in June, when the plant is almost completely covered in blossoms, but flowering continues to the end of September. The shrub has a bushy, upright growth habit and needs very little spring pruning of deadwood. It is resistant to powdery mildew and blackspot.

## George Vancouver
*Modern Shrub Rose*

**184**

**Height:** 3 feet (0.9 m)
**Flower size:** 2.5 inches (6 cm)
**Number of petals:** 24
**Climatic zone:** 3
(Agriculture Canada 1994)

An upright shrub produces deep red buds that open to pretty medium-red flowers which fade to pink when fully open. Blooms appear singly and in clusters of up to six continuously from June through September. 'George Vancouver' resembles 'Champlain' in color and foliage but is hardier, more fertile and more resistant to mildew. Resistant to powdery mildew and blackspot. Explorer series.

## Hawkeye Belle
*Modern Shrub Rose*

**185**

**Height:** 3.5–4 feet (1.2 m)
**Flower size:** 4–4.5 inches (11 cm)
**Number of petals:** 35–40
**Climatic zone:** 4
(Buck 1975)

The lovely flowers of 'Hawkeye Belle' have been described as "honeysuckle white with a slight pink blush" that intensifies with age. They grow in clusters of up to 10 and have an intense sweet fragrance. Blooming is continuous until frost. The vigorous, erect, bushy shrubs have an abundance of large, leathery dark green leaves tinted with copper when young.

# Henry Kelsey
*Modern Shrub Rose / Climber*

**186**

**Height:** 6.5–8 feet (2–2.5 m)
**Flower size:** 2.5–3 inches
(6–8 cm)
**Number of petals:** 25
**Climatic zone:** 3
(Svejda 1984)

The flat medium-red blooms of 'Henry Kelsey' have a spicy scent and grow in clusters of 9 to 18. Throughout the summer, flowering is abundant and continuous. The vigorous shrub has a trailing growth habit and is very winter-hardy. It is resistant to powdery mildew but only moderately resistant to blackspot, so it is best planted where air circulation is good. Explorer series.

25

# Hope for Humanity
*Modern Shrub Rose*

**187**

**Height:** 20 inches (0.5 m)
**Flower size:** 3 inches (8 cm)
**Number of petals:** 15–25
**Climatic zone:** 3
(Agriculture Canada 1995)

Named in honor of the 100th anniversary of the Canadian Red Cross Society, 'Hope for Humanity' has deep wine-red flower buds that turn blood-red when they open into pretty cup-shaped flowers borne in clusters of 2 to 15. Continuous flowering begins in late June. A low-growing shrub, it has good resistance to powdery mildew and rust, fair-to-good resistance to blackspot. Parkland series.

# J.P. Connell
*Modern Shrub Rose*

**188**

**Height:** 3.25–5 feet (1–1.5 m)
**Flower size:** 2.75–3.5 inches
(7–9 cm)
**Number of petals:** 50
**Climatic zone:** 3
(Svejda 1987)

Soft yellow flowers with high centers grace this Explorer series rose. Blooms are borne in clusters of three to eight. Young plants (up to two years) flower sparsely, but mature plants flower heavily in June and then sporadically afterward. The shrubs have good resistance to powdery mildew but are somewhat susceptible to blackspot.

# John Davis
*Modern Shrub Rose / Climber*

**189**

**Height:** 6.5–8 feet (2–2.5 m)
**Flower size:** 3–3.5 inches
(8–9 cm)
**Number of petals:** 40
**Climatic zone:** 3
(Svejda 1986)

The medium-pink flowers, borne in clusters of up to 17, have a light, spicy fragrance and are often quartered as many old-fashioned roses are. The vigorous, well-foliated shrub flowers freely and continuously. Makes a good pillar rose. Resistance to powdery mildew and blackspot is high. Explorer series.

# John Franklin
*Modern Shrub Rose*

**190**

**Height:** 4 feet (1.2 m)
**Flower size:** 2.5 inches (6 cm)
**Number of petals:** 25
**Climatic zone:** 3
(Svejda 1980)

The double medium-red flowers of 'John Franklin' are fringed like carnations and grow in clusters of up to 30. The vigorous, bushy shrub flowers freely throughout the summer. It is very winter-hardy, although deadwood needs to be pruned away in spring. Moderate resistance to powdery mildew and blackspot. Explorer series.

# Lambert Closse
*Modern Shrub Rose*

**191**

**Height:** 32–36 inches (0.85 m)
**Flower size:** 3 inches (8 cm)
**Number of petals:** 53
**Climatic zone:** 3
(Ogilvie 1994)

Deep pink hybrid-tea-like buds open to a lovely medium pink blend that fades to pale pink when the flowers are fully open. Blooms are borne in clusters of up to three. Upright, bushy shrubs flower from June through September. Resistant to powdery mildew and blackspot. Explorer series.

# Louis Jolliet

*Modern Shrub Rose / Climber*

192

**Height:** 4 feet (1.2 m)
**Flower size:** 2.75 inches (7 cm)
**Number of petals:** 38
**Climatic zone:** 3
(Ogilvie 1990)

Very full medium-pink flowers with a spicy fragrance are borne in clusters of 3 to 10 from June through September when grown in full sun. 'Louis Jolliet' is a vigorous climbing rose with a trailing growth habit and is resistant to powdery mildew and blackspot. Explorer series.

# Morden Amorette

*Modern Shrub Rose*

193

**Height:** 12–20 inches
(0.3–0.5 m)
**Flower size:** 3 inches (7–8 cm)
**Number of petals:** 25–30
**Climatic zone:** 3
(Marshall 1977)

This low-growing shrub produces carmine-red to deep pink flowers with inside petals that roll inward to hide the center. Deadheading is advised to promote continued blooming, and the plant needs some spring pruning of deadwood. Moderate resistance to powdery mildew and blackspot. Parkland series.

# Morden Blush
*Modern Shrub Rose*

194

**Height:** 1.5–3 feet (0.5–1 m)
**Flower size:** 2.75 inches (7 cm)
**Number of petals:** 52
**Climatic zone:** 3
(Collicutt 1988)

The flowers of 'Morden Blush' vary in color according to temperature—light pink in cool weather, ivory to white in hot weather. An excellent bloomer, it flowers from June to freeze-up and tolerates high summer temperatures. It is quicker to rebloom if deadheaded. Very winter-hardy. Moderate-to-good resistance to powdery mildew and blackspot. Parkland series.

# Nicolas
*Modern Shrub Rose*

195

**Height:** 2.5 feet (0.75 m)
**Flower size:** 2.5 inches (6 cm)
**Number of petals:** 18–20
**Climatic zone:** 3
(Agriculture Canada 1996)

The pretty medium-red flowers of 'Nicolas' grow abundantly in clusters of up to three from June through September. The shrub has a compact growth habit and needs only light pruning of deadwood in spring. Resistant to powdery mildew; tolerates blackspot. Explorer series.

## Quadra
*Modern Shrub Rose / Climber*

196

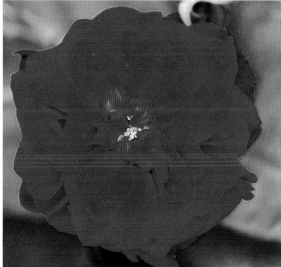

**Height:** 6 feet (1.8 m)
**Flower size:** 3 inches (8 cm)
**Number of petals:** 66
**Climatic zone:** 3
(Ogilvie 1994)

This climber's many-petaled deep red flowers make it unique among hardy roses. The very dark red buds become a deep red as they open, then fade to a lighter shade when fully open. They grow in clusters of up to four. The shrub has a spreading growth habit, and new leaves have a reddish tinge. Resistant to powdery mildew and black-spot. Explorer series.

## Royal Edward
*Modern Shrub Rose / Groundcover*

197

**Height:** 18 inches x 24 inches wide (0.45 x 0.55 m)
**Flower size:** 2–2.5 inches (5.5 cm)
**Number of petals:** 18
**Climatic zone:** 3
(Ogilvie 1994)

The flower buds of this pretty little Explorer series rose are deep pink, then open to medium pink. They grow in clusters of up to seven from June through September. This semiminiature spreading shrub has a trailing habit and is suitable for rock gardens or plantings in small spaces. Resistant to powdery mildew and blackspot.

## Simon Fraser
*Modern Shrub Rose*

198

**Height:** 2 feet (0.6 m)
**Flower size:** 2 inches (5 cm)
**Number of petals:** 5/22
**Climatic zone:** 3
(Ogilvie 1992)

The medium-pink flowers of 'Simon Fraser,' borne in clusters of up to four, appear steadily from June through September if the plant is grown in full sun. Single five-petaled flowers bloom first, but later, the plant produces semidoubles with about 22 petals. A low shrub rose with an upright habit, it has dark green semiglossy foliage. Disease-resistant. Explorer series.

257

## Winnipeg Parks
*Modern Shrub Rose*

199

**Height:** 16–28 inches (0.4–0.7 m)
**Flower size:** 3 inches (8 cm)
**Number of petals:** 22
**Climatic zone:** 3
(Collicutt 1990)

The dense bushes of 'Winnipeg Parks' produce medium-red to deep pink cupped flowers that grow in clusters of up to four throughout the season and have a mild tea fragrance. The very attractive foliage is tinged with red in fall. Good as a bedding rose or specimen plant. Moderate-to-good resistance to powdery mildew and blackspot. Parkland series.

# GLOSSARY

**Alternate (of leaves):** arranged singly along a branch at different heights, first on one side, then on the other. Compare with Opposite.

**Blind shoot:** a mature cane that produces no flowers.

**Bract:** a specialized leaf usually situated at the base of a flower and often the same color as the flower.

**Chlorosis:** a condition marked by yellowing of the leaves; usually a symptom of poor chlorophyll production.

**Climber:** a type of rose with long, rigid canes, usually with large blooms, that flowers several times a year.

**Climbing:** term added to the name of a variety to indicate the climbing form obtained through genetic mutation (for example, 'Iceberg' Climbing or Cl.).

**Compost:** decaying organic material such as dead leaves or manure that is used to fertilize the soil.

**Corymb:** type of inflorescence in which the flower-bearing stems grow from different places on the branch to reach the same height and form clusters.

**Cross:** a plant produced by crossbreeding or cross-pollination.

**Cross-pollination:** the transfer of pollen from the flower of one plant to the flower of a plant with a different genetic composition.

**Cultivar (*cultivated variety*):** a variety created through hybridization.

**Cutting:** piece of a plant (root, stem or leaf) cut from the plant and used for propagation.

**Deciduous:** a plant that sheds its leaves annually.

**Flower shape:** flowers are classified according to the number of petals; very double, more than 50 petals; double, 25–50 petals; semidouble, 8–20 petals; simple, 5–7 petals.

**Fungicide:** chemical agent used to kill fungal diseases.

**Genus:** a group of plants with shared botanical characteristics; the individual members of a genus are species.

**Graft:** insertion of a plant part (bud, shoot or scion) into the stem or stock of another (the rootstock).

**Groundcover:** term for low-growing or trailing plants used to cover the ground.

**Hip:** the ripe fruit of a rose.

**Hybrid:** a plant that results from crossing different species, whether through natural pollination or human manipulation. The same as "variety."

**Insecticide:** a chemical substance or preparation used to kill insects.

**Leaflet:** one of the blades or divisions of a compound leaf.

**Mulch:** layer of material, usually organic, used to cover the ground around a plant to protect it.

**Mutation:** plant or plant part that through a sudden change in genetic code presents traits (color, flower shape, habit, etc.) that differ from those of the parent. Also called a sport.

**Opposite (of leaves):** arranged in pairs along a branch, one on each side at the same height. Compare with Alternate.

**pH:** a measure of the acidity or alkalinity of the soil.

**Rambler:** type of rose with many flexible canes, abundant foliage, usually small flowers in pale colors, usually a single flush of blooms in a year.

**Reflexed:** bent backward; applied to mature flower petals that fold back.

**Reflowering (reblooming):** ability of a rose or other plant to produce more than one flush of blooms each year.

**Sarmentose:** a plant that produces runners.

**Species.** See Genus

**Spore:** reproductive cell of plants that do not have flowers.

**Systemic:** type of fungicide or pesticide that is absorbed and circulated within the plant, thus affecting the entire plant and not just the area to which the agent was applied.

**Sport.** See Mutation.

**Sucker:** a shoot growing from below the point of a graft and thus possessing the characteristics of the rootstock, not those of the grafted plant.

# CLASSIFICATION OF ROSES

Abbreviations and symbols:
*Cl.: Climbing*
*P\*: slight scent; P\*\*: moderate scent; P\*\*\*: strong scent*

## ANTIQUE ROSES
### Gallica Roses (Rosa gallica)
Originally from western Asia and central and southern Europe, the gallicas were the first roses planted in gardens, cultivated by the Medes and Persians and then by the Greeks and Romans. These are thus truly antique roses, but they are also the parents of other important kinds, including, probably, the damask and alba roses, and they show up in the chromosomes of the centifolias. These are red roses par excellence, although there are a few stupendous varieties with pink flowers. The red of the gallicas is heavy with magenta, purple and cherry tones. The beauty and intensity of their color and their scent are among their most attractive qualities; they are also very easy to grow. Upright, robust and compact, covered with big, opaque, somewhat rough leaves, resistant to cold and with full, spherical buds and pretty blossoms, they have a single flowering each year, usually in early summer.

Aside from the species, other early forms include *Rosa gallica officinalis,* known as the 'Apothecary's Rose' because of its presumed medicinal properties, most of all as an astringent, and *R. gallica versicolor,* or 'Rosa Mundi,' which probably originated in England in the Middle Ages and has variegated petals. There have been many other varieties. John Parkinson described only a dozen in the 17th century, but in the 19th century, largely because of the passion of Empress Josephine, this class of rose was highly promoted by French hybridizers. They put into circulation as many as 1,000 different types. Today's garden catalogs list about fifty.

'Alain Blanchard' (Vibert 1839), 4 feet (1.2 m); large, almost simple flowers, purple-crimson; P\*\*
'Anaïs Ségalas' (Vibert 1837), 3 feet (0.9 m); large double flowers, crimson-cherry; P\*\*\*

'Assemblage des Beautés' (1823), 4 feet (1.2 m); medium double flowers, brilliant cherry; P\*
'Belle de Crécy' (prior to 1829), 4 feet (1.2 m); medium double flowers, cherry with lavender-purple shading; P\*\*\*
'Belle Isis' (Parmentier 1845), 4 feet (1.2 m); medium double flowers, pale pink; P\*\*\*
'Camaieux' (Vibert 1830), 3 feet (0.9 m); double flowers, striped white, pink, lavender; P\*\*\*
'Cardinal de Richelieu' (Laffay 1840), 4 feet (1.2 m); large double flowers, dark purple; P\*\*
'Charles de Mills', 4-5 feet (1.2-1.5 m); medium-large double flowers, purple-crimson; P\*
'Cramoisi Picoté' (Vibert 1834), 3.25 feet (1 m); medium double flowers, pink-crimson
'D'Aguesseau' (Vibert 1837), 4 feet (1.2 m); large double flowers, bright crimson with purple tones; P\*
'Duc de Guiche' (Prevost 1835), 4 feet (1.2 m); large double flowers, purple-crimson; P\*
'Duchesse d'Angoulême' (Vibert 1835), 3.25 feet (1 m); medium double flowers, soft pink; P\*
'Duchesse de Buccleugh' (Robert 1846), 6.5 feet (2 m); large double flowers, bright lavender-crimson
'Duchesse de Montebello' (Laffay 1929), 4.25 feet (1.3 m); medium double flowers, pink; P\*
'Empress Josephine,' syn. 'Francofurtana' (prior to 1824), 5 feet (1.5 m); large double flowers, intense pink; P\*
'George Vibert' (Robert 1853), 3 feet (0.9 m); large double flowers, striped white and crimson-purple
'Gloire de France' (prior to 1819), 3 feet (0.9 m); medium double flowers, pale pink; P\*
'Hippolyte' (early 1800s), 5 feet (1.5 m); small double flowers, purple-magenta
'James Mason' (Beales 1982), 5 feet (1.5 m); large semidouble flowers, brilliant crimson; P\*
'La Belle Sultane,' syn. 'Violacea' (1795), 5 feet (1.5 m); large, slightly more than simple flowers, purple-crimson
'La Plus Belle des Ponctuées,' 6 feet (1.8 m); double flowers, dark pink speckled pale pink
'Oeillet Parfait' (Foulard 1841), 3.25 feet (1 m); medium double flowers, pink striped crimson-white

'Pompon Panachée' (Robert & Moreau 1858), 3 feet (0.9 m); double flowers, cream speckled and striped pink

'Président de Sèze' (prior to 1836), 5 feet (1.5 m); double flowers, magenta with gray-lilac

*Rosa complicata*, 10 feet (3 m); large simple flowers, brilliant pink; P*

'Rose du Maître d'École' (Miellez 1849), 3 feet (0.9 m); very large double flowers, magenta-pink and lilac

'Scharlachglut' (Kordes 1952), 10 feet (3 m); large simple flowers, brilliant red

'Sissinghurst Castle' ('Rose des Maures'), 3 feet (0.9 m); large semidouble flowers, crimson-purple and brown; P*

'Surpasse Tout' (prior to 1832), 4 feet (1.2 m); double flowers, crimson-pink

'Tricolore de Flandre' (Van Houtte 1846), 3 feet (0.9 m); small double flowers, pink streaked mauve-purple

'Tuscany' (prior to 1820), 3 feet (0.9 m); medium semidouble flowers, purple-black-crimson

'Tuscany Superb' (Paul 1848), 3 feet (0.9 m); large semidouble flowers, purple-black-crimson; P***.

## Damask Roses (Rosa x damascena)

This is not a true species but a hybrid. One of the parents is presumed to have been *Rosa gallica*. The damask roses probably originated in the Middle East and were certainly known in the classical world. They reigned as queen in Persian and Arabian gardens and, as indicated by the Islamic philosopher and physician Avicenna, were widely cultivated from Syria to Egypt for the manufacture of attar, the base of many of the cosmetics and scents used in antiquity. There are two known forms. One is the summer damask, a shrub 6.5 feet (2 m) high with long branches that tend to bend and are covered with stiff setules and thorns, pale leaves with five leaflets, elegant flowers between white and pink, semidouble, with a strong spicy scent. The other is the autumn damask, of obscure origin, but which Virgil called *Rosa* x *bifera* because it possessed the quality, unique for a Western rose, of flowering twice a year. It has soft, semidouble flowers with long petals of a silky pink and is intensely scented. It is also known by the name 'Quatre Saisons.' Some

authors claim it was being cultivated as early as 1000 B.C. on the island of Samos and dedicated to the cult of the goddess Aphrodite.

This is an important rose because, in the 19th century, it was used in crosses that led to roses such as the Portlands and the Bourbons. Unquestionable references to the damask rose can be found in the 16th century, when it was always referred to as the Damascus rose because it was believed to have come from the vicinity of that Syrian city.

Several varieties of damask roses enjoyed great favor in the past. They are a less homogeneous class than the gallicas: some are thorny, others are not; some are compact, and others have such a loose habit, they need support. They are valued for the elegant softness of their flowers, which tend to fold, and they are celebrated for their scent. These are romantic roses that require fertile soil to give their best. They are best when used in informal settings or borders. They have one flowering, early in the summer, and it is ephemeral.

'Blue Damask' (prior to 1759), 4 feet (1.2 m); medium double flowers, lilac

'Botzaris' (1856), 4 feet (1.2 m); large double flowers, creamy white; P***

'Celsiana' (prior to 1750), 5 feet (1.5 m); large semidouble flowers, pale pink, aromatic leaves; P***

'Coralie' (prior to 1848), 4 feet (1.2 m); semidouble flowers, delicate pink

'Gloire de Guilan' (Hilling 1949), 5 feet (1.5 m); medium double flowers, pale pink; P***

'Ispahan' (prior to 1832), 5 feet (1.5 m); medium double flowers, bright pink; P***

'Kazanlik,' syn. *Rosa trigintipetala*, 5 feet (1.5 m); medium semidouble flowers, pink; P***

'La Ville de Bruxelles' (Vibert 1849), 5 feet (1.5 m); large double flowers, pure pink; P***

'Leda,' syn. 'Painted Damask,' 3 feet (0.9 m); medium double flowers, pale pink edged red; P*

'Madame Hardy' (1832), 6 feet (1.8 m); medium very double flowers, pure white; P***

'Madame Zöetmans' (Marest 1830), 4 feet (1.2 m); large double flowers, cream suffused with pink; P***

'Marie Louise' (prior to 1813), 4 feet (1.2 m); large double flowers, mauve pink; P***

'Omar Khayyám' (introduced 1893), 3 feet (0.9 m); medium double flowers, pale pink; P**

'St. Nicholas' (R. James 1950), 3 feet (0.9 m); medium semidouble flowers, pink

'York and Lancaster' (prior to 1629), 6 feet (1.8 m); semidouble flowers, pink and white striped; P*.

## Alba Roses (Rosa x alba)

More than any others, these are the roses of myth and legend, the roses that have struck the fancy of poets and painters. The softness of their colors, the sweetness of their scent and the delicacy of their flowers are qualities that make falling in love with them only too easy. Born on sea foam with Venus, watered by the tears of Muhammad, the colors of their petals reflections of the glow of Paradise—no attribute seems excessive for their beauty.

It is unclear whether they were known to the ancient world; sure references to them show up only in the 13th century, and by the 16th, they were in widespread cultivation. By that time, they had been exhaustively described by William Turner.

Genetic studies performed by Hurst in the 19th century established that the albas are not a species but are instead most probably the outcome of a spontaneous cross between *Rosa canina* and *R. gallica* or *R. damascena*. *Rosa* x *alba* has glaucous leaves and simple flowers of pure white, which is why it represented England's House of York. There are two other forms: *alba maxima*, almost 6.5 feet (2 m) high, with double flowers, large and creamy white; and *semiplena*, with semidouble flowers that are highly scented; its variety *suaveolens* is even more so.

Resistant to cold, disease and pests, the albas are long-lived, the roses best suited to northern gardens, where the brevity of summer makes it easier to forgive the fact that they flower only once. Albas are also the best roses for shady spots, places beneath trees, and they can take far more severe pruning than other antique roses. The blooms are spectacular and usually begin toward the end of June.

'Amelia' (Vibert 1823), 4 feet (1.2 m), large semidouble flowers, pink; P***

'Belle Amour' (discovered 1950), 5 feet (1.5 m); large semidouble flowers, salmon pink; P* (also classified as a damask)

'Celestial,' syn. 'Celeste' (prior to 1800), 5 feet (1.5 m); large semidouble flowers, shell-pink; P**

'Chloris' (prior to 1848), 5 feet (1.5 m); semidouble flowers, pink; P***

'Félicité Parmentier' (1834), 3.25 feet (1 m); small double flowers, pink-white; P**

'Great Maiden's Blush' (15th century), 6.5 feet (2 m); very double flowers, pink-white; P***

'Jeanne d'Arc' (Vibert 1818), 6 feet (1.8 m); large double flowers, cream

'Madame Legras de Saint Germain' (1846), 6.5 feet (2 m); medium very double flowers, ivory; P***

'Madame Plantier' (Plantier 1835), 11.5 feet (3.5 m); medium very double flowers, pure white; P***

'Pompon Blanc Parfait' (1876), 5 feet (1.5 m); medium double flowers, pink; P**

'Queen of Denmark,' syn. 'Königin von Dänemark' (1826), 5 feet (1.5 m); small very double flowers, pink; P***

'Small Maiden's Blush' (15th century), 3.25 feet (1 m); medium very double flowers, pink-white; P***.

## Centifolia Roses (Rosa x centifolia)

Of all roses, the centifolias have the most uncertain origin. Experts claim they were not known to antiquity; cytological examinations reveal them to be highly complex hybrids involving *Rosa gallica, R. moschata, R. phoenicia, R. canina* and probably the autumn damask and alba roses as well. They are sterile because their reproductive system has been transformed into petals; their existence is recorded only from the end of the 16th century. They enjoyed great fortune until the end of the 19th.

Shrubs with a very open habit, they send out long branches that should be cut back by half after the flowers are gone. They are medium sized and have rough, opaque, gray-green leaves; the flowers are rounded, packed full of petals and heavy ("cabbage roses" is an old name for them). The larger petals fold back on the smaller ones, and the entire flower has a languid air. The flowering begins around the second half of June and is magnificent, but it occurs only once. French and Dutch hybridizers dedicated themselves to these roses and are responsible for creating most of the varieties.

These are the roses that inspired so many artists, who fixed their images in paintings, fabrics and ceramics. Beloved of the 19th century—a very floral century—they slowly fell out of favor and have not survived competition from the new breeds of reflowering roses.

'Blanchefleur' (Vibert 1835), 5 feet (1.5 m); very double flowers, cream white; P**

*Rosa centifolia* (prior to 1800), 5 feet (1.5 m); very double flowers, luminous pink; P**

*Rosa centifolia bullata* (1801), 5 feet (1.5 m); double flowers, luminous pink; P**

'Chapeau de Napoléon' (*Rosa centifolia cristata*) (Vibert 1826), 4.25 feet (1.3 m); medium-large double flowers, silvery pink; P***

'Fantin-Latour,' 5-5.5 feet (1.5-1.7 m); medium-large very double flowers, flesh-pink; P***

'Juno' (1832), 4.6 feet (1.4 m); medium-large double flowers, luminous pink; P*

'Paul Ricault' (Portemer 1845), 5 feet (1.5 m); very double flowers, intense pink; P***

'Petite de Hollande' (ca. 1800), 4 feet (1.2 m); small double flowers, pale pink with dark center; P*

'Petite Lisette' (Vibert 1817), 3 feet (0.9 m); very small double flowers, pink

'Pompon de Bourgogne' (prior to 1664), 32 inches (0.8 m); very small double flowers, silvery pink; P*

'Reine des Centefeuilles' (1824), 5 feet (1.5 m); large double flowers, intense pink; P**

'Robert Le Diable,' 3 feet (0.9 m); small very double flowers, purple-crimson with lilac shadows

'Rose de Meaux' (Sweet 1789), 2 feet (0.6 m); very small double flowers, pink; P*

'Rose de Meaux White,' like the preceding but with white flowers

'Rose des Peintres,' syn. *Rosa x centifolia major* (prior to 1800), 6 feet (1.8 m); large very double flowers, pink

'Spong' (Spong 1805), 4 feet (1.2 m); very double flowers, intense pink, lighter at the sides; P*

'The Bishop,' 4 feet (1.2 m); very double flowers, cherry with lilac reverse; P*

'Tour de Malakoff' (Soupert & Notting 1856), over 6.5 feet (2 m); large very double flowers, very dark mauve; P*

'Unique Blanche,' syn. 'White Provence' (1775), 4 feet (1.2 m); large very double flowers, creamy, rosy white; P**

'Village Maid,' syns. 'Centifolia Variegata,' 'Cottage Maid,' 'La Rubanée' (Vibert 1845), 5 feet (1.5 m); large double flowers, ivory striped pink; P*.

## Moss Roses (Rosa x centifolia muscosa)

The most important genetic mutation of the centifolias, which also led to such dwarf mutations as 'Rose de Meaux' and 'Pompon de Bourgogne,' was *Rosa x centifolia muscosa*, easily recognized by the more or less abundant mosslike growth that encrusts the buds and the bases of the flowers and exudes a distinctive intensely aromatic scent from special glands. First mentioned around the end of the 17th century, the moss roses knew great fortune in the second half of the 19th. About 30 varieties enjoyed the most success, and these are today cultivated by passionate collectors.

'Alfred de Dalmas' (Portemer 1855), 3.25 feet (1 m); medium-large double flowers, rosy cream, reflowering; P**

'Blanche Moreau' (Moreau-Robert 1880), 4 feet (1.2 m); very double flowers, medium, rosy white; P*

'Capitaine John Ingram' (Laffay 1854), 5 feet (1.5 m); very double flowers, purple-cherry; P***

'Common Moss,' syn. 'Old Moss' (prior to 1700), 4 feet (1.2 m); medium very double flowers, pale pink; P***

'Comtesse de Murinais' (Vibert 1843), 6 feet (1.8 m); very double flowers, very pale pink; P***

'Deuil de Paul Fontaine' (Fontaine 1873), 3 feet (0.9 m); very double flowers, brown-purple; P***

'Dresden Doll' (Moore 1975), miniature, 10 inches (0.25 m); small very double flowers, pale pink

'Duchesse de Verneuil' (Portemer 1856), 5 feet (1.5 m); very double flowers, flesh-pink

'Eugénie Guinoisseau' (Guinoisseau 1864), 6 feet (1.8 m); large double flowers, purple-violet with gray tones, reflowering; P*

'Général Kleber' (Robert 1856), 5 feet (1.5 m); large double flowers, lilac-pink; P***

'Gloire des Mousseux' (Laffay 1852), 5 feet (1.5 m); very large double flowers, pink; P***

'Henry Martin' (Laffay 1863), 6 feet (1.8 m); medium double flowers, purple-crimson; P*

'James Mitchell' (Verdier 1861), 5 feet (1.5 m); medium double flowers, luminous pink; P*

'Japonica,' syn. 'Mousseux du Japon,' 3 feet (0.9 m); small semidouble flowers, silvery lavender-pink

'Jeanne de Monfort' (Robert 1851), 6-6.5 feet (1.8–2 m); large semidouble flowers, pale pink; P**

'Little Gem' (Paul 1880), miniature, 2 feet (0.6 m); small double flowers, crimson

'Louis Gimard' (Pernet Père 1877), 5 feet (1.5 m); large very double flowers, silvery crimson-pink

'Madame Louis Lévèque' (Lévèque 1898), 5 feet (1.5 m); medium-large double flowers, pale pink; P***

'Maréchal Davoust' (Robert 1853), 4 feet (1.2 m); medium semidouble flowers, mauve-purple; P***

'Mousseline' (Moreau-Robert 1881), 3 feet (0.9 m); medium double flowers, flesh-pink, almost white, reflowering; P*. Often confused with 'Alfred de Dalmas.'

'Nuits de Young' (Laffay 1845), 4 feet (1.2 m); medium-small double flowers, purple-brown; P**

'René d'Anjou' (Robert 1853), 4 feet (1.2 m); small double flowers, pale pink; P***

'Salet' (Lacharme 1854), 4 feet (1.2 m); large very double flowers, pink, reflowering; P**

'Shailer's White Moss' (Shailer 1788), 4 feet (1.2 m); medium very double flowers, white; P*

'Soupert & Notting' (Pernet Père 1874), 3 feet (0.9 m); small double flowers, lilac-pink, reflowering

'William Lobb' (Laffay 1855), over 6.5 feet (2 m); medium-large double flowers, violet-purple; P***.

## China Roses

Between the end of the 18th century and the early years of the 19th, four roses arrived in Europe from China that the geneticist Hurst came to call "the stud roses." These roses were of enormous historical importance because they led to fundamental changes in the evolution of the rose; while not in cultivation themselves, they came to play a part in all the various classes of modern everblooming roses. The China roses that came to be cultivated in the West were not really very numerous. Different from European roses, their principal characteristics are small, shiny leaves; delicate, fresh, brilliant colors; slight fragrance; an open, light habit; and regular reblooming. Easy to cultivate, elegant in appearance

and not overly large, they can accompany any other rose or shrub and bring a note of color to the garden without creating a sense of overcrowding.

'Anne-Marie de Montravel' (Rambaux 1880), 2 feet (0.6 m); small very double flowers, pure white

'Comtesse du Cayla' (Guillot 1902), 3 feet (0.9 m); very small semidouble flowers, pink-orange; P***

'Cécile Brünner' (Veuve Ducher, Pernet Ducher 1881), 4 feet (1.2 m); very small double flowers, pale pink; P**

'Cécile Brünner' Cl. (Hosp 1894), 13-26 feet (4–8 m); small double flowers, pale pink; P**

'Cramoisi Superieur' (Coquereau 1832), small semidouble flowers, pale crimson

'Cramoisi Superieur' Cl. (Coutourier 1885), 10 feet (3 m); small semidouble flowers, pale crimson

'Fabvier' (Laffay 1832), 3 feet (0.9 m); small semidouble flowers, crimson

'Fellenberg' (Fellenberg 1857), 6.5 feet (2 m); small semidouble flowers, crimson cherry

'Gloire des Rosomanes' (Vibert 1825), 4 feet (1.2 m); medium double flowers, cherry crimson

'Grüss an Teplitz' (Geschwind 1897), 6 feet (1.8 m); medium-large double flowers, crimson; P***

'Hermosa' (Marqueseau 1840), 3 feet (0.9 m); small double flowers, pink, delicate lilac-red; P*

'Irène Watts' (Guillot 1890), 2 feet (0.6 m); small double flowers, peach-pink

'Le Vésuve' (Laffay 1825), 3 feet (0.9 m); medium double flowers, cream pink with crimson shadings; P*

'Louis Philippe' (Guérin 1834), 2 feet (0.6 m); medium semidouble flowers, crimson and white

'Louis XIV' (Guillot Fils 1859), 2 feet (0.6 m); medium double flowers, dark crimson; P***

'Madame Laurette Messimy' (Guillot Fils 1887), 2 feet (0.6 m); large semidouble flowers, salmon-pink

'Old Blush China,' syn. 'Parson's Pink China' (1789), up to 6 feet (1.8 m); medium semidouble flowers, pink; P*

'Perle d'Or' (Dubreuil 1884), up to 6 feet (1.8 m); small very double flowers, gilt apricot

'Viridiflora' (1855), 4 feet (1.2 m); double flowers with green sepals; a mutation of 'Old Blush China.'

## Portland Roses

In 1848, fully 84 types of Portland roses were growing in Kew Gardens. Of those, only a very small group has survived. These roses descended from a brilliant red rose, the famous 'Duchess of Portland,' whose genetic background most probably included 'Slater's Crimson China' and an autumn damask. They began with a rose created by the director of the imperial gardens in Paris that he called 'Rosa Lelieur' (later renamed 'Rose du Roi'). That rose certainly involved a gallica. Small, compact shrubs, similar to a gallica but reblooming and with the scent of a damask, they produce flowers that are usually crimson or pink but also white. These roses are still interesting in the modern garden.

'Arthur de Sansal' (Cartier or Cochet 1855), 3 feet (0.9 m); medium double flowers, purple crimson; P**

'Blanc de Vibert' (Vibert 1847), 3 feet (0.9 m); double flowers, pure white; P***

'Comte de Chambord' (Moreau-Robert 1863), 3.25 feet (1 m); medium very double flowers, pink; P***

'Jacques Cartier' (Moreau-Robert 1868), 3.25 feet (1 m); medium very double flowers, pink; P***

'Madame Knorr' (Verdier 1855), 3.25 feet (1 m); large semidouble flowers, luminous pink with pale reverse; P***

'Marbrée' (Robert et Moreau 1858), 4 feet (1.2 m); large very double flowers, marbled pink

'Portland Rose,' syn. 'Duchess of Portland' (ca. 1790), 3 feet (0.9 m); medium semidouble flowers, scarlet-cherry; P***

'Rose de Rescht,' 3.25 feet (1 m); medium very double flowers, purple-fuchsia; P***

'Rose du Roi' (Lelieur 1815), 3 feet (0.9 m); medium double flowers, purple-crimson; P***

'Rose du Roi à Fleurs Pourpres' (1819), 3 feet (0.9 m); medium double flowers, violet-purple-red; P***

'Yolande d'Aragon' (Vibert 1843), 4 feet (1.2 m); large double flowers, lively purple-pink; P***.

## Bourbon Roses

Queens of 19th-century gardens, these highly romantic roses are still much loved and cultivated today. They came into being as the result of a spontaneous cross between the China rose 'Parson's Pink China' and an autumn damask but were then the subject of much complex crossing, primarily at the hands of French gardeners. They boast the best qualities of their parents: stupendous soft flowers; strong, sweet scent; long flowering that begins early in the summer, even earlier in temperate climates, with an autumn bloom that is particularly good. Compact or climbing shrubs, they have large leaves and form luxuriant bushes; the climbers reach beyond 13 feet (4 m). The colors are usually pale, but there are also purples and crimsons. They prefer a sunny, warm position but are not delicate; what they like least is dampness and rain. In some varieties, a malformation of the flower may occur if the weather is cold at the onset of flowering, but this occurs only early in the season.

'Adam Messerich' (Lambert 1920), 5 feet (1.5 m); large semidouble flowers, red-pink; P***

'Boule de Neige' (Lacharme 1867), 4 feet (1.2 m); small very double flowers, ivory tinted pink; P***

'Blairii n. 1' (Blair 1845), 11.5 feet (3.5 m); medium-large double flowers, pink; P*

'Blairii n. 2' (Blair 1845), 11.5 feet (3.5 m); medium-large double flowers, pink with dark shadows; P*

'Bourbon Queen,' syns. 'Queen of Bourbons,' 'Souvenir de la Princesse de Lamballe' (Mauget 1834), 6-10 feet (1.8-3 m); medium-large semidouble flowers, pink with darker veining and pale edges; P***

'Champion of the World' (1894), 3.25 feet (1 m); medium double flowers, lilac-pink; P***. Also classified among the hybrid perpetuals.

'Commandant Beaurepaire' (Moreau-Robert 1874), 5 feet (1.5 m); large double flowers, crimson streaked purple, mauve and pink; P***

'Coupe d'Hebé' (Laffay 1840), 6.5 feet (2 m); medium double flowers, pale pink; P**

'Gipsy Boy,' syn. 'Zigeunerknabe' (Lambert 1909), 6 feet (1.8 m); medium double flowers, purple-black-crimson

'Great Western' (Laffay 1840), 5 feet (1.5 m); large double flowers, dark purple; P***

'Honorine de Brabant,' 6 feet (1.8 m); large double flowers, pink streaked crimson and purple; P**

'Kathleen Harrop' (Dickson 1919), 8 feet (2.5 m); medium-large double flowers, shell-pink with dark reverse; P*

'La Reine Victoria' (Schwartz 1872), 5 feet (1.5 m); medium double flowers, lilac-pink; P**

'Louise Odier' (Margottin 1851), 5 feet (1.5 m); medium double flowers, bright pink; P***

'Madame Ernest Calvat' (Veuve Schwartz 1888), 6 feet (1.8 m); very double flowers, pink; P***

'Madame Isaac Pereire' (Garcon 1881), 6.5-8 feet (2-2.5 m); large double flowers, magenta-crimson; P***

'Madame Lauriol de Barny' (Trouillard 1868), 6 feet (1.8 m), large very double flowers, silvery pink; P***

'Madame Pierre Oger' (A. Oger 1878), 5 feet (1.5 m); medium double flowers, creamy pink; P***

'Mrs. Paul' (Paul 1891), 5 feet (1.5 m); large very double flowers, rosy white; P***

'Paul Verdier' (Verdier 1866), 6.5 feet (2 m); medium-large double flowers, bright pink; P**

'Prince Charles' (1842), 5-6 feet (1.5-1.8 m); large double flowers, purple veined crimson; P*

'Souvenir de la Malmaison' (Béluze 1843), 4 feet (1.2 m); large double flowers, flesh-pink; P**

'Souvenir de la Malmaison' Cl. (Bennett 1893), 11.5 feet (3.5 m); large double flowers, flesh-pink; P**

'Souvenir de St. Anne's' (1950), 6.5 feet (2 m); large semidouble flowers, very pale pink; P***

'Variegata di Bologna' (Bonfiglioli 1909), 4.25-10 feet (1.3-3 m); large very double flowers, cream streaked purple-crimson; P***

'Zéphirine Drouhin' (Bizot 1868), 8-10 feet (2.5-3 m); medium semidouble flowers, cherry-pink; P***.

## Noisette Roses

This group of roses is descended from *Rosa moschata* crossed with a China rose, either 'Old Blush' or 'Parson's Pink China'. These are all climbing or rambling roses with copious flowering, but they should be divided into two groups, beginning with a very interesting group created in the early years of the 19th century. These roses are resistant to cold and, like the musk roses, produce large bunches of small flowers, scented and in pale colors. The second group, composed of roses created later, has larger, more showy flowers with splendid blossoms, but they suffer from cold weather and are therefore better suited to a veranda or a temperate climate. The Noisettes give magnificent results, and having a robust constitution, they do not require anything more than the care given any antique rose.

'Aimée Vibert' (Vibert 1828), 11.5-16.5 feet (3.5-5 m); medium double flowers, pure white; P*

'Alister Stella Gray' (Gray 1894), 8-15 feet (2.5-4.5 m); medium double flowers, creamy yellow; P***

'Blush Noisette' (Noisette 1817), up to 6.5 feet (2 m); small double flowers, lilac-pink; P**

'Bouquet d'Or' (Ducher 1872), 10 feet (3 m); large double flowers, bronze-salmon; P*

'Céline Forestier' (Trouillard 1842), 6 feet (1.8 m); large very double flowers, primrose-yellow; P***

'Claire Jacquier' (Bernaix 1888), 15 feet (4.5 m); medium double flowers, yellow; P***

'Champneys' Pink Cluster' (Champneys 1802), 10 feet (3 m); small double flowers, pink; P***

'Cloth of Gold,' syn. 'Chromatella' (Coquereau 1843), 16.5 feet (5 m); large double flowers, pale yellow; P*

'Crépuscule' (Dubreuil 1904), 11.5 feet (3.5 m); large double flowers, orange-apricot

'Desprez à Fleurs Jaunes' (Desprez 1835), 20 feet (6 m); medium double flowers, peach-yellow; P***

'Lamarque' (Maréchal 1830), 11.5 feet (3.5 m); medium double flowers, white with lemon center; P***

'Madame Alfred Carrière' (Schwartz 1879), 11.5 feet (3.5 m); large double flowers, very pale pink; P***

'Maréchal Niel' (Pradel 1864), 15 feet (4.5 m); large double flowers, golden yellow; P***

'Rêve d'Or' (Veuve Ducher 1869), 11.5 feet (3.5 m); large double flowers, pinkish yellow-ocher; P*

'William Allen Richardson' (Richardson-Ducher 1878), 15 feet (4.5 m); medium-large double flowers, orange-apricot.

## Tea Roses

'Hume's Blush Tea-Scented China' and 'Park's Yellow Tea-Scented China' trace their origin back to Chinese roses that arrived in Europe at the beginning of the

19th century. These in turn led to the modern roses most cultivated in the entire world, the hybrid teas. The parent plant of this family was 'Safrano,' created in 1839. Many varieties followed, the results of crosses done primarily with Bourbons and Noisettes. Shrubs and climbers (the latter the more interesting), these are roses of great beauty but little tolerance, which may be why they fell into disfavor after the arrival of more resistant, easier-to-cultivate roses. The flowers are pretty, with the typical high center shaped like a cone in pale hues, almost always pastels. Best suited to cultivation in a greenhouse, on a veranda or in a well-protected site. The flowering is always long and lasts the full season.

'Adam' (Adam 1833), 6.5 feet (2 m); large very double flowers, apricot-amber

'Anna Oliver,' syn. 'Olivier' (Ducher 1872), 3.25 feet (1 m); double flowers, pale salmon-pink with darker reverse; P*

'Archiduc Joseph' (Nabonnand 1872), 5 feet (1.5 m); double flowers, pink with orange-purple shadings

'Baronne Henriette de Snoy' (Bernaix 1897), 6.5 feet (2 m); double flowers, flesh-pink with darker reverse; P**

'Belle Lyonnaise' (Levet 1870), 10 feet (3 m); large double flowers, creamy yellow; P*

'Cathérine Mermet' (Guillot Fils 1869), 4 feet (1.2 m); large semidouble flowers, lilac-pink; P**

'Clementina Carbonieri' (Bonfiglioli 1913), 3 feet (0.9 m); very double flowers, yellowish pink-orange; P**

'Devoniensis,' syn. 'Magnolia Rose' (Foster 1838), 11.5 feet (3.5 m); large very double flowers, cream; P***

'Dr. Grill' (Bonnaire 1886), 3 feet (0.9 m); large double flowers, coppery pink; p*

'Duchesse de Brabant' (Bernède 1857), 3 feet (0.9 m); large double flowers, pale and dark pink; P***

'Général Gallieni' (Nabonnand 1899), 4 feet (1.2 m); coppery red flowers

'Général Schablikine' (Nabonnand 1878), 3 feet (0.9 m); very double flowers, coppery cherry-red

'Gloire de Dijon' (Jacotot 1853), up to 13 feet (4 m); large double flowers, golden ocher-pink; P***

'Lady Hillingdon' (Lowe and Shawer 1910), 3 feet (0.9 m); large double flowers, apricot-yellow; P***

'Lady Hillingdon' Cl. (Hicks 1917), 15 feet (4.5 m); large double flowers, apricot-yellow; P***

'Lady Plymouth' (Dickson 1914), 3 feet (0.9 m); large double flowers, ivory with cream and pink shadings; P*

'Maman Cochet' (Cochet 1893), 3.25 feet (1 m); large double flowers, pale pink; P**

'Madame de Tartas' (Bernède 1859), 3 feet (0.9 m); large double flowers, pale pink with yellow center; P**

'Madame Jules Gravereux' (Soupert & Notting 1901), 10 feet (3 m); large very double flowers, peach-yellow; P*

'Madame Lombard' (Lacharme 1878), 3 feet (0.9 m); large very double flowers, salmon; P**

'Marie van Houtte' (Ducher 1871), 3 feet (0.9 m); large very double flowers, creamy orange-pink; P**

'N-iphetos' (Bougère 1843), 4 feet (1.2 m); very large double flowers, white; P***

'Niphetos' Cl. (Keynes 1889), 10 feet (3 m); very large double flowers, white; P***

'Papa Gontier' (Nabonnand 1883), 3 feet (0.9 m); large semidouble flowers, crimson-pink; P*

'Paul Lédé' (Lowe 1913), 13 feet (4 m); large semidouble flowers, pink-yellow; P***

'Perle des Jardins' (Levet 1874), 3 feet (0.9 m); very double flowers, straw-yellow; P**

'Rosette Delizy' (Nabonnand 1922), 3 feet (0.9 m); large double flowers, crimson-apricot-pink

'Safrano' (Beauregard 1839), 3 feet (0.9 m); large semidouble flowers, saffron-yellow-apricot; P**

'Sombreuil' (Robert 1850), 8 feet (2.5 m); medium very double flowers, creamy pink; P***

'Souvenir de Madame Léonie Viennot' (Bernaix 1898), 13 feet (4 m); double flowers, primrose-yellow with copper and orange shadings; P*

'Souvenir d'un Ami' (Bélot-Defougère 1846), 8 feet (2.5 m); large very double flowers, salmon-pink; P***

'Triomphe de Luxembourg' (Hardy 1840), 3 feet (0.9 m); large very double flowers, salmon-pink.

## Hybrid Perpetual Roses

The hybrid perpetuals came into being following a series of very elaborate crosses among the types of

roses most popular in the 19th century: Bourbons, Portlands, teas and hybrids of the China roses. France was the center of production and Laffay the most prolific breeder, but several interesting varieties came from Britain, the creations of William Paul. The roses were produced in the hundreds, and because of their excellent qualities—the reflowering, the intoxicating fragrance, the intensity of their colors, the opulence and enormous size of their blooms, their robustness and resistance to cold—they were the most popular roses through the second half of the 19th century, dominating gardens and rose contests until the advent of the hybrid teas.

Vigorous shrubs, upright but also untidy, perhaps lacking in true elegance, almost all of them have flowers in tones based on red, usually very solid, such as purple, cherry and crimson; yellow is completely missing from this category. The oldest varieties form a somewhat homogeneous group; those of more recent vintage tend to present very different traits. Some can be used as climbers; others can be cultivated using a technique worked out expressly for them in Victorian gardens: They can be "pegged" by fixing the tips of the branches to stakes arranged in a sunburst around the shrub so that they grow into arches that will display the flowers to best advantage. Of the nearly 4,000 varieties produced, about a hundred are still with us today.

'American Beauty' (Lédéchaux 1875), 3 feet (0.9 m); large semidouble flowers, crimson; P***

'Anna de Diesbach,' syn. 'Gloire de Paris' (Lacharme 1858), 4 feet (1.2 m); large double flowers, crimson; P***

'Archiduchess Elizabeth d'Autriche' (Moreau-Robert 1881), 5 feet (1.5 m); very double flowers, pink

'Ardoisée de Lyon' (Damaizin 1858), 4 feet (1.2 m); large very double flowers, cherry-purple-violet; P***

'Baron Girod de l'Ain' (Reverchon 1897), 4 feet (1.2 m); large double flowers, dark crimson edged with white; P***

'Baronesse Rothschild,' syn. 'Baronne Adolph de Rothschild' (Pernet Père 1868), 4-5 feet (1.2-1.5 m); large double flowers, pale pink; P**

'Baronne Prévost' (Desprez 1842), 4-5 feet (1.2-1.5 m); large very double flowers, pink; P*

'Black Prince' (Paul 1866), 5 feet (1.5 m); large double flowers, black-crimson; P***

'Charles Lefèbvre' (Lacharme 1861), 4 feet (1.2 m); large very double flowers, brown-crimson; P**

'Duke of Edinburgh' (Paul 1868), 3 feet (0.9 m); semidouble flowers, crimson-scarlet; P**

'Duke of Wellington' (Granger 1864), 4 feet (1.2 m); large double flowers, crimson; P***

'Dupuy Jamain' (Jamain 1868), 4 feet (1.2 m); large double flowers, cherry; P***

'Emperor du Maroc' (Guinoisseau 1858), 4 feet (1.2 m); medium-large very double flowers, dark crimson; P***

'Eugène Fürst' (Soupert & Notting 1875), 4 feet (1.2 m); large double flowers, purple-crimson; P***

'Ferdinand de Lesseps,' syn. 'Maurice Bernardin' (Verdier 1869), 4 feet (1.2 m); large double flowers, purple with lavender shadows; P***

'Ferdinand Pichard' (Tanne 1921), 5 feet (1.5 m); striped crimson pink and white; P**

'Fisher Holmes' (Verdier 1865), 3 feet (0.9 m); large double flowers, crimson-scarlet; P**

'Frau Karl Druschki' (Lambert 1901), 5 feet (1.5 m); large double flowers, white

'Frau Karl Druschki' Cl. (Lawrenson 1906), 15 feet (4.5 m); large double flowers, white

'Général Jacqueminot' (Roussel 1853), 5 feet (1.5 m); large double flowers, crimson; P**

'Georg Arends' (Hinner 1910), 5 feet (1.5 m); large double flowers, pink and pale pink; P***

'Gloire du Ducher' (Ducher 1965), 6 feet (1.8 m); large very double flowers, crimson-purple; P***

'Gloire Lyonnaise' (Guillot fils 1885), 4 feet (1.2 m); large very double flowers, cream; P**

'Hugh Dickson' (Dickson 1905), 8 feet (2.5 m); large double flowers, crimson-scarlet; P***

'John Hopper' (Ward 1864), 5-6 feet (1.5-1.8 m); large very double flowers, pink edged with lavender; P***

'La Reine' (Laffay 1842), 3 feet (0.9 m); large double flowers, silvery pink; P**

'Mabel Morrison' (Broughton 1978), 4 feet (1.2 m); large double flowers, white; P**

'Mrs. John Laing' (Bennett 1887), 4 feet (1.2 m); large very double flowers, silvery pink; P***

'Paul Neyron' (Levet 1869), 3.25 feet (1 m); very large double flowers, crimson-pink; P***

'Pierre Notting' (Portemer 1863), 4 feet (1.2 m); large double flowers, dark crimson; P***

'Prince Camille de Rohan' (Verdier 1861), 4 feet (1.2 m); medium very double flowers, black-crimson; P*

'Reine des Violettes' (Millet Malet 1860), 5 feet (1.5 m); medium double flowers, violet-purple; P***

'Roger Lambelin' (Schwartz 1890), 4 feet (1.2 m); medium double flowers, brown-crimson edged with white; P***

'Sidonie' (Vibert 1847), 3 feet (0.9 m); large very double flowers, bright pink; P**

'Souvenir du Dr. Jamain' (Lacharme 1865), 10 feet (3 m); large almost double flowers, ruby-red; P***

'Ulrich Brünner Fils' (Levet 1882), 4 feet (1.2 m); large double flowers, crimson-pink; P**

'Vick's Caprice' (Vick 1891), 4 feet (1.2 m); very large double flowers, pink striped lilac and white; P***.

## SPECIES ROSES AND THEIR HYBRIDS
### Rosa arvensis and Hybrids

This is the common European wild rose that wraps around hedges and climbs the branches of trees. It is indigenous to all of Europe except for southern Spain and Scandinavia. Its leaves are composed of five to seven leaflets, the scented flowers are simple and pure white, 1-1.2 inches (2.5-3 cm) in diameter; they grow in corymbs in June to July. The hips are small, ovoid and bright red. This rose is the parent of a small group of hybrids called the Ayrshire roses, created in Scotland, which have the perfume of myrrh. Today, they are forgotten.

'Bennett's Seedling' (Bennett 1840), 20 feet (6 m); small double flowers, white; P*

'Dundee Rambler' (Martin 1850), 20 feet (6 m); small double flowers, white

'Ruga' (prior to 1830), 33 feet (10 m); medium semidouble flowers, pink then cream; P*

'Splendens' (prior to 1838), 20 feet (6 m); semidouble flowers, cream suffused with pink; P**.

### Rosa brunonii

This climbing species, which can grow to 23 feet (7 m), came originally from the Himalayas and Nepal and was introduced to Europe in 1822. It has gray-green canes, leaves composed of five to seven leaflets, recurved thorns, cream flowers 1-2 inches (2.5-5 cm) in diameter that are simple and very fragrant and grow in large corymbs in June to July; it produces ovoid brown hips. It needs a well-protected site because it does not do well in cold. The variety 'La Mortola' (La Mortola Gardens 1939) is an improved and more vigorous form.

### Rosa californica

Indigenous to California, this 10-foot (3 m) shrub has branches with flat, recurved thorns and leaves composed of five to seven leaflets. The pink flowers are simple and small and grow in corymbs from June to August; the hips are small and spherical. There is also a form with double flowers, *Rosa californica plena*, with colors in pink to crimson; scented.

### Rosa canina and Hybrids

This is the dog rose, the common European wild rose found throughout that continent all the way to Scandinavia. Its central canes grow upright, the laterals arch, all furnished with strong recurved thorns. The leaves have five to seven leaflets. The sweetly scented flowers grow in groups of three in pink to white; they are 1.5 to 2 inches (4-5 cm) in diameter and bloom in June. The plant produces an abundance of red-orange hips. The species is highly variable and was once used as rootstock; today, it has been replaced in that role by *Rosa iaxa*. There is a form without thorns, *Rosa canina inermis*.

'Abbotswood' (Hilling 1954), 10 feet (3 m); spontaneous hybrid, double flowers, pink; P*

'Andersonii' (Hillier 1912), 6.5 feet (2 m); medium simple flowers, deep pink, scarlet hips

'Kiese' (Kiese 1910), 8 feet (2.5 m); flowers slightly more than simple, flame-red with yellow centers.

### Rosa carolina

This rose is indigenous to northeastern North America and has been in cultivation since 1826. The shrub is 3.25 feet (1 m) tall, has thin branches and produces abundant suckers; it has shiny, glaucous leaves composed of five leaflets; small, simple bright pink flowers that bloom in July-August; round red hispid hips later on. The several forms include *Rosa*

*carolina plena*, with double flowers, also called the Pennsylvanian rose, and *R. alba*, with white flowers.

## Rosa caudata
Originally from western China, *Rosa caudata* was introduced in Europe in 1896. The shrub grows up to 13 feet (4 m) tall and has strong, wide thorns, long leaves composed of seven to nine leaflets and simple red flowers 2 inches (5 cm) in diameter that grow in corymbs; it flowers in June. It is interesting for its oblong orange hips with elongated necks.

## Rosa davidii
This shrub species from western China was introduced in 1908. It has a luxuriant, upright habit, wide thorns, leaves with seven to eleven leaflets, simple pink flowers 0.6 inch (1.5 cm) in diameter that grow in corymbs in June to July; hips are elongated and scarlet.

## Rosa ecae
Indigenous to Turkestan and Afghanistan and introduced in Europe in 1880, this is an upright shrub that does not exceed 3.25 feet (1 m) in height. Very thorny, it is dense with red-brown canes and small fernlike leaves composed of five to nine leaflets; the flowers are small and simple, 1-1.2 inches (2.5-3 cm) in diameter, deep yellow and bloom in May to June; the hips are obovate. It is the basis of two splendid varieties.

'Golden Chersonese' (Allen 1963), 6 feet (1.8 m); small simple flowers, golden yellow; P*

'Helen Knight' (Knight 1966), 5 feet (1.5 m); large simple flowers, deep yellow; P*.

## Rosa eglanteria (Rosa rubiginosa) and Hybrids
Commonly known as the eglantine or sweetbriar rose, this is often found in woodlands; it is indigenous to all of Europe, Asia Minor and the Caucasus. It is very similar to the better-known dog rose but with smaller leaflets, flowers 2 inches (5 cm) in diameter, a darker pink with more accentuated sepals, branches thick with thorns, and bright red ovoid hips. It has one peculiar characteristic: The foliage gives off the scent of apples when touched or after rain. Known as early as the 17th century, it was only in the 19th that several of its varieties

appeared in gardens. They acquired far greater fame when an English lawyer, Lord Penzance, driven by his passion for roses, created several hybrids that became enormously famous as the Penzance briars, also known as sweetbriars and the roses of Penzance. They are derived from crosses with Bourbons and hybrid perpetuals and several species from the Middle East, *Rosa foetida*, *R. foetida persiana* and *R. bicolor*, from which they took their vivid yellow and flame colors.

The varieties of *Rosa eglanteria* have a single, splendid and rather short-lived flowering at the beginning of summer. Because of this and because they are large, open shrubs, they are most often used in areas of the garden where they can be left on their own to create a sense of nature unspoiled.

'Amy Robsart' (Penzance 1894), 10 feet (3 m); small semidouble flowers, deep pink; P**

'Anne of Geierstein' (Penzance 1894), 10 feet (3 m); simple flowers, dark crimson, numerous scarlet hips

'Greenmantle' (Penzance 1894), 8 feet (2.5 m); simple flowers, pink with white eyes; P*

'Hebe's Lip,' syn. 'Rubrotincta' (Paul 1912), 4 feet (1.2 m); almost simple flowers, white tinted red, numerous hips; P**

'Herbsfeuer,' syn. 'Autumn Fire' (Kordes 1961), 6 feet (1.8 m); semidouble flowers, dark red, orange hips; P*

'Janet's Pride' (Paul 1892), 6 feet (1.8 m); semidouble flowers, ivory edged with pink; P*

'Julia Mannering' (Penzance 1895), 6 feet (1.8 m); medium semidouble flowers, pearly pink with darker veining; P*

'La Belle Distinguée,' 5 feet (1.5 m); very double flowers, scarlet

'Lady Penzance' (Penzance 1894), 6.5 feet (2 m); small simple flowers, coppery salmon-pink, red hips; P**

'Lord Penzance' (Penzance 1894), 6.5 feet (2 m); small simple flowers, yellow suffused with pink; P**

'Lucy Ashton' (Penzance 1894), 6 feet (1.8 m); simple flowers, white edged with pink

'Magnifica' (Hesse 1916), 6 feet (1.8 m); large semidouble flowers, purple-red; P*

'Manning's Blush' (1800), 5 feet (1.5 m); small double flowers, rosy white

'Meg Merrilies' (Penzance 1890), 8 feet (2.5 m); small semidouble flowers, crimson, scarlet hips; P**.

## Rosa fedtschenkoana

This shrub is found in southeastern Europe and Asia. It is 5 feet (1.5 m) high and has light gray-green foliage, simple white flowers 1.5 inches (3.8 cm) in diameter and pear-shaped hips bristling with setules. After the first copious flowering, the shrub produces occasional flowers throughout the summer.

## Rosa foetida and Hybrids

Originally from Asia Minor, Persia, Afghanistan and the northwestern Himalayas, this is a shrub of 10 feet (3 m) with thin canes, few but long thorns and leaves composed of five to nine leaflets. The small flowers, 2 inches (5 cm) in diameter, are a bright but deep yellow and appear in June; the scent is unpleasant. *Rosa foetida* is important to the evolution of the rose because it provided the basis for the Pernettian roses (Pernet-Ducher 1880), transmitting its strong yellow color, which was lacking in modern roses.

*Rosa foetida persiana* (southwestern Asia 1837), 6 feet (1.8 m); very double flowers, golden yellow
*Rosa foetida bicolor* (Asia prior to 1500), 5 feet (1.5 m); simple flowers, scarlet-orange with yellow reverse
'Lawrence Johnston,' syn. 'Hidcote Yellow,' 26 feet (8 m); large semidouble flowers, yellow; P*
'Le Rêve' (Pernet-Ducher 1920), 20 feet (6 m); large semidouble flowers, bright yellow; P***.

## Rosa glauca (Rosa rubrifolia) and Hybrids

This rose is native to the chain of mountains running across Europe from the Pyrenees to the Balkans. The shrub grows up to 10 feet (3 m) high and is particularly interesting for the purplish color of its canes and for its glaucous leaves, which are tinged with purple. The flowers are solid pink, simple, and appear in June; the hips are globular and red.

'Carmenetta' (Central Exp. Farm 1923), 6.5 x 13 feet (2 x 4 m); simple flowers, pale pink; P*
'Sir Cedric Morris' (Morris introduced by Beales 1979), 30 feet (9 m); small simple flowers in enormous bunches, white, small orange hips; P**.

## Rosa helenae and Hybrids

Originally from central China and introduced by E.H. Wilson in 1907, this is a climbing species that reaches up to 16.5 feet (5 m). Its branches are well furnished with recurved thorns, its leaves are composed of seven to nine leaflets, and it produces numerous 1.5-inch (3.8 cm) scented white flowers that grow in flat corymbs in June to July; ovoid red hips.

'Lykkefund' (Olsen 1930), 26 feet (8 m); semidouble medium-size flowers, creamy yellow with pink shading; P***.

## Rosa x kordesii

This hybrid was created by the Kordes nursery, Germany's leading producer of roses, on the basis of a sport of the rugosa 'Max Graf.' It has never been sold but has served as the basis for a series of highly successful varieties.

'Dortmund' (Kordes 1955), 10 feet (3 m); large simple flowers, bright red with white eyes; P*
'Ilse Krohn Superior' (Kordes 1964), 10 feet (3 m); large double flowers, pure white; P***
'Leverkusen' (Kordes 1954), 10 feet (3 m); medium double flowers, lemon yellow; P*
'Parkdirektor Riggers' (Kordes 1957), 13 feet (4 m); medium semidouble flowers, blood-red; P*.

## Rosa laevigata and Hybrids

Originally from China and introduced in Europe in 1759, this rose was brought to North America and has become thoroughly naturalized in the southeastern United States. Known as the Cherokee Rose, it is the state flower of Georgia. A climber, it can grow to 20 feet (6 m); it has glossy, almost evergreen leaves composed of only three leaflets; it is not cold-resistant, so is best suited to temperate climates. The flowers are simple, pure white, up to 3.5 inches (9 cm) in diameter and scented; flowering is May to June. It produces hispid hips, first yellow then reddish. Its descendants are splendid—roses with a singular fascination and the single defect of being somewhat delicate, but planted in a warm, protected site, they become the jewels of any garden.

'Anemone Rose,' syn. *Rosa x anemoides* (Schmidt 1895), 10 feet (3 m); large simple flowers, pink; P**

'Cooper's' (Burmese 1927), 20 feet (6 m); very large simple flowers, cream; P**

'Ramona' (Dietrich & Turner 1913), 10 feet (3 m); large simple flowers, crimson; P**

'Silver Moon' (Van Fleet 1910), 21.3 feet (6.5 m); large semidouble flowers, cream on an amber background; P**.

## Rosa longicuspis var. sinowilsonii (Rosa sinowilsonii) and Hybrids

This species from southwestern China was introduced in 1904. A climber, it is not resistant to cold and grows up to 16.5 feet (5 m). The leaves are semievergreen, the thorns short and recurved. The flowers are white, 1.5 inches (3.8 cm) in diameter and grow in open corymbs in June to July; elliptical red hips.

'Wedding Day' (Stern 1950), 26 feet (8 m); small simple flowers in large bunches, ivory-pink; P***.

## Rosa x macrantha and Hybrids

Created in France in the 18th century, one of its two parents was Rosa gallica. The shrub grows to 5 feet (1.5 m) and has green, flexible canes with few recurved thorns; leaves are composed of five to seven leaflets. It is interesting for its somewhat large flowers, in sprays, semidouble, pale pink then white; the large, globular hips are a dull red. The scent is intense; flowering is May to June.

'Chianti' (Austin 1967), 5 feet (1.5 m); large semidouble flowers, dark crimson then purple; P***

'Daisy Hill' (Kordes 1906), 8 feet (2.5 m); large simple flowers, pink; red hips; P**

'Raubritter' (Kordes 1967), 3 feet (0.9 m); small semidouble flowers, pale pink

'Scintillation' (Austin 1967), 4 x 6 feet (1.2 x 1.8 m); small semidouble flowers, pale pink; P***.

## Rosa x micrugosa

In cultivation since 1905, this shrub grows to 6.5 feet (2 m). It has upright, well-thorned canes, folded leaves with prominent wrinkles as do the rugosa species. The flowers are simple, 3-3.5 inches (8-9 cm) in diameter and a light pearly pink; they appear in May. Hips are round, hispid and orange-green. There is also a form with white flowers, an alba, 'Dr. Hurst.'

## Rosa moschata and Hybrid Musk Roses

Of obscure origin, Rosa moschata is a shrublike climber 10-13 feet (3-4 m) high, probably from India or China and brought to Asia Minor and then to southern Europe in the 17th century. The leaves are composed of five to seven leaflets that tend to fall, few hooked thorns, simple flowers of a creamy white that are 1.2 inches (3 cm) in diameter and grow in large bunches at the ends of the canes; strong moss scent; small oval hips. The flowering is late, beginning in August and lasting until the first frost.

The category of hybrid musk roses, a name that is not completely appropriate, is applied to a large number of popular roses still in widespread use although they were created in the first 30 years of the 20th century. The breeder most responsible for them was an English minister, the Reverend Joseph Pemberton (later followed by his assistant Ann Bentall). He worked in particular with two roses, 'Aglaia' and 'Trier,' created by a German breeder, Peter Lambert; the origin of these roses goes back to Rosa multiflora and the moss roses by way of the Noisette 'Rêve d'Or.' Very useful in any garden, these grow as large, graceful shrubs with arching branches and large corymbs of flowers as fresh as splashing water. They create highly theatrical effects. The bloom is long and repeated; the flowers come in many colors and are small, medium and, in a few cases, large.

'Autumn Delight' (Bentall 1933), 3 feet (0.9 m); almost simple flowers, cream; P***

'Ballerina' (Bentall 1937), 5 feet (1.5 m); small simple flowers, magenta with white centers, copious small hips; P*

'Belinda' (Bentall 1936), 5 feet (1.5 m); small semidouble flowers, intense pink with lilac shadings; P**

'Buff Beauty' (Bentall 1939, perhaps earlier), 5 feet (1.5 m); large double flowers, apricot; P***

'Cornelia' (Pemberton 1925), 5 feet (1.5 m); semidouble flowers, ocher-yellow; P**

'Danaë' (Pemberton 1913), 5 feet (1.5 m); medium semidouble flowers, pale coral-pink; P**

'Daybreak' (Pemberton 1918), 3.25 feet (1 m); semidouble flowers, pale yellow; P***

'Eva' (Kordes 1938), 6 feet (1.8 m); large almost simple flowers, crimson with white centers; P***

'Felicia' (Pemberton 1928), 5 feet (1.5 m); medium semidouble flowers, silvery flesh-pink; P***

'Francesca' (Pemberton 1928), 6.5 feet (2 m); large semidouble flowers, apricot; P***

'Kathleen' (Pemberton 1922), 8 feet (2.5 m); small almost simple flowers, rosy cream; P***

'Lavender Lassie' (Kordes 1960), 4-5 feet (1.2-1.5 m); medium double flowers, lavender-pink; P**

'Moonlight' (Pemberton 1913), 8 feet (2.5 m); small semidouble flowers, white; P***

'Nur Mahal' (Pemberton 1923), 4 feet (1.2 m); medium semidouble flowers, mauve-cherry; P**

'Pax' (Pemberton 1918), 6 feet (1.8 m); large semidouble flowers, cream white; P**

'Penelope' (Pemberton 1924), 5 feet (1.5 m); medium semidouble flowers, apricot then cream; P**

'Pink Prosperity' (Bentall 1931), 4 feet (1.2 m); small double flowers, pale pink; P***

'Prosperity' (Pemberton 1919), 5 feet (1.5 m); medium double flowers, creamy white; P***

'Robin Hood' (Pemberton 1927), 4 feet (1.2 m); medium semidouble flowers, crimson-scarlet

'Thisbe' (Pemberton 1918), 4 feet (1.2 m); small semidouble flowers, straw-yellow; P***

'Vanity' (Pemberton 1920), 6 feet (1.8 m); large flowers, slightly more than simple, cherry-pink; P**

'Wilhelm' (Kordes 1934), 5-6 feet (1.5-1.8 m); small semidouble flowers, dark crimson with white centers

'Will Scarlet' (Hilling 1947), 6 feet (1.8 m); medium semidouble flowers, bright scarlet.

Other hybrids based on *Rosa moschata*:

'Francis E. Lester' (Lester Rose Garden 1946), 15 feet (4.5 m); medium simple flowers, white with touches of pink, red hips; P***

'Paul's Himalayan Musk' (Paul ca. 1800), 33 feet (10 m); small semidouble flowers, pink; P***

'Princess of Nassau', syn. 'Princesse de Nassau' (early 1800s), perpetual, 10 feet (3 m); double flowers, pale yellow suffused with pink; P**

'The Garland' (Wills 1835), 15 feet (4.5 m); small semidouble flowers, creamy white suffused with pink; P***. Also classified among the hybrid multifloras.

## Rosa moyesii and Hybrids

Originally from western China, the species was introduced in 1894. The shrub is vigorous, up to 9 feet (3 m) high, and has straight thorns, leaves with seven to thirteen leaflets, rigid canes and dark crimson flowers 2-2.5 inches (5-6 cm) in diameter that bloom in June. It is cultivated mainly for its pretty hips, which are pendulous, oranged-red and flask shaped. Since it tends to grow thin at the bottom, it must be pruned back.

'Eddie's Crimson' (Eddie 1956), 10 feet (3 m); small double flowers, dark blood-red

'Eddie's Jewel' (Eddie 1962), 8 feet (2.5 m); small double flowers, brick-red, round red hips

'Eos' (Ruys 1950), 8 feet (2.5 m); medium semidouble flowers, orange-red with white centers; P*

'Fargesii' (Veitch 1913), 10 feet (3 m); small simple flowers, dark pink, flask-shaped orange hips

'Geranium' (R.H.S. 1938), 8 feet (2.5 m); small simple flowers, scarlet; crimson hips

'Highdownensis' (Hillier 1928), 8 feet (2.5 m); simple flowers, crimson with white centers, flask-shaped plum hips

'Hillieri' (Hillier 1920), 8 feet (2.5 m); small simple flowers, dark red, orange flask-shaped hips

'Marguerite Hilling,' 8 feet (2.5 m); large simple flowers, brilliant pink

'Nevada' (Dot 1927), 6 feet (1.8 m); large simple flowers, white. Also classified among the Pimpinellifolias.

## Rosa multiflora (Rosa polyantha) and Hybrids

Originally from Japan, Korea and eastern China, this is a shrub of about 10 feet (3 m), highly branched and moderately thorny; its leaves are composed of nine leaflets. The small flowers are white and simple, have a fruity scent and grow in corymbs; small red hips. Also used as a rootstock, it has been the basis for a large number of ramblers and has been part of the creation of such important classes of roses as the Noisettes and the polyanthas.

*Rosa multiflora carnea* (introduced 1804), 20 feet (6 m); small very double flowers, pale pink

*Rosa multiflora platyphylla*, syn. 'Seven Sisters Rose' (introduced 1817), 20 feet (6 m); medium double flowers, pink, cherry, mauve, lilac, purple; P**

'Aglaia' (Lambert 1896), 8 feet (2.5 m); small semidouble flowers, primrose-yellow then white; P*

'Apple Blossom' (Burbank 1932), 10 feet (3 m); small double flowers, pink with pale centers; P*

'Bleu Magenta', 16.5 feet (5 m); small double flowers between violet and cherry; P*

'Blush Rambler' (Cant 1903), 11.5 feet (3.5 m); small semidouble flowers, pale pink; P**

'Crimson Rambler' (Japan 1893), 16.5 feet (5 m); small semidouble flowers, crimson

'Ghislaine de Féligonde' (Turbat 1916), 8 feet (2.5 m); small double flowers, apricot suffused with pink; P**

'Goldfinch' (Paul 1907), 8 feet (2.5 m), small semidouble flowers, golden yellow then cream; P*

'Hiawatha' (Walsh 1904), 16.5 feet (5 m); small simple flowers, bright pink; P**

'Phyllis Bide' (Bide 1923), 10 feet (3 m); small semidouble flowers, pink, cream and yellow; P*

'Rambling Rector' (prior to 1912), 20 feet (6 m); small semidouble flowers, cream; P*

'Rose Marie Viaud' (Igoult 1924), 16.5 feet (5 m); small very double flowers, blue-violet

'Russelliana', syns. 'Old Spanish Rose', 'Russell's Cottage Rose' (introduced 1840), 10 feet (3 m); small very double flowers, cherry-purple; P*

'Seagull' (Pritchard 1907), 16.5-23 feet (5-7 m); small semidouble flowers, white; P***

'Tausendschön', syn. 'Thousand Beauties' (Schmidt 1906), 11.5 feet (3.5 m); large double flowers, pink

'Tea Rambler' (Paul 1904), 11.5 feet (3.5 m); small double flowers, pale coral-pink; P*

'Thalia' (Schmidt 1895), 13 feet (4 m); small double flowers, white; P***

'Trier' (Lambert 1904), perpetual, 8 feet (2.5 m); small almost simple flowers, cream suffused with pink; P**

'Veilchenblau' (Schmidt 1909), 15 feet (4.5 m); small semidouble flowers, blue-violet; P**

'Violette' (Turbat 1921), 15 feet (4.5 m); small almost double flowers, violet-purple; P*.

## Rosa pendulina

A shrub species 3.25 to 5 feet (1-1.5 m) high, this came originally from the mountainous areas of central-southern Europe. It has purplish or green canes, often thornless, leaves composed of seven to nine leaflets, simple flowers up to 2 inches (5 cm) in diameter in purple or pink that grow in bunches of five; blooms May to June. The hips are pendulous and flask-shaped. There is also *Rosa pendulina plena*, also called 'Morlettii,' up to 8 feet (2.5 m) high, with magenta double flowers and leaves that take on pretty shades in the fall.

## Rosa pimpinellifolia and Hybrids

Until a few years ago, this was called *Rosa spinosissima*; its new name refers to the resemblance of its foliage to that of the *Sanguisorba* and *Pimpinella* genera. Indigenous to Asia and Europe, from Scotland to Siberia, it is highly resistant to cold. The plant is dense with thorns of every type and has splendid leaves with seven to nine small fernlike leaflets. It has the habit of a dense shrub; height is variable, 5-6 feet (1.5-1.8 m). The single flowering occurs between May and June; the flowers, 1-2 inches (2.5-5 cm) in diameter, are creamy white and grow along the branches. In the fall, the species and its several varieties produce highly decorative and characteristic hips shaped like billiard balls, brown and black.

Spontaneous forms other than the species are *Rosa pimpinellifolia altaica*, from western Asia, with larger white flowers and large purple-brown hips; *R. pimpinellifolia hispida*, from northeast Asia, with medium pale yellow flowers; and *R. pimpinellifolia lutea*, originally from Asia, with simple bright yellow flowers.

The breeder who first brought attention to these roses, which are known as Scotch or burnet roses, was Robert Brown, of Perth, Scotland. At the beginning of the 19th century, and working with his brother, he created various hybrids, some of which, such as 'Mrs. Colville' and 'William III,' are still in cultivation. In recent years, the most successful varieties have come from the German nursery Kordes.

'Andrewsii' (1806), 4 feet (1.2 m); small semidouble flowers, dark pink

'Double Blush,' 3.25 feet (1 m); medium double flowers, pale pink, large round, brown-black hips; P**

'Double Yellow' (1828), 5 feet (1.5 m); medium double flowers, yellow; P*

'Double White,' 5 feet (1.5 m); medium double flowers, creamy white; P**

'Dunwich Rose,' 5 feet (1.5 m); small simple flowers, creamy yellow, small brown hips

'Falkland,' 4 feet (1.2 m); semidouble flowers, lilac-pink, wine-colored hips

'Frühlingsanfang' (Kordes 1950), 10 feet (3 m); large simple flowers, ivory; brown hips; P*

'Frühlingsduft' (Kordes 1949), 10 feet (3 m); large double flowers, lemon-yellow suffused with pink; P***

'Frühlingsgold' (Kordes 1937), 6.5 feet (2 m); large almost simple flowers, golden yellow; P**

'Frühligsmorgen' (Kordes 1942), 6 feet (1.8 m); simple flowers, cherry-pink with white center; P**

'Frühlingsschnee' (Kordes 1954), 6 feet (1.8 m); large simple flowers, pure white

'Frühlingstag' (Kordes 1949), 6.5 feet (2 m), large semidouble flowers, golden yellow; P***

'Frühlingszauber' (Kordes 1942), 6.5 feet (2 m); large almost simple flowers, cherry-pink

'Golden Wings' (Shepherd 1956), 5 feet (1.5 m); large simple flowers, saffron-yellow

'Maigold' (Kordes 1953), 11.5 feet (3.5 m); medium semidouble flowers, yellow suffused with orange; P***

'Mary Queen of Scots,' 3 feet (0.9 m); small double flowers, plum with lilac reverse

'Mrs. Colville,' 32 inches (0.8 m); simple flowers, dark purple-crimson with white center, purple hips

'Ormiston Roy' (Doorenbos 1938), 4 feet (1.2 m); simple flowers, bright yellow, brown-black hips

'Robbie Burns' (Austin 1985), 6 feet (1.8 m); medium simple flowers, pale pink; P**

*Rosa* x *harisonii*, syn. 'Harison's Yellow' (1846), 6 feet (1.8 m); large very double flowers, yellow

'Single Cherry,' 3 feet (0.9 m); small simple flowers, cherry-red, black hips; P**

'Stanwell Perpetual' (Lee 1838), 5 feet (1.5 m); medium double flowers, pale pink; P**

'William III,' 2 feet (0.6 m); small semidouble flowers, crimson-purple, almost black hips; P*.

## Rosa primula

This is an upright shrub about 6.5 feet (2 m) high, originally from northern China and Turkestan. It has thin canes armed with thorns, small pretty leaves composed of three to eight leaflets with the strong aroma of incense, small simple flowers, pale yellow, arranged along the length of the branches. The scent is intense. Flowering is in May.

## Rosa x richardii

Because it is commonly planted near churches and cemeteries in regions where it is indigenous, this is called the Holy Rose of Ethiopia. A low shrub, 2 feet (0.6 m) high, it has many unequal thorns; the small rugose leaves are composed of three to five leaflets; pale pink medium-size flowers grow in small corymbs; blooms June to July.

## Rosa roxburghii

This shrub species from China was brought from Calcutta to England in 1814. It has a wide habit, is up to 8 feet (2.5 m) high and has gray canes that peel at maturity; leaves have seven to fifteen leaflets. The double bright pink flowers, 2-2.5 inches (5-6 cm) in diameter, bloom in June. The buds are very spiny and look like horse chestnuts, hence the common name chestnut rose. *Rosa roxburghii normalis* has simple flowers, white or pale pink.

## Rosa rugosa and Hybrids

Introduced in Europe in 1796, this species is originally from Japan and northern Asia. The shrub has large, simple flowers of a brilliant pink and is highly robust, almost immune to mistreatment and intense cold. Aside from the trembling beauty of the blossoms, the distinctive sign of the species and almost all of its hybrids is its leaves, which are deeply wrinkled. The leaves are a bright green that takes on gold and bronze tones in the fall. The hips are usually large, much like shiny billiard balls, tomato-red in color, and they sometimes appear while the plant is still bearing flowers. An early group of hybrids appeared at the end of the 19th century, others were created later, and some are quite recent. Very spiny, dense with branches and practically immune to disease, they make perfect roses for impassible hedges and are always pretty in the least formal part of a garden. Spontaneous forms of *Rosa rugosa* include *alba*, with white flowers and large orange hips that appear at the same time as the flowers, and *rubra*, with purple-crimson flowers.

'Agnes' (Saunders 1922), 6.5 feet (2 m); large double flowers, amber-yellow; P***

'Belle Poitevine' (Bruant 1894), 6 feet (1.8 m); large double flowers, mauve-pink; P*

'Blanc Double de Coubert' (Cochet-Cochet 1892), 5 feet (1.5 m); medium semidouble flowers, pure white; P***

'Carmen' (Lambert 1907), 4 feet (1.2 m); medium simple flowers, dark crimson

'Conrad Ferdinand Meyer' (Müller 1899), 10 feet (3 m); large double flowers, silvery pink; P***

'Dr. Eckener' (Berger 1931), 10 feet (3 m); large semidouble flowers, bronze-yellow; P***

'Fimbriata' (Morlet 1891), 4 feet (1.2 m); small double flowers, white shaded with pink; P*

'F.J. Grootendorst' (De Goey 1918), 4 feet (1.2 m); small double flowers, crimson

'Frau Dagmar Hastrup,' syn. 'Hartopp' (Hastrup 1914), 2.7-4 feet (0.8-1.2 m); large simple flowers, silvery pink; P*

'Grootendorst Supreme' (Grootendorst 1936), small double flowers, garnet-red

'Hansa' (Schaum and Van Tol 1905), 4 feet (1.2 m); large very double flowers, purple, red hips; P***

'Lady Curzon' (Turner 1901), 8 feet (2.5 m); large simple flowers, pearly pink; P*

'Madame Georges Bruant' (Bruant 1887), 5 feet (1.5 m); large semidouble flowers, creamy white; P*

'Martin Frobisher' (Canada 1968), 4 feet (1.2 m); medium double flowers, pale pink; P***

'Max Graf' (Bowditch 1919), 2 x 8 feet (0.6 x 2.5 m), prostrate; medium simple flowers, intense pink

'Mrs. Anthony Waterer' (Waterer 1898), 5 feet (1.5 m); large double flowers, crimson-magenta ; P***

'Nova Zembla' (Mees 1907), 10 feet (3 m); large double flowers, pure white; P***

'Parfum de l'Hay,' syn. 'Rose à Parfum de l'Hay' (Gravereaux 1901), 4 feet (1.2 m); large double flowers, cherry; P***

'Pink Grootendorst' (Grootendorst 1923), 4 feet (1.2 m); small double flowers, pink

'Pink Robusta' (Kordes 1986), 6.5 feet (2 m); medium semidouble flowers, pure pink; P*

'Robusta' (Kordes 1979), 6.5 feet (2 m); large simple flowers, scarlet

*Rosa* x *paulii*, prostrate, 3 x 10 feet (0.9 x 3 m); medium simple flowers, pure white

*Rosa* x *paulii rosea*, prostrate, 3 x 8 feet (0.9-2.5 m); medium simple flowers, pure pink

'Roseraie de l'Hay' (Cochet-Cochet 1901), 6 feet (1.8 m); large double flowers, dark crimson; P***

'Ruskin' (Van Fleet 1928), 5 feet (1.5 m); large semidouble flowers, pink; P***

'Sarah van Fleet' (Van Fleet 1926), 5 feet (1.5 m); large semidouble flowers, pink; P***

'Scabrosa' (Harkness 1960), 4-5 feet (1.2-1.5 m); large simple flowers, bright magenta, abundant orange hips; P**

'Schneezwerg' (Lambert 1912), 5 feet (1.5 m); medium semidouble flowers, pure white, orange hips

'Souvenir de Philémon Cochet' (Cochet-Cochet 1899), 5 feet (1.5 m); large very double flowers, white

'Thérèse Bugnet' (Bugnet 1950), 6 feet (1.8 m); large double flowers, pink-red; P*

'Vanguard' (Steverns 1932), 8 feet (2.5 m); semidouble flowers, bronze-salmon; P***

'White Grootendorst' (Eddy 1962), 4 feet (1.2 m); small double flowers, pure white.

## Rosa sempervirens and Hybrids

This southern European species, 15 feet (4.5 m) high, has thin, flexible canes and leaves, evergreen in milder climates, that are composed of three to five leaflets. The simple white flowers are 2 inches (5 cm) in diameter and scented; they grow in corymbs; hips are red-orange and globular. A few of the hybrids created in France in the 19th century by A.A. Jacques, gardener to the duc d'Orléans (later King Louis Philippe), are still quite popular today. As suggested by such rose experts as Peter Beales, this rose seems to have played an important role in the creation of many modern climbers.

'Adélaïde d'Orléans' (Jacques 1826), 15 feet (4.5 m); small semidouble flowers, rosy cream then white

'Félicité et Perpétue' (Jacques 1827), 15 feet (4.5 m); small double flowers, white with pink touches; P**

'Flora' (Jacques 1829), 11.5 feet (3.5 m); small double flowers, lilac-pink; P**

'Princesse Louise' (Jacques 1829), 11.5 feet (3.5 m); medium double flowers, cream and lilac-pink in large bunches

'Princesse Marie' (Jacques 1829), 15 feet (4.5 m); intense pink with lilac tones in enormous bunches

'Spectabilis' (ca. 1850), 8 feet (2.5 m); small double flowers, creamy pink then white

## Rosa sericea and Hybrids

Originally from the Himalayan region, this shrub grows up to 8 feet (2.5 m) high; it is upright and has gray or brown canes, tiny decorative leaves composed of seven to eleven leaflets and large flattened thorns, cuneate, straight and recurved. Small white flowers, usually with four petals, bloom in May; small, yellow-to-orange hips. *Rosa sericea* ssp. *omiensis* f. *pteracantha* is cultivated for the beauty of its large thorns, a transparent ruby-red when young, and for its fernlike foliage.

'Heather Muir' (Sunningdale Nurseries 1957), 8 feet (2.5 m); small simple flowers, white; orange hips

'Hidcote Gold' (Hilling 1948), 8 feet (2.5 m); small simple flowers, bright yellow.

## Rosa setigera and Hybrids

The Prairie Rose of the Great Plains (introduced in Europe in 1810), this species is indigenous to North America. Although a shrub, it produces long runners that tend to be prostrate. The leaves are light green, with three to five leaflets; the flowers are simple, 2 inches (5 cm) in diameter, a dark pink that turns to white, and they grow in open corymbs between June and August; hips are small, round and red. No fragrance.

'Baltimore Belle' (Feast 1843), 13 feet (4 m); small double flowers, pink then cream; P*

'Erinnerung an Brod,' syn. 'Souvenir de Brod' (Geschwind 1886), 11.5 feet (3.5 m); double flowers, magenta-purple; P*

'Jean Lafitte' (Horvath 1934), 11.5 feet (3.5 m); large double flowers, intense pink; P**

'Long John Silver' (Horvath 1934), 20 feet (6 m); large double flowers, white; P**.

## Rosa soulieana and Hybrids

Originally from China, this rose was introduced in France by Father Soulié; it arrived in England in 1899. This climbing shrub is 10 feet (3 m) in height, very dense and has thin, flexible canes, gray-green leaves with nine leaflets and yellowish unciate thorns. The simple white flowers are about 1.5 inches (3.5-3.8) cm in diameter and grow in bunches in July; the scent is fruity. In the fall, it produces abundant ovoid orange hips. It is not particularly resistant to cold.

'Kew Rambler' (Kew 1919), 16.5 feet (5 m); small simple flowers, pink with white eyes; P**

'Ohio' (Shepherd 1949), perpetual, up to 6.5 feet (2 m); semidouble flowers, bright red.

## Rosa sweginzowii

This climbing species from northern China was introduced in 1909. It grows to 16.5 feet (5 m) in height and has angular canes well armed with large, triangular, flattened thorns, abundant foliage, bright pink flowers 1.5 inches (4 cm) in diameter that bloom in June; flask-shaped bright red hips. The variety *Rosa sweginzowii macrocarpa* is cultivated in gardens for the decorative value of its flowers but primarily for its large, waxy, meaty hips.

## Rosa tomentosa

This species grows over a vast area from Europe to the Balkans, the Caucasus and Asia Minor. The shrub is 6.5 feet (2 m) high and has zigzagging canes, robust thorns and leaves composed of five to seven leaflets; pale pink scented flowers are 1.5 inches (4 cm) in diameter; bright red oval hips.

## Rosa villosa (Rosa pomifera)

A species indigenous to the mountain regions of Europe, this shrub grows to 6.5 feet (2 m) and generates lateral shoots; glaucous leaves are composed of five to six leaflets; straight thorns; pink flowers 1.2 to 2 inches (3-5 cm) in diameter bloom June to July; large, applelike hispid hips, orange-red.

## Rosa virginiana

Species native to northeastern North America and introduced to gardens before 1807. An upright shrub, 5 feet (1.5 m) high, it grows even in sand. It has recurved thorns and leaves that take on splendid coloration in the fall. The flowers are simple, pink, 2 inches (5 cm) in diameter and bloom June to July; good scent; the round, orange hips remain for the entire winter. There is also a form with double flowers, *Rosa virginiana plena*, or 'Rose d'Amour.'

## Rosa wichuraiana and Hybrids

Originally from Japan, Korea and eastern China, this robust climbing species tends to remain prostrate but can grow to 20 feet (6 m). The leaves are composed of seven to nine leaflets; unciate thorns; white flowers are 1.2-2 inches (3-5 cm) in diameter and grow in small terminal corymbs in June to July; dark red ovoid hips.

'Albéric Barbier' (Barbier 1900), 20-23 feet (6-7 m); medium double flowers, white with lemon centers; P**

'Albertine' (Barbier 1921), 15 feet (4.5 m); large double flowers, lobster-red; P***

'Alexander Girault' (Barbier 1909), 11.5 feet (3.5 m); large double flowers, strawberry with copper and pink shadings; P***

'Alida Lovett' (Van Fleet 1905), 11.5 feet (3.5 m); large double flowers, shell-pink on yellow; P*

'American Pillar' (Van Fleet 1909), 15 feet (4.5 m); simple flowers, crimson-pink with white centers

'Auguste Gervais' (Barbier 1918), 20 feet (6 m); medium-large semidouble flowers, bronze-salmon; P***

'Aviateur Blériot' (Fauque 1910), 13 feet (4 m); double flowers, apricot then cream; P*

'Breeze Hill' (Van Fleet 1926), 20 feet (6 m); large very double flowers, flesh-pink tinted apricot; P*

'Chaplin's Pink' Cl. (Chaplin Bros. 1928), 16.5 feet (5 m); medium semidouble flowers, silvery pink; P*

'Crimson Shower' (Norman 1951), 11.5 feet (3.5 m); small double flowers, purple-crimson; P*

'Débutante' (Walsh 1902), 11.5 feet (3.5 m); small very double flowers, pale pink; P*

'Dorothy Perkins' (Jackson & Perkins 1901), 13 feet (4 m); small semidouble to double flowers, pink; P*

'Dr. W. Van Fleet' (Van Fleet 1910), 20 feet (6 m); medium semidouble flowers, pearly pink; P*

'Emily Gray' (William 1918), 10-16.5 feet (3-5 m); almost double flowers, golden yellow then lemon; P*

'Evangeline' (Walsh 1906), 16.5 feet (5 m); small simple flowers, pale pink; P*

'Excelsa,' syn. 'Red Dorothy Perkins' (Walsh 1909), 16.5 feet (5 m); small double flowers, crimson

'François Juranville' (Barbier 1906), 20-26 feet (6-8 m); large double flowers, salmon-pink; P***

'Gardenia' (Manda 1899), 20 feet (6 m); medium very double flowers, creamy white; P*

'Gerbe Rose' (Fauque 1904), 10-13 feet (3-4 m); medium-large double flowers, pink on a cream base; P*

'Jersey Beauty' (Manda 1899), 16.5 feet (5 m); medium simple flowers, creamy yellow; P***

'Léontine Gervais' (Barbier 1903), 20-26 feet (6-8 m); large double flowers, salmon-yellow and orange; P***

'Mary Wallace' (Van Fleet 1924), 13 feet (4 m); large semidouble flowers, warm pink; P**

'May Queen' (Manda 1898), 20 feet (6 m); large double flowers, lilac-pink; P***

'Minnehaha' (Walsh 1905), 16.5 feet (5 m); small double flowers, pink then white

'Paul Transon' (Barbier 1900), 16.5 feet (5 m); medium double flowers, rosy salmon; P***

'Sanders White' (Sanders & Sons 1912), 13 feet (4 m); small double and simple flowers, pure white; P**

'Thelma' (Easlea 1927), 13 feet (4 m); medium semidouble flowers, coral suffused with crimson with yellow centers; P*.

## Rosa willmottiae

Originally from western China and introduced in 1904, this is a splendid shrub with arching plum-colored canes covered with a gray pruinose bloom, aromatic gray-green leaves, similar to those of a fern, dark lilac flowers 1.5 inches (3.5 cm) in diameter with cream stamens; small pear-shaped reddish orange hips.

## Rosa xanthina and Hybrids

Originally from northern China and Korea and introduced in Europe in 1906, this wide shrub grows to 10 feet (3 m). It has dark leaves and yellow semidouble solitary flowers 1.5 inches (4 cm) in diameter; blooms in spring. Only one variety is planted in gardens, 'Canary Bird,' *Rosa xanthina spontanea*, which many believe to be a sport of *R. xanthina*.

'Canary Bird' (1907), 8 feet (2.5 m); small simple flowers, bright yellow; P**.

## Rosa xanthina f. hugonis (Rosa hugonis)

Originally from China, this upright shrub of 8 feet (2.5 m) has brown canes and flat thorns mixed with sharp setules. The fernlike leaves are composed of seven to thirteen leaflets that take on gold and bronze tones in the autumn. The flowers, very abundant, are bright yellow, 2 inches (5 cm) in diameter and bloom in May to June. The hips are small and very dark red.

MODERN ROSES

## Hybrid Tea Roses

These are the best-known roses, the ones most widely cultivated, the ones used to fill beds, the ones florists sell, the ones people exchange on all festive occasions. The earliest date back to 1867, and since then, they have slowly but surely imposed themselves on every other kind of rose, coming to dominate the market. Nurseries come out with dozens of new ones every year, and one year's selections often end up canceling all memory of the previous year's. The salient characteristic is the shape of the large flower, with its tall, cone-shaped center, especially pretty when in bud. These are robust roses that owe their success to their astonishing reflowering, their striking flowers and their vast color range.

An enormous number of varieties was created in the 20th century; those listed here are the ones that have won the most fame and success and, in many cases, the most prestigious awards. Many of the oldest varieties are still being planted in gardens or deserve to be brought back. They are arranged by color.

**Red:** 'Alec's Red' (Cocker 1970), bright crimson, scented; 'Alexander' (Harkness 1972), vermilion; 'Baronne Edmond de Rothschild' (Meilland 1968), dark crimson with silvery underside, intense scent; 'Black Lady' (Tantau 1976), very dark red, intense scent; 'Black Night' (Hilloch 1934), almost black red; 'Blue Moon' (Tantau 1965), mauve-purple, intense scent; 'Catherine Deneuve' (Meilland 1982), vermilion; 'Charles Mallerin' (Meilland 1951), dark crimson, strong scent; 'Christian Dior' (Meilland 1958), velvety scarlet; 'Chrysler Imperial' (Lammerts 1952), dark crimson, scented; 'Crimson Glory' (Kordes 1935), velvety crimson, intense scent; 'Ena Harkness' (Norman/Harkness 1946), bright red, scented; 'Fragrant Cloud,' (Tantau 1963), purple, intensely scented; 'Gloria di Roma' (Aicardi 1937), cherry, scented; 'Ingrid Bergman' (Poulsen 1984), intense red; 'Le Rouge et le Noir' (Delbard 1982), very dark red, scented; 'Loving Memory' (1981), medium red; 'Mary Pope' (Kordes 1993), fuchsia, antique shape; 'Mister Lincoln' (Swim 1964), dark red; 'Papa Meilland' (Meilland 1963), velvety crimson, strong scent; 'Soraya' (Meilland 1955), orange-red with crimson reverse; 'Shot Silk' (Dickson 1924), cherry and orange, intense scent; 'Royal William' (Kordes 1987), dark crimson, intense scent.

**Pink:** 'Confidence' (Meilland 1951), luminous pink, scented; 'Eden Rose' (Meilland 1950), strong red with darker veining, very scented; 'Frédéric Mistral' (Meilland 1994), flesh-pink, very scented; 'Grace de Monaco' (Meilland 1950), pale pink, scented; 'Helen Traubel' (Swim 1951), apricot-pink, scented; 'Johann Strauss' (Meilland 1994), pale pink, scented; 'Kordes Perfecta' (Kordes 1957), pink on yellow base, scented; 'Lady Sylvia' (Stevens 1926), creamy pink, scented; 'Michèle Meilland' (Meilland 1945), pale salmon-pink, scented; 'Manou Meilland' (Meilland 1979), pink, intensely scented; 'Maria Callas' (Meilland 1965), peach-pink, strong scent; 'Madame Butterfly' (Hill 1918), tender pink, strong scent; 'Madame Caroline Testout' (Pernet-Ducher 1890), pale pink with dark center, strong scent; 'Ophelia' (Paul 1912), pale pink almost white, scented; 'Paul Shirville' (Harkness 1983), coral-pink; 'Pink Favourite' (Von Abrams 1956), pink with darker reverse, scented; 'Pink Peace' (Meilland 1959), pink, highly scented;

'Prima Ballerina' (Tantau 1957), pale pink, intense scent; 'Pure Bliss' (Dickson 1994), pale pink, intense scent; 'Savoy Hotel' (Harkness 1989), pale pink; 'Silver Jubilee' (Cocker 1978), pink, peach and cream; 'Tiffany' (Lindquist 1954), salmon pink, strong scent; 'Wendy Cussons' (Gregory 1963), strong pink, intense scent; 'Yves Piaget' (Meilland 1984), pink, intense scent.

**Cream, yellow and orange:** 'Adolf Horstmann' (Kordes 1971), gold, bronze and orange, scented; 'Bettina' (Meilland 1953), yellow-orange, scented; 'Comtesse de Vandal' (Leander 1932), salmon with bronze reverse, scented; 'Diamond Jubilee' (Boerner 1947), cream, scented; 'Diorama' (de Ruiter 1965), gold shaded with apricot, scented; 'Double Delight' (Swim 1976), yellow edged with magenta-pink, spicy scent; 'Elina' (Dickson 1983), ivory with yellow centers, scented; 'Elisabeth Harkness' (Harkness 1969), cream shaded with pink and amber; 'Freedom' (Dickson 1984), yellow; 'Garden Party' (Swim 1959), pale yellow; 'Grandpa Dickson' (Dickson 1966), lemon-yellow, scented; 'Jardins de Bagatelle' (Meilland 1985), rosy apricot, strong scent; 'Just Joey' (Cants of Colchester 1972), orange, strong scent; 'King's Ransom' (Morey 1961), yellow with darker veins, strong scent; 'Mischief' (McGredy 1961), salmon, scented; 'Mojave' (Swim 1954), apricot-orange; 'Peace' (Meilland 1945), gold edged with pink, weak scent; 'Peer Gynt' (Kordes 1968), gold, strong scent; 'Princesse de Monaco' (Meilland 1982), cream edged with pink; 'Remember Me' (Cocker 1984), bronze-orange; 'Sutter's Gold' (Swim 1950), gold with orange and peach shadings, strong scent; 'Super Star' (Tantau 1960), orange-vermilion, strong fruity scent; 'Tournament of Roses' (Warriner 1989), salmon; 'Troika' (Poulsen 1971), bronze-orange; 'Valencia' (Kordes 1989), orange and yellow, strong scent.

**White:** 'Grand Nord' (Delbard 1973), pure white, scented; 'Pascali' (Lens 1963), pure white, scented; 'Rose Gaujard' (Gaujard 1957), silvery white, scented; 'Virgo' (Mallerin 1947); 'Youki-san' (Meilland 1965), very scented.

## Polyantha Roses

In the second half of the 19th century, working with *Rosa multiflora* (or *polyantha*), several breeders created varieties of small shrub roses that were reflowering and had graceful bunches of blooms. The first small group was soon joined by others with larger blossoms and increasingly generous flowerings. Over time, the name polyantha came to be applied to the first group, and after much discussion, the name floribunda came into use for all the new creations. Few polyanthas are offered by nurseries today, but those few are eternal: roses of great generosity, easy to cultivate, healthy and of high quality.

The most popular, almost all of early date, include 'Baby Faurax' (Lille 1924), mauve; 'China Doll' (Lammerts 1946), pink on a yellow base; 'Ellen Poulsen' (Poulsen 1911), dark pink; 'Irene von Dänemark' (Poulsen 1948), pure white, scented; 'Little White Pet' (Henderson 1879), white, scented; 'Mignonette' (Guillot Fils 1880), rosy white; 'Nathalie Nypels' (Leenders 1919), pink; 'Orange Triumph' (Kordes 1937), salmon-orange; 'Orléans Rose' (Le Vavasseur 1909), pink-crimson with white center; 'The Fairy' (Bentall 1937), pink, scented; 'Yvonne Rabier' (Turbat 1910), white.

## Floribunda Roses

Along with the hybrid teas, floribundas are the roses most often cultivated in gardens. They are popular mainly because of their extraordinary reflowering, their undemanding nature, their convenient sizes and their ability to form vivacious multicolored hedges when planted en masse against the green of a garden. The number of floribundas is constantly growing—there are already more varieties than anyone could count—and they can be had in every color. Their only possible drawback is the frequent absence of scent.

**Red:** 'Angel Face' (Swim 1968), mauve; 'Anne Poulsen' (Poulsen 1935), crimson; 'Chorus' (Meilland 1977), vermilion; 'City of Belfast' (McGredy 1968), scarlet; 'Cocorico' (Meilland 1953), geranium-red; 'Ducky Maiden' (Le Grice 1974), crimson with black shadows; 'Europeana' (de Ruiter 1963), blood-red; 'Evelyn Fison' (McGredy 1962), orange-red, scented; 'Frensham' (Norman/Harkness 1946), dark red; 'John Armstrong' (Swim 1961), dark red; 'Lake Como' (Harkness 1968), mauve, intensely scented; 'La Rossa' (Barni 1998), solid bright red; 'Lavender Dream' (Interplant 1984), lavender; 'Lilac Charm' (Le Grice 1962), lavender-lilac; 'Lilli Marlene'

(Kordes 1959), crimson-scarlet; 'Matangi' (McGredy 1974), red on yellow base; 'Paprika' (Tantau 1958), geranium-red; 'Picasso' (McGredy 1971), cherry; 'Regensberg' (McGredy 1979), red-pink with white brushstrokes; 'Sarabande' (Meilland 1957), geranium-red; 'The Times Rose' (Kordes 1984), crimson.

**Pink:** 'Bordure Rose' (Delbard 1985), pink; 'Dainty Maid' (Le Grice 1940), shell-pink with crimson reverse; 'English Miss' (Cants of Colchester 1978), pale pink, intense scent; 'Escapade' (Harkness 1967), mauve; 'Fashion' (Boerner 1949), salmon-pink, strong scent; 'Many Happy Returns' (T.G.C. 1990), pale pink; 'Pinocchio' (Kordes 1940), salmon-pink; 'Sevillana' (Buck 1976), pink suffused with yellow, scented; 'Seventeen' (Boerner 1959), soft pink; 'Yesterday' (Harkness 1974), lavender-pink, scented.

**Yellow and orange:** 'Allgold' (Le Grice 1956), gold; 'Amber Queen' (Harkness 1984), amber, scented; 'Anne Harkness' (Harkness 1980), yellow; 'Arthur Bell' (McGredy 1965), gold; 'Charleston' (Meilland 1963), yellow with crimson shadings; 'Chinatown' (Poulsen 1963), yellow, scented; 'Circus' (Swim 1956), yellow shaded pink and salmon; 'Elizabeth of Glamis' (McGredy 1964), salmon, intense scent; 'First Choice' (Morse 1958), orange with yellow centers; 'Goldilocks' (Boerner 1945), pale yellow; 'Irish Mist' (McGredy 1966), salmon-orange; 'Marie Curie' (Meilland 1996), apricot, orange and pink; 'Masquerade' (Boerner 1949), gold, salmon and red; 'Moonsprite' (Swim 1956), pale gold, very double and very scented; 'Mountbatten' (Harkness 1982), yellow, scented; 'Orange Sensation' (de Ruiter 1961), orange-vermilion; 'Princess Michiko' (Dickson 1966), bronze-orange; 'Rimosa' (Meilland 1958), yellow; 'Southampton' (Harkness 1971), orange-apricot, very scented; 'Sunsprite,' syns. 'Friesia,' 'Kordesia' (Kordes 1973), yellow, intense scent; 'Tip Top' (Tantau 1963), salmon, scented; 'Westerland' (Kordes 1969), yellow with shadings of flame-red; 'Zambra' (Meilland 1961), intense orange, scented.

**White:** 'Class Act' (Warriner 1988), creamy white; 'Iceberg' ('Schneewittchen') (Kordes 1958), pure white, scented; 'Ivory Fashion' (Boerner 1958), ivory, scented; 'Margaret Merril' (Harkness 1977), white, very scented; 'Saratoga' (Boerner 1963), white, very scented.

## Grandiflora Roses

This relatively new category of roses was created by breeders eager to blend the best characteristics of the floribundas and the hybrid teas. Thus these roses produce medium-size flowers in bunches, and the shape of the flower is very much like that of the hybrid teas.

Among those that have met with the greatest success are 'Apricot Nectar' (Boerner 1965), apricot; 'Buccaneer' (Swim 1954), gold; 'Carrousel' (Duehrsen-Elmer 1950), dark red; 'Lucky Lady' (Swim 1986), pale pink; 'Roundelay' (Swim 1954), cardinal red, scented; 'Queen Elizabeth' (Lammerts 1954), pale pink, scented; 'Sonia' (Meilland 1970), pale pink; 'Pink Parfait' (Swim 1960), pink with dark veining.

## Miniature Roses

Miniature roses are truly small and have very thin canes and minuscule flowers and leaves. They were created in the 19th century on the basis of *Rosa chinensis minima* but have met with fortune only in recent years. Their popularity results as much from their ease of cultivation and great adaptability as from their reflowering. These are plants for containers on terraces or balconies, not for gardens. They require little care, minimal pruning beyond a cleaning early in spring and the usual watering and fertilization. They are usually healthy and resistant to disease and cold.

Among the most famous miniatures are 'Angela Rippon' (de Ruiter 1978), crimson-pink; 'Baby Masquerade' (Tantau 1955), yellow tending to red; 'Bordure Nacrée' (Delbard 1985), cream tones; 'Cinderella' (de Vink 1953), rosy white, scented; 'Colibri' (Meilland 1958), orange; 'Lavender Lace' (Moore 1968), lavender; 'Little Buckaroo' (Moore 1956), red with white centers, scented; 'Magic Carrousel' (Moore 1972), pink; 'Orange Sunblaze' (Meilland 1986), orange; 'Para Ti' (Dot 1946), cream; 'Perle de Alcanada' (Dot 1944), crimson; 'Perle de Monserrat' (P. Dot 1945), pink edged with silver; 'Polka Dot' (Moore 1956), ivory; 'Rosmarin' (Kordes 1965), silver pink with crimson eyes; 'Scarlet Gem' (Meilland 1961), scarlet; 'Snow Carpet' (McGredy 1980), white; 'Starina' (Meilland 1965), orange-scarlet; 'Swany' (Meilland 1978), white; 'Sweet Fairy' (de Vink 1976), lilac; 'Tom Thumb' (de

Vink 1936), crimson; 'White Gem' (Meilland 1976), white; 'Zwergkönig' (Kordes 1954), pink. There are also the roses in the Meillandina and Symphonie series by Meilland and the Rampichella series by Nino Sanremo.

## English Roses

In the 1950s, English breeder David Austin began creating a new kind of rose that won immediate acclaim. The popularity of his roses grew steadily, until today, they are known and cultivated throughout the world, highly valued for their special qualities. This should come as no surprise, since Austin's original idea was to cross antique and modern roses with the aim, fully reached, of creating roses that possessed the best qualities of both. From the modern roses, in particular, came the great reflowering and the incredible selection of colors, and from the antique roses came the graceful shapes of the flowers and the scent. Having shown the way, Austin was followed by other breeders in Germany and France (in France, Meilland had only recently followed a similar procedure to create the series of Romantic roses). After long and careful work in selection, Austin put almost a hundred English roses on the market. All are suitable for beds or borders or for planting in small groups in a garden. All have splendidly designed flowers and intense scent. They are available in every possible shade, and they have long and repeated periods of bloom.

The most popular include 'Abraham Darby' (1985), bright apricot; 'Barbara Austin' (1997), pale pink; 'Charity' (1997), apricot-yellow; 'Chaucer' (1970), pale pink, scented of myrrh; 'Constance Spry' (1961), climber 13 feet (4 m) high, strong pink; 'Eglantyne' (1994), pure pink; 'Emily' (1992), pale pink, very scented; 'English Garden' (1986), yellow with pale edges; 'Gertrude Jekyll' (1986), strong pink, highly scented; 'Glamis Castle' (1992), white; 'Golden Celebration' (1992), gold with bronze shadows; 'Graham Thomas' (1983), sun-yellow, tea-scented; 'Jayne Austin' (1990), pale yellow; 'Jude the Obscure' (1995), intense yellow; 'L. D. Braithwaite' (1988), crimson, intense scent; 'Marinette' (1995), semidouble, cream and pastel pink; 'Mary Rose' (1983), bright pink; 'Pat Austin' (1995), orange, yellow and bronze; 'Perdita' (1983),

pale pink on yellow; 'Sharifa Asma' (1989), pale pink; 'Sophie's Rose' (1997), red; 'The Dark Lady' (1991), dark crimson; 'The Pilgrim' (1991), lemon-yellow; 'The Prince' (1990), crimson with black shadows.

## Shrub, Groundcover and Patio Roses

The terms "shrub," "groundcover" and "patio" have come into use only recently and do not refer to roses from any one group; in fact, the roses to which the terms are applied do not share common origins. Rather, the roses in these three groups have been put together for convenience on the basis of the uses they can serve in garden or home. Indeed, the name itself defines two of the groups: groundcover roses are prostrate, well suited to covering ground; patio roses are those best suited to planting in containers on a patio, terrace or balcony. As for the shrub roses, the generic term "shrub," used to indicate any plant of the shrub type, is here used in contrast with the term "bush": A shrub rose has an open habit with long canes, while a bush has a compact habit and grows to a smaller size.

The roses in these groups are neither hybrid teas nor floribundas. As will be obvious, this is a big group, also quite miscellaneous. Many of these roses are the fruit of crosses between species roses and bush roses, many are reflowering, and many stand out for their splendid flowers or their generous flowering. Many roses included in some other group can also be included among the shrub roses. This applies to most of the antique roses, the hybrid moss roses, hybrid rugosas and a large number of modern roses. Among the best known examples are 'Nevada,' 'Golden Wings,' 'Fritz Nobis,' 'Pink Robusta,' 'Red Blanket,' 'Westerland'; among the English roses are 'Graham Thomas,' 'William Morris,' 'Mary Rose,' 'Othello,' 'Red Coat' and 'Dapple Dawn.'

# COMPETITIONS AND PRIZES

The first rose exhibition took place in London in 1858, and just two years later, the famous Crystal Palace became the official headquarters for rose shows. Truly international competitions at which new varieties could be classified and awarded came into being only later. The first took place in the Jardins de Bagatelle, near Paris, in 1907. Before then, it was not possible for roses to win medals or other distinctions.

In 1928, the Royal National Horticultural Society in St. Albans, England, began organizing competitions. Before a rose can participate in this competition, it must pass three years under observation at St. Albans in soil approved by the association. It must show that it possesses the necessary qualities in terms of beauty of flower, resistance to disease, vigor, scent and reflowering. Twenty-one judges, including rose professionals, experts and amateurs, award a gold medal and various certificates and awards of merit. The rose that wins the gold medal can go on to receive the highest honor, the President's International Trophy, when it is declared Rose of the Year. Since 1958, the association has also awarded the Edland Medal for Fragrance.

Many other nations and cities have followed the examples of France and England, setting aside testing grounds to host competing roses, holding competitions and assigning their own gold or silver medals and certificates of merit to the winners; some of these also give out titles such as Rose of Gold and other special honors.

In France, in addition to the event at the Jardins de Bagatelle, rose competitions are held in Paris, Orléans, Lyons, Poitiers and Nantes, where the competition is particularly dedicated to scent; in Switzerland in the Parc de la Grange in Geneva; in Ireland in Dixon Park in Dublin and in Belfast. In Belgium, competitions are held at Le Roeulx Castle in Hainaut and in Courtrai. In The Netherlands, the competition held in the Westbroekpart in The Hague assigns a gold medal and a medal for scent. The leading rose competition in Germany is in Baden-Baden; others take place in Munich and Frankfurt. In Italy, the Roseto di Roma is the most important; other competitions are held at the Villa Reale in Monza and in Genoa. The major Spanish rose competition is at Madrid's Rosaleda Park.

In the United States, the most coveted rose award is the All American Rose Selection. The city of Portland, Oregon, awards a gold medal. Other competitions are held in Tokyo and New Zealand.

# GREAT CREATORS, GREAT BREEDERS

*Aicardi, Domenico*: Italian hybridizer in San Remo. He made his name in 1936 with 'Eterna Giovinezza' and 'Saturnia', gold medal winner at Rome and Portland. In 1937, he consolidated his fame with 'Gloria di Roma', a rose that itself became famous. His other creations include 'Signora Puricelli' and the last 'Cristoforo Colombo'. He specialized in rose varieties best suited for sale as cut flowers. Following his death in 1966, his work was continued by his niece Ada Mansuino.

*Armstrong, D.L.*: California rose grower highly esteemed in the United States, founder of the important Armstrong Nurseries, where several hybridizers have distinguished themselves, including W.E. Lammerts ('Queen Elizabeth', 'Chrysler Imperial'), A.E. Ellis and especially Herbert Swim, winner of innumerable medals and creator of more than 80 rose varieties. Among Swim's most successful roses, mainly hybrid teas, are 'Sutter's Gold', 'Mojave', 'Double Delight', 'Pink Parfait', 'Joseph's Coat', 'Royal Highness' and 'Mister Lincoln'. Today, Swim's place in the nursery has been taken by Jack E. Christensen.

*Austin, David*: Leading authority in the world of roses, ingenious hybridizer, author and creator of a new type of rose, the English rose, of which there are now more than 100. His nursery in Albrighton (Wolverhampton, U.K.) is one of the best stocked in Great Britain.

*Barni, Vittorio*: Head of an important Italian nursery, he has promoted the spread of the rose in Italy and is a successful hybridizer. Among his creations are 'Annabella', 'Ambra', 'Antico Amore', 'Notturno', 'Rita Levi Montalcini' and 'Sans Souci'.

*Beales, Peter*: One of the leading hybridizers in Great Britain, author of one of the fundamental texts on rose cultivation and founder of one of the most dependable nurseries in Europe. His creations include 'Anna Pavlova', 'Sir Frederic Ashton', 'Norwich Castle' and 'Lady Romsey'.

*Cants of Colchester*: Nursery in Essex, England, founded by William Cant in 1765 and specializing in roses since 1847. Cant's grandson Benjamin was among the founders of the National Rose Society. Among the nursery's most successful roses are 'Just Joey' and 'English Miss'.

*Carruth, Tom*: American hybridizer best known in recent years for his 'Fourth of July' ('Crazy for You'), a climber with striped flowers. Carruth works in the important Philadelphia nursery founded by O. Weeks, second only to the Armstrong nursery.

*Clark, Alister*: Prolific Australian hybridizer, creator of more than 100 varieties, many of which are still unknown outside Australia but could be of great interest because of their suitability for temperate climates.

*Cocker, Alexander*: Scottish hybridizer who began his career in 1963 in a nursery in Aberdeen, Scotland, and earned enormous success within a few short years with such varieties as 'Silver Jubilee' and 'Alec's Red', both still used in gardens. His nursery is now associated with that of Harkness.

*Delbard, Georges*: Director of the Delbard-Chabert nursery. He made his name in 1958 with 'Centenaire de Lourdes', still very popular, and furthered his career in 1963 with 'Delbard's Orange' and 'Vol de Nuit', winner of a gold medal at Rome in 1977. The company is still active under the name Georges Delbard.

*De Ruiter, Gijsbert*: In Holland, a leading country for flowers, the de Ruiters, father and son, specialized first in polyantha roses then in floribundas, selling their products primarily in northern Europe. Their 'Orange Sensation' is famous.

*De Vink, Jan*: Dutch hybridizer involved primarily in miniature roses.

*Dickson & Sons*: Long-standing nursery in County Down, Northern Ireland. Both Patrick and Alexander Dickson have worked there, in particular on hybrid teas, including some with simple flowers. Among their numerous creations are 'Grandpa Dickson', 'Shot Silk', 'Red Devil', 'Beautiful Britain' and 'Precious Platinum'.

*Dot, Pedro*: Gardener to the Marquis of Monistrol and the most important hybridizer in Spain. He began his work in 1920 and, assisted by his son Simon, created 120 varieties, including a large number of miniatures ('Para Ti', 'Estrellita de Oro', 'Perla de Alcanada', 'Perla di Monserrat') along with two roses of world fame, 'Madame Grégoire de Staechelin' and 'Nevada'.

*Fumagalli, Niso*: For many years director of the Associazione Italiana della Rosa and founder of the Roseto di Monza. He created 'Gingia' in 1982.

*Gregory, Walter*: Hybridizer in the important group of breeders in Nottinghamshire, England. He began his career in 1952. His introductions include 'Blessings,' 'Pink Perpétue' and 'Wendy Cussons,' which have received five awards.

*Guillot, Jean-Baptiste*: One of the first creators of roses, with headquarters in Lyons, France. His 'La France,' 1867, is considered the parent plant of the hybrid teas; his 'Paquerette' and 'Mignonette' are the parents of the polyanthas. His nursery is still in operation, now run by the fourth generation of Guillots.

*Harkness*: Family of English hybridizers. In 1879, Robert and John Harkness founded a nursery at Bedale in Yorkshire, England, and in 1899, a branch was started in Hertfordshire, R. Harkness and Co., that specialized in roses. The most recent generation is represented by Jack Harkness, an outstanding figure in the world of roses, author of books and expert hybridizer, who has created more than 150 varieties since 1962, many of them floribundas, including the celebrated 'Elizabeth' and 'Anne Harkness,' 'Alexandra,' 'Amber Queen,' 'Escapade,' 'Lake Como,' 'Margaret Merril,' 'Mountbatten,' 'Yesterday' and the hybrid tea 'Compassion.'

*Jackson & Perkins*: Nursery in Oregon famous as the world's largest and best stocked. Many famous hybridizers have worked there, including Eugene Boerner, one of the founders, who created enormously successful floribundas such as 'Goldilocks,' 'Lavender Pinocchio,' 'Masquerade' and 'Fashion.' Today, William Warriner works there.

*Josephine*: French empress, wife of Napoleon I. Beginning in 1799, she assembled one of the most important collections of roses, primarily gallicas, in her chateau Malmaison. These are the roses painted by the famous Redouté. Josephine's efforts and influence contributed to the spread of the rose in Europe and to its recognition as the most important flower.

*Kordes, Wilhelm*: Founder of the nursery in Elmshorn, Germany, who later moved to Sparrieshoop, where his two sons Wilhelm and Hermann (Kordes Söhne) began working in 1919. In 1920, the nursery came under the direction of Wilhelm, a rose breeder to whom the world of roses owes a great deal. By way of his broad program of hybridization, he renewed the various rose classes—hybrid teas, floribundas, climbers, shrubs and groundcover roses—trying to achieve a wider range of colors, better resistance to cold and more dependable reflowering. He was responsible for *Rosa* x *kordesii*, the Frühling group and a great number of famous hybrids, beginning with 'Crimson Glory,' the fortune of which he repeated with 'Kordes Perfecta,' 'Fritz Nobis,' 'Flammentanz,' 'Dortmund,' 'Isle Krohn,' 'Leverkusen,' 'Maigold,' 'Raubritter,' 'Sparrieshoop' and 'Till Eulenspiegel.' Since 1950, the nursery has been in the hands of his son Reimer, who repeated his father's great successes with 'Schneewittchen' (syn. 'Iceberg'), 'Friesia,' 'Lichtkönigin Lucia,' 'Lilli Marlene,' 'Marlena,' 'Tradition' and 'Westerland.' Today, the nursery still achieves good results with conventional roses as well as groundcover and patio roses.

*Laffay, M.*: French hybridizer and a leading figure among hybridizers of the 19th century. In his nursery in Auteuil, he performed important activities of hybridization, creating many varieties and giving names to 350, including 'La Reine,' parent plant of the hybrid perpetuals, 'Cardinal de Richelieu,' 'Nuits de Young,' 'William Lobb' and 'Unique Blanche.'

*Le Grice, Edward*: Important breeder, active in Norfolk, England, since 1977. He specializes in yellow roses, the most famous of which is 'Allgold,' but he has also made many floribundas that are still in cultivation such as 'Dusky Maiden,' 'Dainty Maid,' 'Lilac Charm' and 'My Choice.'

*Lens, Louis*: Active for 50 years in Belgium's most important nursery. His most famous creations are 'Pascali' and 'Dame de Coeur,' much cultivated in Belgium and Holland. His son Victor carries on the work and is primarily involved in improving the hybrid musk roses.

*McGredy*: Family of famous breeders now in its fourth generation. The company was founded in 1880 with headquarters in Northern Ireland and was exclusively commercial. Sam McGredy II enjoyed his first successes in the 1930s with 'McGredy Ivory,' 'McGredy Yellow' and 'McGredy Sunset,' earning 52 medals all told. Since 1972, Sam McGredy IV has been active as a breeder in New Zealand. His name is now attached to many varieties, mostly hybrid teas and floribundas: 'Piccadilly,' 'Mischief,' 'Handel, 'Chanelle,' 'Picasso,' 'Elizabeth of Glamis,' 'Arthur Bell,' 'Evelyn Fison' and 'Trumpeter.'

*Mallerin, Charles*: French hybridizer, master of Francis Meilland, remembered most of all for 'Virgo.'

*Mansuino*: Family of horticulturists in San Remo, Italy. Quinto Mansuino, a student of Aicardi's, did most of his work in the 1950s and 1960s; his name is tied to the Mansuino roses made for sale as cut flowers ('Biancaneve,' 'Miss Italia,' 'Rubino') and to 'Purezza,' a rambler that won a gold medal at Rome in 1960. Derived from a *Rosa banksiae*, it was interesting because it had no thorns and was reflowering. Also important is the work of Domenico Mansuino.

*Meilland*: Family of French cultivators and hybridizers of great importance. Antoine Meilland (Papa Meilland) founded the company with headquarters in Tassin-les-Lyons. His son Francis began the hybridization activity. A skilled businessman, Francis founded the Universal Rose Selection with the object of sending the company's new products to the proving grounds of all the most important international competitions. He also actively promoted the establishment of patents for rose varieties, including guarantees of exclusive rights to production. 'Peace,' with is clamorous success, was only the first of a series of hybrid teas that became famous: 'Baccarat,' the most famous cut rose, 'Bettina,' 'Eden Rose' and 'Grace de Monaco.' His wife Marie-Louise and son Alain continue his work. Marie-Louise is known for 'Clair Matin,' 'Zambra' and 'Polka'; Alain for 'Papa Meilland,' 'Sonia,' 'Pharaoh,' 'Maria Callas' and 'Kalinka.' Today, the Meilland name is particularly tied to miniature roses, the Meillandina and Symphonie series, which are widely available on the Mediterranean market. In addition to Meilland, whose new products bear the name Meilland Selection, there is also the Meilland-Richardier Company, directed by Francis' son Alfred and his daughter Michèle.

*Moore, Ralph S.*: The most active hybridizer in the field of miniatures, with an annual production of more than 700,000 specimens. His California nursery was founded in 1937. Among the successes are 'Little Buckaroo,' 'Magic Carrousel,' 'Lavender Lace,' 'New Penny' and 'Lollipop,' as well as miniature climbers and miniature moss roses such as 'Dresden Doll.'

*Onodera, Susumu*: The best-known Japanese hybridizer, he earned international fame following the success of 'Nozomi,' which was one of the first groundcover roses, if not the very first.

*Pernet-Ducher, Joseph*: Successor of Pernet-Père, he began his career in 1887 and soon put the first hybrid teas on the market; he is most remembered for his Pernettian roses, created through crosses with *Rosa foetida*, which led to later hybrid teas in bright yellow. He signed 52 varieties, including 'Madame Caroline Testout,' 'Madame Abel Chatenay' and 'Souvenir de Claudius Pernet,' all hybrid teas of great quality. In 1919, the company became the property of Jean Gaujard.

*Poulsen*: Family of Danish hybridizers. They have dedicated their efforts to the floribundas in particular, working to create cold-resistant roses suitable for northern Europe. Among Svend Poulsen's major successes are 'Else Poulsen,' 'Kirsten Poulsen' and 'Irene von Dänemark.' Niels Dines, who continued his father's work, is known for 'Chinatown.' Today, the Poulsen name is tied most of all to small-size groundcover and patio roses put on the market by companies such as Mattock. Among these are 'Pink Bells,' 'Red Bells,' 'White Bells' and the many groundcover roses in the series named for English counties as well as 'Crystal Palace,' 'Pink Hit' and 'Sun Hit.'

*Rivers, Thomas*: Founder, in 1725, of the first nursery in England and editor of the first rose book, *The Rose Amateur Guide*, which lists more than 700 varieties.

*Tantau, Mathias*: German hybridizers, father and son, whose Uetersen company has specialized in roses since 1919. They do most of their work with hybrid teas. By 1946, they were presenting 60 roses for the market, all signed by the father, to which those created by the son must be added. They achieved international success with the dazzling 'Super Star,' the highly scented 'Duftwolke' (syn. 'Fragrant Cloud'), 'Prima Ballerina,' 'Whisky Mac' and an almost blue rose, 'Blue Moon.'

*Thomas, Graham Stuart*: Figure of outstanding importance in the world of roses, consultant to the National Trust and many public and private gardens, journalist and writer, author of important texts on climbing and shrub roses. Thanks to his efforts, many antique roses were retrieved from abandoned gardens and saved from oblivion.

*Vibert, J.P.*: One of the leading experts on roses in the 19th century. In 1815, he founded a nursery in Chenevières-sur-Marnes that came to host 10,000 plants of 300 different varieties. A skilled hybridizer, he named more than 600 varieties, including 'Aimée Vibert', 'Camaieux', 'Duchesse d'Angoulême', 'La Ville de Bruxelles', 'Comtesse de Murinais' and 'Yolande d'Aragon'.

*Warriner, William A.*: After setting up a nursery in Tustin, California, he joined the Jackson & Perkins company as hybridizer and consultant. Winner of many medals, he has signed 'Love', 'Honor', 'Cherish', and 'Red Masterpiece' as well as the more famous 'Pristine', 'Pure Bliss' and 'Sun Flare'.

# ROSE ASSOCIATIONS

Canada: Canadian Rose Society
110 Fairfax Crescent
Scarborough, Ontario M1L 1Z8
www.mirror.org/groups/crs

United States: American Rose Society
PO Box 30,000
Shreveport, LA 71130-0030
www.ars.org

# SPECIALIZED NURSERIES

CANADA

Au Jardin de Jean-Pierre
1070 RR 1 Ouest
Sainte-Christine, QC J0H 1H0
819-858-2142

Cornhill Nursery Ltd.
2700 Route 890
Cornhill, NB E4Z 1M2
506-756-3635

Hortico, Inc.
723 Robson Road
Waterdown, ON L0R 2H1
905-689-6984

Carl Pallek & Son Nursery
1567 Niagara Stone Road
Virgil, ON L0S 1T0
905-468-7262

Pickering Nurseries, Inc.
670 Kingston Road
Pickering, ON L1V 1A6
905-839-2111

UNITED STATES

The Antique Rose Emporium
7561 East Evans Road
San Antonio, TX 78266
210-651-4565

Bay Laurel Nursery
2500 El Camino Real
Atascadero, CA 93422
805-466-3406

Bridges Roses
2734 Toney Road
Lawndale, NC 28090
704-538-9412

W. Atlee Burpee & Co.
300 Park Avenue
Warminster, PA 18991
800-333-5808

Carroll Gardens
444 East Main Street
Westminster, MD 21157
800-638-6334

Chamblee's Rose Nursery
10926 U.S. Highway 69 North
Tyler, TX 75706
800-256-7673

Edmund's Roses
6235 SW Kahle Road
Wilsonville, OR 97070
888-481-7673

Garden Valley Ranch Rose Nursery
498 Pepper Road
Petaluma, CA 94952
707-795-0919

Heirloom Old Garden Roses
24062 Riverside Drive NE
St. Paul, OR 97137
503-538-1576

Heritage Rosarium
211 Haviland Mill Road
Brookeville, MD 20833
301-774-6890

Howerton Rose Nursery
1656 Weaverville Road
Northampton, PA 18067
610-262-5412

Jackson & Perkins Co.
1310 Center Drive, #J
Medford, OR 97501
800-872-7673

Sam Kedem Nursery & Garden
12414 191st Street East
Hastings, MN 55033
651-437-7516

Mary's Plant Farm
2410 Lanes Mill Road
Hamilton, OH 45013
513-894-0022

Michigan Miniature Roses
45951 Hull Road
Belleville, MI 48111
734-699-5814

The Old Mill Nursery
806 South Belt Highway
St. Joseph, MO 64507
800-344-8107

Petaluma Rose Co.
582 Gossage Avenue
Petaluma, CA 94952
707-769-8862

Regan's Nursery
4268 Decoto Road
Fremont, CA 94555
800-249-4680

The Rose Ranch
2877 Torre Drive
La Grange, CA 95329
209-852-9220

The Roseraie at Bayfields
670 Bremen Road
Waldoboro, ME 04572
207-832-6330

Roses of Yesterday & Today
803 Brown's Valley Road
Watsonville, CA 95076
831-728-1901

Sequoia Nursery
2519 East Noble Avenue
Visalia, CA 93292
559-732-0190

Teas Nursery Co., Inc.
4400 Bellaire Boulevard
Bellaire, TX 77401
713-664-4400

Vintage Gardens
2833 Old Gravenstein Highway South
Sebastopol, CA 95472
707-829-2035

## Historical Background

Jekyll, Gertrude, and Edward Mawley. *Roses for English Gardens*. New York: Charles Scribner's Sons, 1902.

Paul, William. *The Rose Garden*. London: Kent & Co., 1875.

Thomas, Graham Stuart. *Climbing Roses, Old and New*. London: Phoenix House, 1965. Reprint, J. M. Dent & Sons, 1974.

_____. *The Old Shrub Roses*. London: Phoenix House, 1961.

_____. *Shrub Roses of Today*. London: Phoenix House, 1962.

Willmott, Ellen Ann. *The Genus Rosa*. London: John Murray, 1914.

## General

Anderson, Frank J. *Redouté Roses*. New York: Abbeville Press, 1981.

Austin, David. *David Austin's English Roses*. London: Conran Octopus, 1993.

_____. *Old Roses and English Roses*. Woodbridge, Suffolk: Antique Collectors' Club, 1992.

_____. *Shrub Roses and Climbing Roses*. Woodbridge, Suffolk: Antique Collectors' Club, 1993.

Beales, Peter. *Classic Roses*. New York: Henry Holt, 1985.

_____. *Twentieth-Century Roses*. Collins Harvill-Harper & Row, 1988.

Buczacki, Stefan. *Roses*. London: Hamlyn Reed International Books, 1996.

Christopher, Tom. *Easy Roses for North American Gardens*. Pleasantville, NY: Reader's Digest Association, 1999.

Essayon, D.G. *The Rose Expert*. Transworld Publishers, 1993.

Gault, S. Millar, and Patrick M. Synge. *The Dictionary of Roses*. London: Ebury Press, 1970.

Gibson, M. *The Book of the Rose*. MacDonald General Books, 1980.

_____. *Growing Roses*. Croom Helm, 1984.

_____. *Growing Roses for Small Gardens*. Christopher Helm, 1990.

Goss, M. *Miniature Roses: Their Care and Cultivation*. Jean McCann Cassel, 1991.

Green, Douglas. *Tender Roses for Tough Climates*. Chapters Publishing Ltd., 1997.

Griffiths, T. *The Best of Modern Roses*. Péacific, 1987.

_____. *The Book of Old Roses*. Michael Joseph, 1984.

_____. *My World of Old Roses*. 2 vols. Whitcoules, 1983.

Harkness, J.L. *Growing Roses*. J.M. Dent & Sons, 1967.

_____. *The Makers of Heavenly Roses*. Souvenir Press, 1985.

_____. *Roses*. J.M. Dent & Sons, 1978.

_____. *The World's Favorite Roses and How to Grow Them*. New York: McGraw Hill, 1979.

Kordes, W. *Rosen*. Studio Vista, 1964.

Krussman, G. *Roses*. Batsford B.T., 1982.

Le Grice, E. *Rose Growing Complete*. Faber & Faber, 1976.

MacFarland, H. *Modern Roses*. Harrisburg, PA, 1980.

Martin, Clair G. *100 Old Roses for the American Garden*. New York: Workman, 1999.

Mattock, John. *Reader's Digest Gardener's Guide to Growing Roses.* Pleasantville, NY: Reader's Digest Association, 1996.

\_\_\_\_\_ et al. *The Complete Book of Roses.* London: Ward Lock, 1994.

Olson, J., and J. Whitman. *Growing Roses in Cold Climates.* Chicago: Contemporary Books, 1998.

Paterson, A. *The History of the Rose.* Hearn Stephenson, 1983.

\_\_\_\_\_. *Taylor's Guide to the Roses.* Houghton Mifflin, 1995.

Phillips, R., and M. Rix. *Roses.* Pan Books, 1988.

Ross, B.V. *Modern Roses in Australia.* Mitchell & Casey, 1930.

\_\_\_\_\_. *Shrub Roses in Australia.* Deane Ross, 1981.

Warner C. *Climbing Roses.* Cassel, 1987.

## Reference Publications

*The American Rose Annual,* American Rose Society, PO Box 30,000, Shreveport, LA 71130-0030.

*Find That Rose,* American English Rosaists, 303 Mile End Road, Colchester, Essex CO4 5EPJ, England. Lists a great number of varieties with the addresses of nurseries where they can be found.

*The Rose Annual,* Royal National Rose Society, Chiswell Green, St. Albans, Hertfordshire, England, AL2 3NR. The annual lists species and antique roses and an exhaustive number of modern varieties.

# PHOTOGRAPH CREDITS

Associazione Italiana della Rosa, Roseto Niso Fumagalli: 242-243.
D. Austin: 12, 52, 86 (1), 109 (1), 110, 124, 141 (1), 148 (1), 149 (1), 157, 208 (2), 226 ('Charlotte'), 226 (1), 233.
P. Beales: 99, 117, 163 (1), 225 (1), 234 (1).
BMR Imperia: 41.
Kordes: 154 (1), 268.
Paroli Galperti: 1-7, 67, 158, 245, 248, 255, 260, 265, 271.
A. Pennati: 54 (*Rosa banksiae alba plena*), 59 (1), 161, 168, 198, 237.
Rose Barni: 18, 55, 77, 91, 95, 97, 100, 106, 114, 122 (1), 162, 274.
Agricultural and Agri-Food Canada, Morden Research Station: 248 (lower), 249 (both), 250 (upper), 251 (lower), 253 (lower), 257 (upper)
Dave Galbraith: 255 (upper)
Claire Laberge: 250 (lower), 254 (lower)
George Pagowski: 246 (lower), 247 (lower), 248 (upper), 253 (upper), 257 (lower)
Beth Powning: 245 (both), , 246 (upper), 247 (upper), 251 (upper), 252 (both), 254 (upper), 255 (lower), 256 (both)